The COKESBURY WORSHIP HYMNAL

ISBN 0-687-08863-1 Cloth Edition
ISBN 0-687-08865-8 Paper Edition
ISBN 0-687-08866-6 Accompanist Edition

ABINGDON PRESS
Nashville

Manufactured in the United States of America

1 Gloria Patri

CHARLES MEINEKE

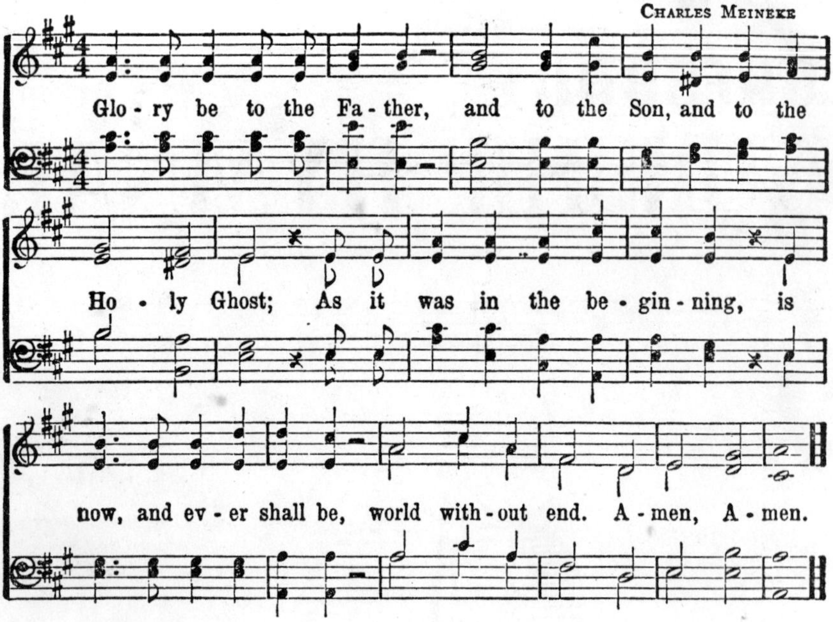

Glo - ry be to the Fa - ther, and to the Son, and to the Ho - ly Ghost; As it was in the be - gin - ning, is now, and ev - er shall be, world with - out end. A - men, A - men.

2 Doxology

THOS. KEN

G. FRANC

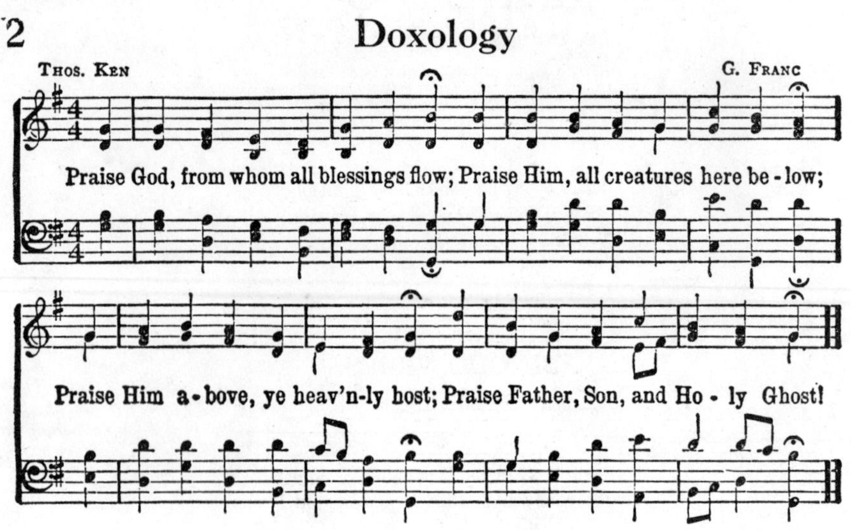
Praise God, from whom all blessings flow; Praise Him, all creatures here be - low;
Praise Him a - bove, ye heav'n-ly host; Praise Father, Son, and Ho - ly Ghost!

Favorite Gospel Hymns is also published as *The Cokesbury Worship Hymnal*

3 Hail, Thou Once Despised Jesus

AUTUMN. 8. 7. 8. 7. D.
John Bakewell, 1721–1819
Arr. from François H. Barthélémon, 1741–1808
1. Hail, Thou once de - spis - ed Je - sus! Hail, Thou Gal - i - le - an King!
2. Pas - chal Lamb, by God ap - point - ed, All our sins on Thee were laid:
3. Je - sus, hail! en-throned in glo - ry, There for ev - er to a - bide;
4. Wor - ship, hon - or, power, and bless - ing Thou art wor - thy to re - ceive;
Thou didst suf - fer to re - lease us; Thou didst free sal - va - tion bring.
By al-might - y love a - noint - ed, Thou hast full a - tone-ment made.
All the heaven-ly hosts a - dore Thee, Seat - ed at Thy Fa-ther's side.
Loud - est prais - es, with - out ceas - ing, Meet it is for us to give.
Hail, Thou ag - o - niz - ing Sav - iour, Bear - er of our sin and shame!
All Thy peo - ple are for - giv - en, Thro' the vir - tue of Thy blood;
There for sin - ners Thou art plead - ing, There Thou dost our place pre - pare,
Help, ye bright an - gel - ic spir - its, Bring your sweet-est, no - blest lays;
By Thy mer - its we find fa - vor; Life is giv - en thro' Thy Name.
O - pened is the gate of heav - en, Peace is made 'twixt man and God.
Ev - er for us in - ter - ced - ing Till in glo - ry we ap - pear.
Help to sing our Sav-iour's mer - its, Help to chant Im-man-uel's praise! A - MEN.

4 Come, Let Us Tune Our Loftiest Song

DUKE STREET. L. M.

ROBERT A. WEST, 1809–1865 JOHN HATTON, d. 1793

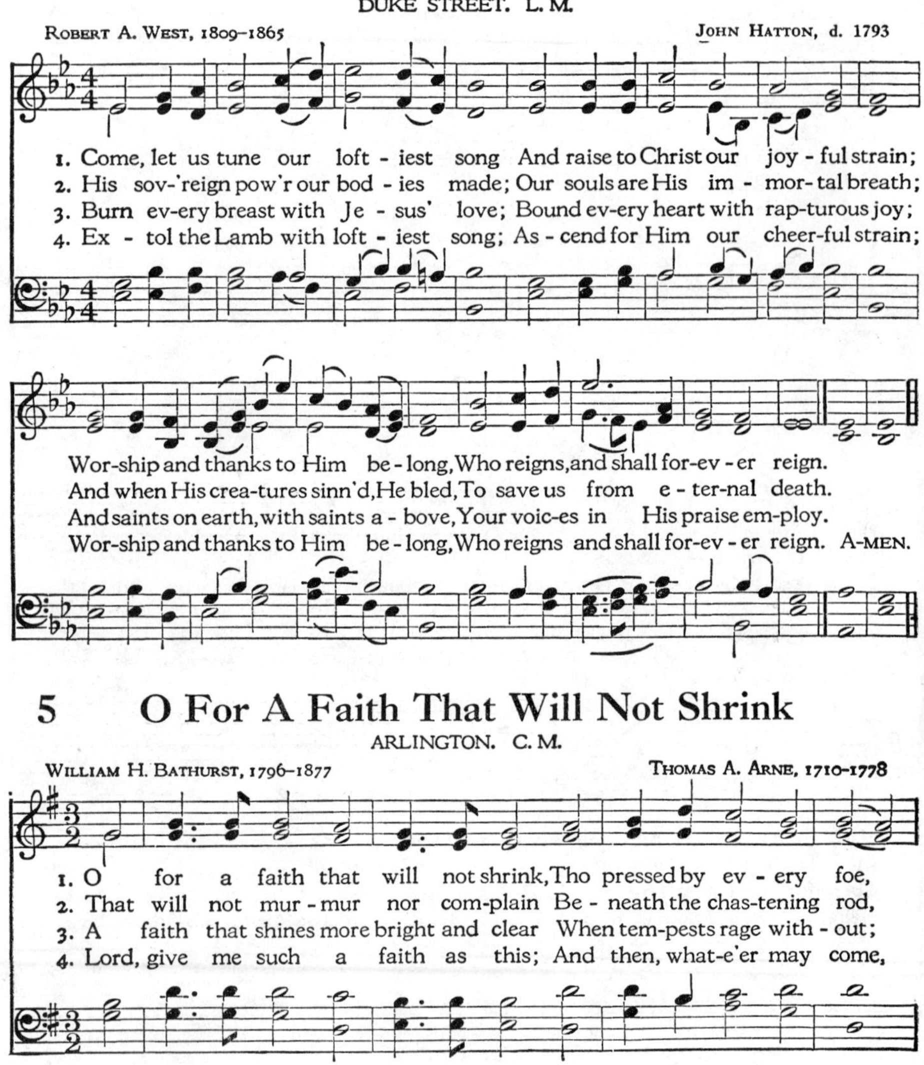
1. Come, let us tune our loft - iest song And raise to Christ our joy - ful strain;
2. His sov-'reign pow'r our bod - ies made; Our souls are His im - mor-tal breath;
3. Burn ev-ery breast with Je - sus' love; Bound ev-ery heart with rap-turous joy;
4. Ex - tol the Lamb with loft - iest song; As - cend for Him our cheer-ful strain;
Wor-ship and thanks to Him be - long, Who reigns, and shall for-ev - er reign.
And when His crea-tures sinn'd, He bled, To save us from e - ter-nal death.
And saints on earth, with saints a - bove, Your voic-es in His praise em-ploy.
Wor-ship and thanks to Him be - long, Who reigns and shall for-ev - er reign. A-MEN.

5 O For A Faith That Will Not Shrink

ARLINGTON. C. M.

WILLIAM H. BATHURST, 1796–1877 THOMAS A. ARNE, 1710–1778

1. O for a faith that will not shrink, Tho pressed by ev - ery foe,
2. That will not mur - mur nor com-plain Be - neath the chas-tening rod,
3. A faith that shines more bright and clear When tem-pests rage with - out;
4. Lord, give me such a faith as this; And then, what-e'er may come,

That will not trem - ble on the brink Of an - y earth - ly woe!
But, in the hour of grief or pain, Will lean up - on its God;
That when in dan - ger knows no fear, In dark-ness feels no doubt:
I'll taste, e'en now, the hal-lowed bliss Of an e - ter - nal home. A-MEN.

6 Holy, Holy, Holy

Reginald Heber — Rev. John B. Dykes

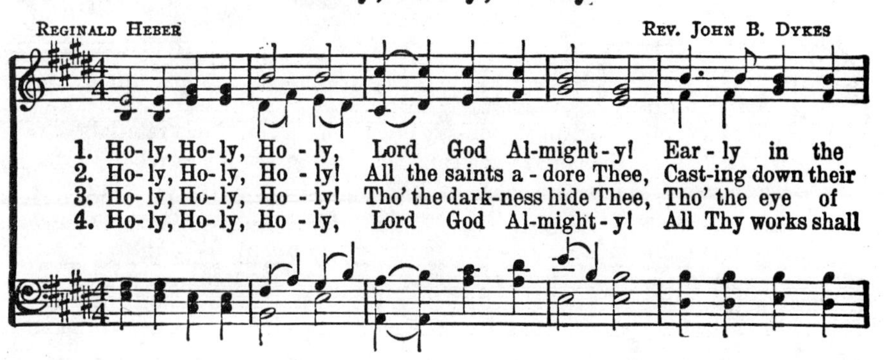
1. Ho-ly, Ho-ly, Ho - ly, Lord God Al-might - y! Ear - ly in the
2. Ho-ly, Ho-ly, Ho - ly! All the saints a - dore Thee, Cast-ing down their
3. Ho-ly, Ho-ly, Ho - ly! Tho' the dark-ness hide Thee, Tho' the eye of
4. Ho-ly, Ho-ly, Ho - ly, Lord God Al-might - y! All Thy works shall

morn - ing our song shall rise to Thee; Ho - ly, Ho - ly, Ho - ly!
gold-en crowns a-round the glass - y sea; Cher-u - bim and ser-a-phim
sin-ful man Thy glo - ry may not see, On - ly Thou art ho - ly;
praise Thy name, in earth, and sky, and sea; Ho - ly, Ho - ly, Ho - ly!

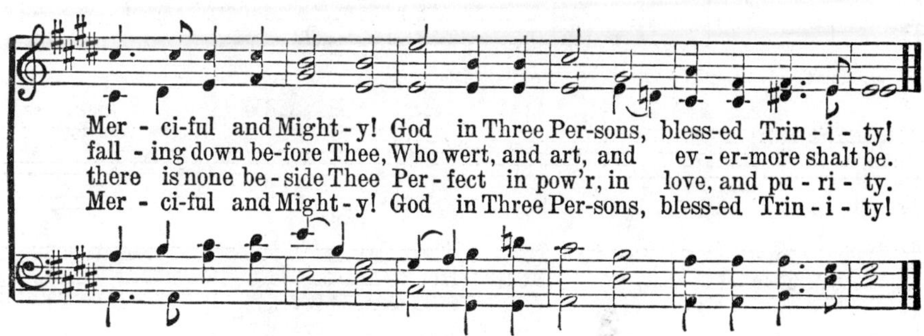
Mer - ci-ful and Might - y! God in Three Per-sons, bless-ed Trin - i - ty!
fall - ing down be-fore Thee, Who wert, and art, and ev - er-more shalt be.
there is none be - side Thee Per - fect in pow'r, in love, and pu - ri - ty.
Mer - ci-ful and Might - y! God in Three Per-sons, bless-ed Trin - i - ty!

7
O Worship The King
Sir Robert Grant
Francis Joseph Haydn
1. O worship the King all-glorious above, And gratefully sing His wonderful love; Our Shield and Defender, the Ancient of days, Pavilioned in splendor, and girded with praise.
2. O tell of His might and sing of His grace Whose robe is the light, whose canopy space; His chariots of wrath the deep thunder-clouds form, And dark is His path on the wings of the storm.
3. Thy bountiful care what tongue can recite? It breathes in the air, it shines in the light, It streams from the hills, it descends to the plain, And sweetly distills in the dew and the rain.
4. Frail children of dust, and feeble as frail, In Thee do we trust, nor find Thee to fail; Thy mercies how tender! how firm to the end! Our Maker, Defender, Redeemer and Friend. A-men.
8
I Love Thy Kingdom, Lord
Timothy Dwight
Aaron Williams
1. I love Thy kingdom, Lord, The house of Thine abode, The
2. I love Thy Church, O God! Her walls before Thee stand, Dear
3. For her my tears shall fall; For her my pray'rs ascend; To
4. Beyond my highest joy I prize her heav'nly ways, Her
5. Sure as Thy truth shall last, To Zion shall be giv'n The

I Love Thy Kingdom, Lord
Church our blest Re-deem - er saved With His own pre-cious blood.
as the ap - ple of Thine eye, And grav - en on Thy hand.
her my cares and toils be giv'n, Till toils and cares shall end.
sweet com - mun-ion, sol - emn vows, Her hymns of love and praise.
bright - est glo - ries earth can yield, And bright-er bliss of heav'n. A-men.
9
Come, Thou Almighty King
Anonymous
Felice De Giardini
1. Come, Thou Al - might - y King, Help us Thy name to sing,
2. Come, Thou In - car - nate Word, Gird on Thy might - y sword,
3. Come, Ho - ly Com - fort - er, Thy sa - cred wit - ness bear
4. To the great One in Three E - ter - nal prais - es be
Help us to praise: Fa - ther, all - glo - ri - ous, O'er all vic -
Our pray'r at - tend: Come, and Thy peo - ple bless, And give Thy
In this glad hour: Thou who al - might - y art, Now rule in
Hence ev - er - more. His sov-'reign maj - es - ty May we in
to - ri - ous, Come, and reign o - ver us, An - cient of Days.
word suc - cess: Spir - it of ho - li - ness, On us de - scend.
ev - 'ry heart, And ne'er from us de - part, Spir - it of pow'r.
glo - ry see, And to e - ter - ni - ty, Love and a - dore.

10 O Day Of Rest And Gladness

C. WORDSWORTH

Arr. by L. MASON

1. O day of rest and glad - ness, O day of joy and light,
2. On thee, at the cre - a - tion, The light first had its birth;
3. To - day on wear - y na - tions The heav'n-ly man - na falls;
4. New gra - ces ev - er gain - ing From this our day of rest,
O balm of care and sad - ness, Most beau - ti - ful, most bright;
On thee, for our sal - va - tion, Christ rose from depths of earth.
To ho - ly con - vo - ca - tions The sil - ver trump-et calls,
We reach the rest re - main - ing To spir - its of the blest.
On thee, the high and low - ly, Bend - ing be - fore the throne, Sing,
On thee our Lord vic - to - rious The Spir - it sent from Heav'n; And
Where gos - pel light is glow - ing With pure and ra - diant beams, And
To Ho - ly Ghost be prais - es, To Fa - ther and to Son; The
Ho - ly, Ho - ly, Ho - ly, To the great Three in One.
thus on thee most glo - rious A tri - ple light was given.
liv - ing wa - ter flow - ing With soul - re - fresh-ing streams.
Church her voice up - rais - es To Thee, blest Three in One. A - MEN.

11 Ancient Of Days

ANCIENT OF DAYS. 11. 10. 11. 10.

WILLIAM C. DOANE, 1832-1913 — J. ALBERT JEFFERY, 1851-1928

In unison
1. An - cient of Days, who sit - test throned in glo - ry,
2. O Ho - ly Fa - ther, who hast led Thy chil - dren
3. O Ho - ly Je - sus, Prince of Peace and Sav - iour,
4. O Ho - ly Ghost, the Lord and the Life - giv - er,
5. O Tri - une God, with heart and voice a - dor - ing,
To Thee all knees are bent, all voic - es pray;
In all the a - ges, with the fire and cloud,
To Thee we owe the peace that still pre - vails,
Thine is the quick - 'ning power that gives in - crease;
Praise we the good - ness that doth crown our days;
Thy love has blessed the wide world's won - drous sto - ry
Through seas dry - shod, through wea - ry wastes be - wil - dering;
Still - ing the rude wills of men's wild be - hav - ior,
From Thee have flowed, as from a pleas - ant riv - er,
Pray we that Thou wilt hear us, still im - plor - ing
With light and life since E - den's dawn - ing day.
To Thee, in rev - erent love, our hearts are bowed.
And calm - ing pas - sion's fierce and storm - y gales.
Our plen - ty, wealth, pros - per - i - ty, and peace.
Thy love and fa - vor kept to us al - ways. A - MEN.

12 Sweet Hour Of Prayer
W. W. Walford
Wm. B. Bradbury
1. Sweet hour of prayer! sweet hour of prayer! That calls me from a world of care,
2. Sweet hour of prayer! sweet hour of prayer! Thy wings shall my pe - ti - tion bear
3. Sweet hour of prayer! sweet hour of prayer! May I thy con - so - la - tion share,
And bids me at my Fa-ther's throne Make all my wants and wish - es known;
To Him whose truth and faith-ful-ness En-gage the wait-ing soul to bless;
Till, from Mount Pisgah's loft - y height, I view my home, and take my flight:
In sea - sons of dis-tress and grief, My soul has oft - en found re - lief,
And since He bids me seek His face, Be-lieve His word and trust His grace,
This robe of flesh I'll drop, and rise To seize the ev - er - last - ing prize;
And oft es - caped the tempter's snare By thy re - turn, sweet hour of prayer.
I'll cast on Him my ev - 'ry care, And wait for thee, sweet hour of prayer.
And shout, while passing thro' the air, Farewell, farewell, sweet hour of prayer.
13 Jesus Shall Reign
Isaac Watts
John Hatton
1. Je - sus shall reign wher-e'er the sun Does his suc-ces-sive jour - neys run;
2. From north to south the prin - ces meet To pay their homage at His feet;
3. To Him shall end-less pray'r be made, And endless praises crown His head;
4. Peo - ple and realms of ev - 'ry tongue Dwell on His love with sweetest song,

Jesus Shall Reign

His kingdom spread from shore to shore, Till moons shall wax and wane no more.
While western em - pires own their Lord, And sav-age tribes at-tend His word.
His name like sweet per - fume shall rise With ev-'ry morn-ing sac - ri - fice.
And in-fant voic - es shall pro - claim Their earthly blessings on His name.

14 All Hail The Power Of Jesus' Name

EDWARD PERRONET — OLIVER HOLDEN

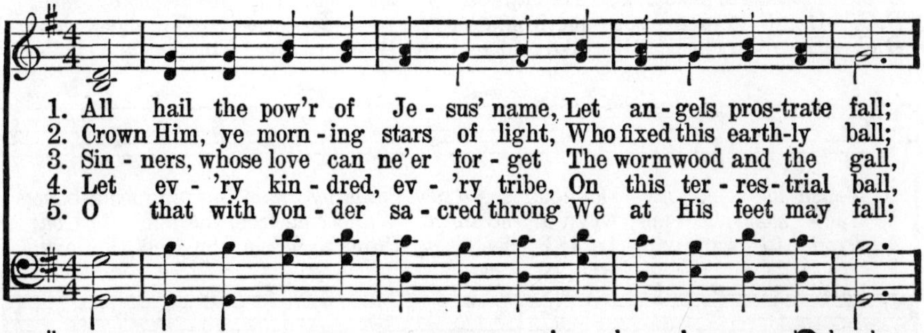

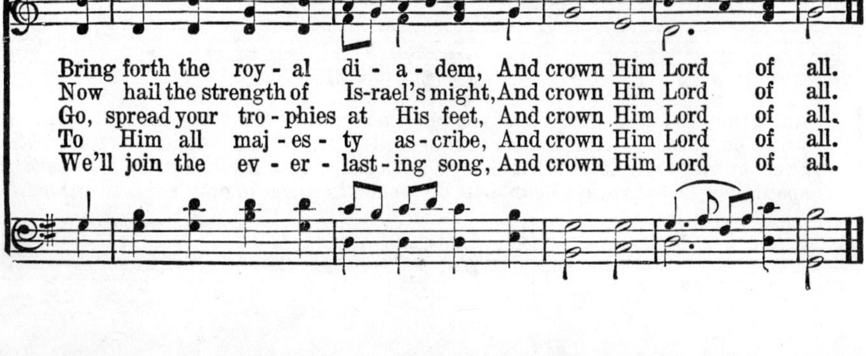

1. All hail the pow'r of Je - sus' name, Let an - gels pros-trate fall;
2. Crown Him, ye morn - ing stars of light, Who fixed this earth-ly ball;
3. Sin - ners, whose love can ne'er for - get The wormwood and the gall,
4. Let ev - 'ry kin - dred, ev - 'ry tribe, On this ter - res - trial ball,
5. O that with yon - der sa - cred throng We at His feet may fall;

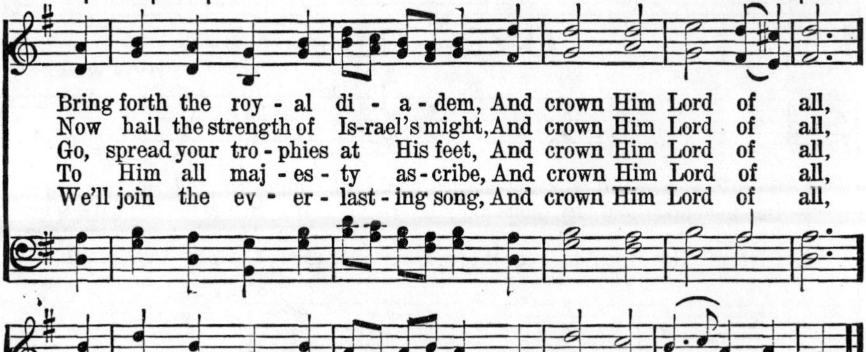

Bring forth the roy - al di - a - dem, And crown Him Lord of all,
Now hail the strength of Is-rael's might, And crown Him Lord of all,
Go, spread your tro - phies at His feet, And crown Him Lord of all,
To Him all maj - es - ty as - cribe, And crown Him Lord of all,
We'll join the ev - er - last - ing song, And crown Him Lord of all,

Bring forth the roy - al di - a - dem, And crown Him Lord of all.
Now hail the strength of Is-rael's might, And crown Him Lord of all.
Go, spread your tro - phies at His feet, And crown Him Lord of all.
To Him all maj - es - ty as - cribe, And crown Him Lord of all.
We'll join the ev - er - last - ing song, And crown Him Lord of all.

15 Come, Thou Fount
Robert Robinson
John Wyeth
Fine.
1. {Come, Thou Fount of ev - 'ry bless-ing, Tune my heart to sing Thy grace;
Streams of mer - cy, nev - er ceas-ing, Call for songs of loud- est praise.}
2. {Here I'll raise my Eb - en - e - zer, Hith-er by Thy help I'll come;
And I hope, by Thy good pleasure, Safe - ly to ar - rive at home.}
3. {Oh, to grace How great a debt - or Dai - ly I'm constrained to be!
Let Thy good-ness, like a fet - ter, Bind my wand' - ring heart to Thee:}
D.C.—Praise the mount, I'm fixed up - on it! Mount of Thy re- deem-ing love.
D.C.—He, to res - cue me from dan-ger, In - ter-posed His pre-cious blood.
D.C.—Here's my heart, O take and seal it, Seal it for Thy courts a - bove.
D. C.
Teach me some me - lo-dious son - net, Sung by flam-ing tongues a-bove;
Je - sus sought me when a stran-ger, Wand'ring from the fold of God;
Prone to wan - der, Lord, I feel it, Prone to leave the God I love;
16 O Zion, Haste
Mary A. Thomson
James Walch
1. O Zi - on, haste, thy mis-sion high ful - fill - ing, To tell to all the
2. Be - hold how ma - ny thousand still are ly - ing, Bound in the dark-some
3. Proclaim to ev - 'ry peo-ple, tongue and na-tion That God in whom they
4. Give of thy sons to bear the message glo-rious; Give of thy wealth to
world that God is Light; That He who made all na-tions is not will - ing
pris - on-house of sin, With none to tell them of the Sav-ior's dy - ing,
live and move is love: Tell how He stooped to save His lost cre - a - tion,
speed them on their way; Pour out thy soul for them in pray'r vic - to - rious;

O Zion, Haste

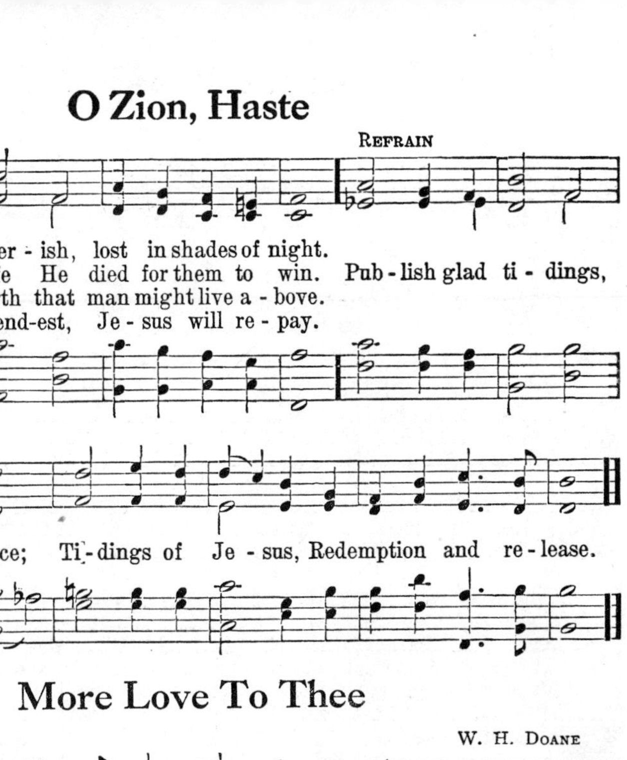

Refrain
One soul should per - ish, lost in shades of night.
Or of the life He died for them to win. Pub - lish glad ti - dings,
And died on earth that man might live a - bove.
And all Thou spend-est, Je - sus will re - pay.
Ti-dings of peace; Ti-dings of Je - sus, Redemption and re - lease.

17 More Love To Thee

Elizabeth Prentiss — W. H. Doane

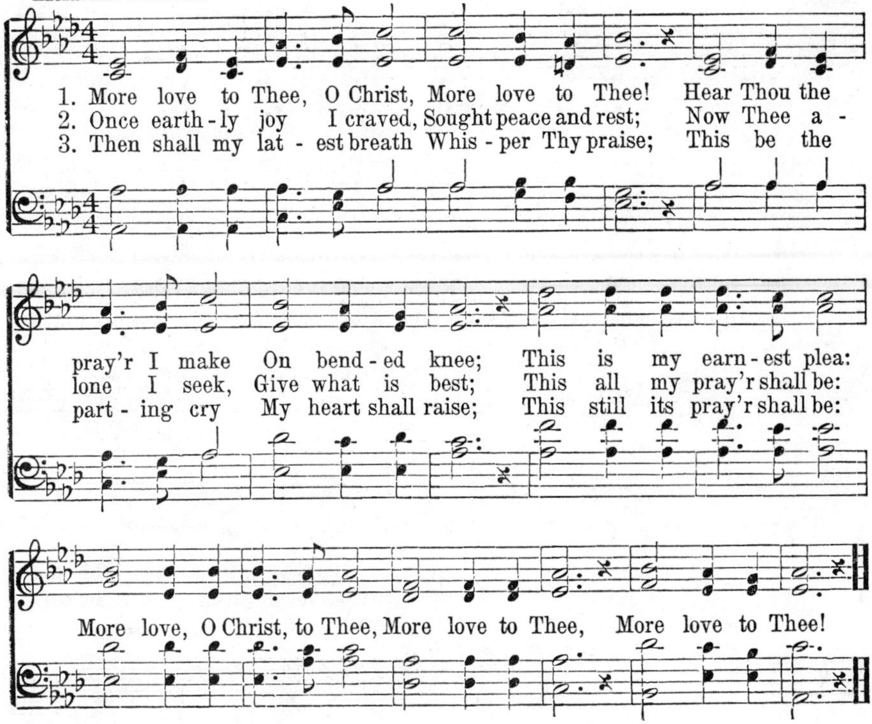

1. More love to Thee, O Christ, More love to Thee! Hear Thou the pray'r I make On bend - ed knee; This is my earn - est plea:
2. Once earth - ly joy I craved, Sought peace and rest; Now Thee a - lone I seek, Give what is best; This all my pray'r shall be:
3. Then shall my lat - est breath Whis - per Thy praise; This be the part - ing cry My heart shall raise; This still its pray'r shall be:

More love, O Christ, to Thee, More love to Thee, More love to Thee!

18 There's A Wideness

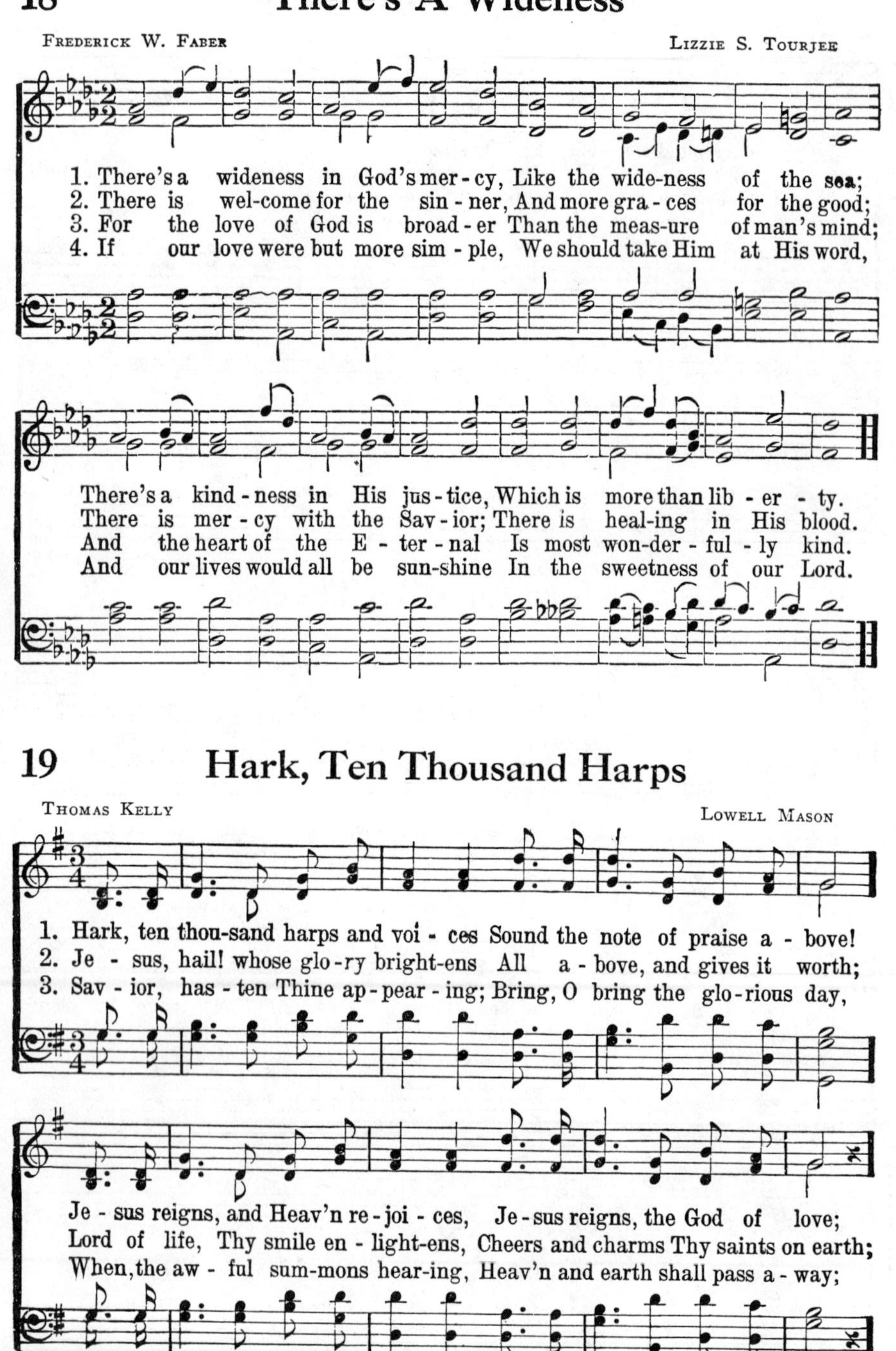
FREDERICK W. FABER
LIZZIE S. TOURJEE
1. There's a wideness in God's mer - cy, Like the wide-ness of the sea;
2. There is wel-come for the sin - ner, And more gra - ces for the good;
3. For the love of God is broad - er Than the meas-ure of man's mind;
4. If our love were but more sim - ple, We should take Him at His word,
There's a kind - ness in His jus - tice, Which is more than lib - er - ty.
There is mer - cy with the Sav - ior; There is heal-ing in His blood.
And the heart of the E - ter - nal Is most won-der - ful - ly kind.
And our lives would all be sun-shine In the sweetness of our Lord.
19
Hark, Ten Thousand Harps
THOMAS KELLY
LOWELL MASON
1. Hark, ten thou-sand harps and voi - ces Sound the note of praise a - bove!
2. Je - sus, hail! whose glo - ry bright-ens All a - bove, and gives it worth;
3. Sav - ior, has - ten Thine ap - pear - ing; Bring, O bring the glo-rious day,
Je - sus reigns, and Heav'n re - joi - ces, Je - sus reigns, the God of love;
Lord of life, Thy smile en - light-ens, Cheers and charms Thy saints on earth;
When, the aw - ful sum-mons hear-ing, Heav'n and earth shall pass a - way;

Hark, Ten Thousand Harps

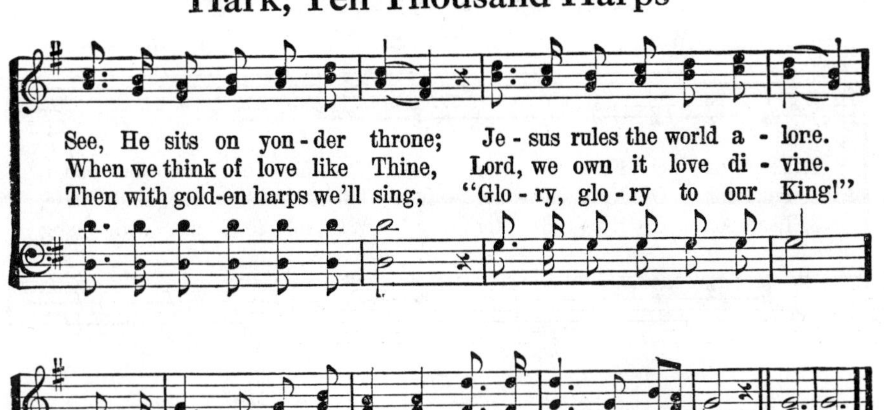
See, He sits on yon - der throne; Je - sus rules the world a - lone.
When we think of love like Thine, Lord, we own it love di - vine.
Then with gold-en harps we'll sing, "Glo - ry, glo - ry to our King!"

Hal - le - lu - jah! hal - le - lu - jah! Hal - le - lu - jah! A - men! A - MEN.

20 Holy Spirit, Truth Divine

7. 7. 7. 7.

Samuel Longfellow, 1819-1892 — Arr. from Louis M. Gottschalk, 1829-1869

1. Ho - ly Spir - it, Truth di - vine, Dawn up - on this soul of mine;
2. Ho - ly Spir - it, Love di - vine, Glow with-in this heart of mine;
3. Ho - ly Spir - it, Pow'r di - vine, Fill and nerve this will of mine;
4. Ho - ly Spir - it, Right di - vine, King with-in my con-science reign;
Word of God, and in - ward Light, Wake my spir-it, clear my sight.
Kin - dle ev - 'ry high de - sire; Per - ish self in Thy pure fire.
By Thee may I strong-ly live, Brave-ly bear, and no - bly strive.
Be my Lord, and I shall be Firm - ly bound, for-ev - er free. A - MEN.

21 Lead On, O King Eternal

ERNEST W. SHURTLEFF
LANCASHIRE
HENRY SMART
1. Lead on, O King E - ter - nal, The day of march has come;
2. Lead on, O King E - ter - nal, Till sin's fierce war shall cease,
3. Lead on, O King E - ter - nal, We fol - low, not with fears;
Henceforth in fields of con - quest Thy tents shall be our home.
And ho - li - ness shall whis - per The sweet A - men of peace;
For glad-ness breaks like morn - ing Wher-e'er Thy face ap - pears;
Thro' days of prep - a - ra - tion Thy grace has made us strong.
For not with swords loud clash-ing, Nor roll of stir - ring drums;
Thy cross is lift - ed o'er us; We jour - ney in its light:
And now, O King e - ter - nal, We lift our bat - tle song.
With deeds of love and mer - cy, The heav'n-ly king - dom comes.
The crown a - waits the con - quest; Lead on, O God of might.

22 Love Divine

Charles Wesley | John Zundel

1. Love di - vine, all loves ex - cel-ling, Joy of Heav'n, to earth come down!
2. Breathe, O breathe Thy lov-ing Spir - it In - to ev - 'ry troub - led breast!
3. Come, Al-might - y to de - liv - er, Let us all Thy life re - ceive;
4. Fin - ish then Thy new cre - a - tion; Pure and spot - less let us be;
Fix in us Thy hum - ble dwell - ing; All Thy faith - ful mer - cies crown.
Let us all in Thee in - her - it, Let us find that sec - ond rest.
Sud-den - ly re - turn, and nev - er, Nev - er - more Thy tem - ples leave:
Let us see Thy great sal - va - tion, Per - fect - ly re-stored in Thee:
Je - sus, Thou art all com-pas-sion, Pure, un-bound-ed love Thou art;
Take a - way our bent to sin-ning, Al - pha and O - me - ga be;
Thee we would be al - ways blessing, Serve Thee as Thy hosts a - bove,
Changed from glo - ry in - to glo - ry, Till in Heav'n we take our place,
Vis - it us with Thy sal - va - tion; En - ter ev - 'ry trem - bling heart.
End of faith, as its be - gin-ning, Set our hearts at lib - er - ty.
Pray, and praise Thee with - out ceas - ing, Glo - ry in Thy per - fect love.
Till we cast our crowns be - fore Thee, Lost in won - der, love, and praise.

23

Holy Spirit, Faithful Guide

HOLY SPIRIT, FAITHFUL GUIDE. 7. 7. 7. 7. D.

MARCUS M. WELLS, 1815-1895 MARCUS M. WELLS, 1815-1895

1. Ho - ly Spir - it, faith - ful Guide, Ev - er near the Chris-tian's side;
2. Ev - er pres - ent, tru - est Friend, Ev - er near Thine aid to lend,
3. When our days of toil shall cease, Wait - ing still for sweet re - lease,

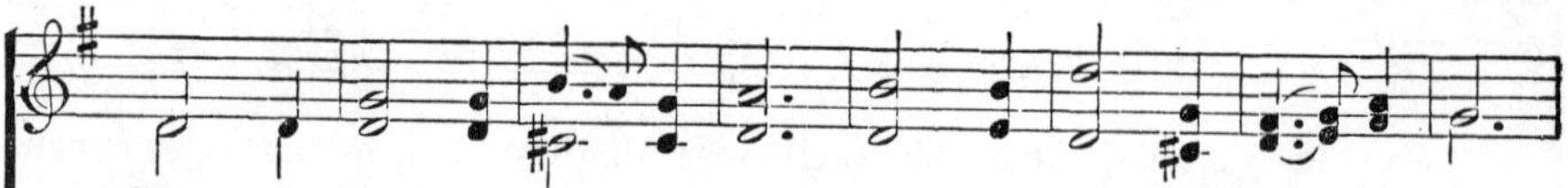

Gen - tly lead us by the hand, Pil - grims in a des - ert land;
Leave us not to doubt and fear, Grop - ing on in dark-ness drear;
Noth - ing left but heav'n and prayer, Wondering if our names are there;

Wea - ry souls for - e'er re - joice, While they hear that sweet-est voice,
When the storms are rag - ing sore, Hearts grow faint and hopes give o'er,
Wad - ing deep the dis - mal flood, Plead - ing naught but Je - sus' blood,

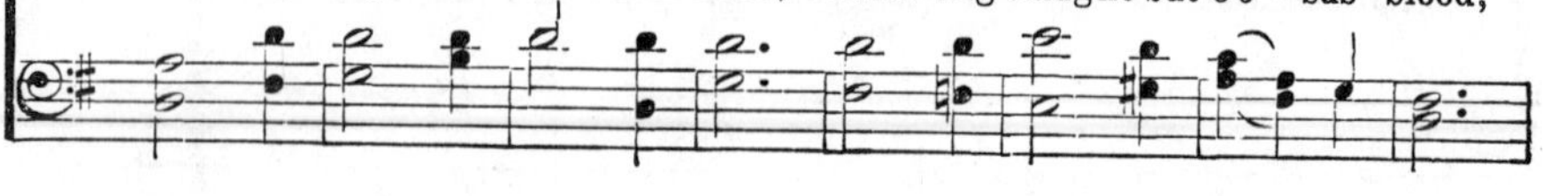

Whisp'ring soft-ly, "Wand'rer, come! Follow me, I'll guide thee home."
Whis - per soft-ly, "Wand'rer, come! Follow me, I'll guide thee home."
Whis - per soft-ly, "Wand'rer, come! Follow me, I'll guide thee home." A-MEN.

24 Rejoice, Ye Pure In Heart

Edward A. Plumtre
Arthur H. Messiter
1. Re - joice, ye pure in heart, Re - joice, give thanks and sing; Your fes - tal ban - ner wave on high,— The cross of Christ your King.
2. Bright youth and snow-crowned age, Strong men and maid - ens fair, Raise high your free, ex - ult - ing song, God's won - drous praise de - clare.
3. With all the an - gel choirs, With all the saints on earth, Pour out the strains of joy and bliss, True rap - ture, no - blest mirth!
4. With voice as full and strong As o - cean's surg - ing praise, Send forth the hymns our fa - thers loved, The psalms of an - cient days.
5. Yes, on thro' life's long path, Still chant - ing as ye go; From youth to age, by night and day, In glad - ness and in woe.
6. Still lift your stan - dard high, Still march in firm ar - ray, As war - riors thro' the dark-ness toil, Till dawns the gold - en day.
Refrain
Re - joice, re - joice, Re - joice, give thanks and sing! A - men.
Re - joice, re - joice,

25

Above The Hills Of Time

LONDONDERRY. 11. 10. 11. 10. D.

WORDS USED BY PERMISSION OF THOMAS TIPLADY

THOMAS TIPLADY, 1882–

Irish Traditional Melody

1. A - bove the hills of time the cross is gleam-ing, Fair as the sun when night has turned to day; And from it love's pure light is rich - ly stream-ing, . . To cleanse the heart and ban - ish sin a - way. To this dear cross the eyes of men are turn - ing . . To - day as

2. The cross, O Christ, Thy won-drous love re - veal - ing, A - wakes our hearts as with the light of morn, And par - don o'er our sin - ful spir - its steal - ing . . Tells us, that we, in Thee, have been re - born. Like ech - oes to sweet tem - ple bells re - ply - ing, . . Our hearts, O

in the a-ges lost to sight; And so for Thee, O Christ, men's hearts are
Lord, make an-swer to Thy love; And we will love Thee with a love un-

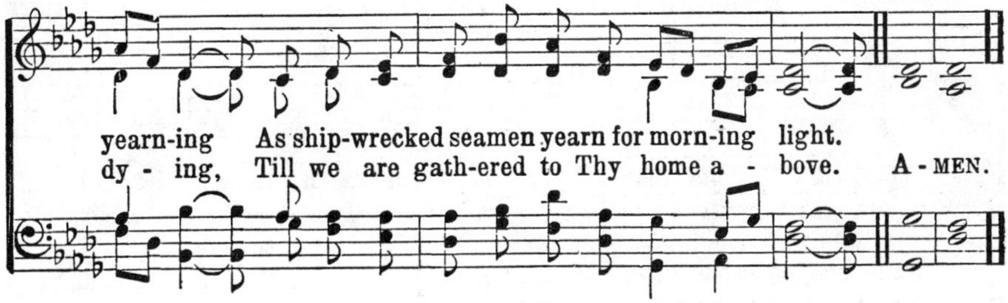

yearn-ing As ship-wrecked seamen yearn for morn-ing light.
dy-ing, Till we are gath-ered to Thy home a-bove. A-MEN.

26 O For A Closer Walk With God

NAOMI. C. M.

WILLIAM COWPER, 1731–1800 HANS G. NÄGELI, 1768–1836

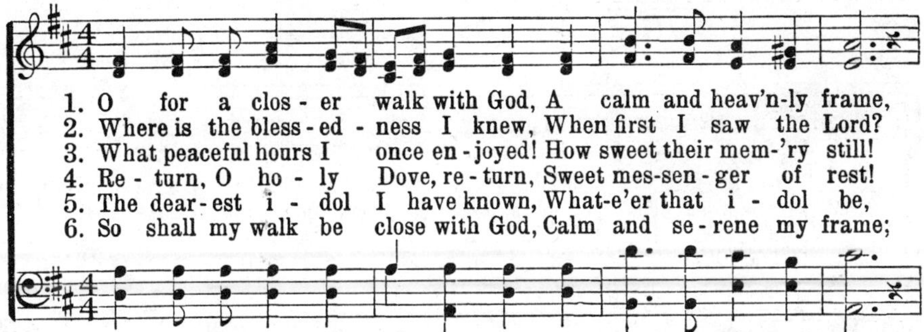

1. O for a clos-er walk with God, A calm and heav'n-ly frame,
2. Where is the bless-ed-ness I knew, When first I saw the Lord?
3. What peaceful hours I once en-joyed! How sweet their mem-'ry still!
4. Re-turn, O ho-ly Dove, re-turn, Sweet mes-sen-ger of rest!
5. The dear-est i-dol I have known, What-e'er that i-dol be,
6. So shall my walk be close with God, Calm and se-rene my frame;

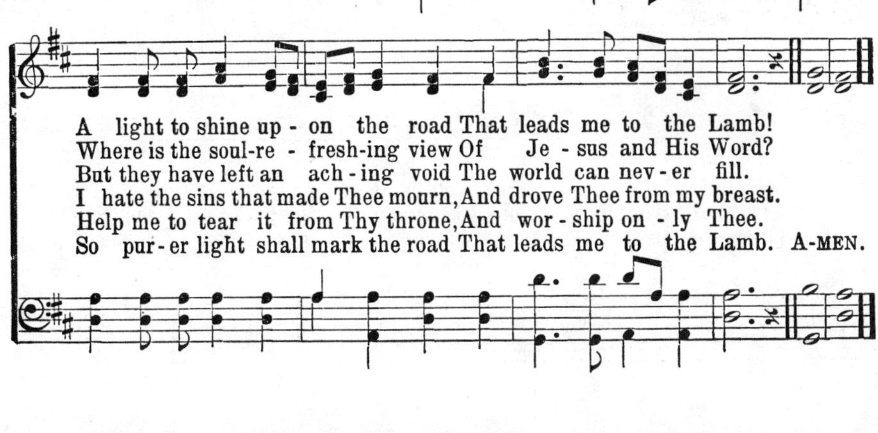

A light to shine up-on the road That leads me to the Lamb!
Where is the soul-re-fresh-ing view Of Je-sus and His Word?
But they have left an ach-ing void The world can nev-er fill.
I hate the sins that made Thee mourn, And drove Thee from my breast.
Help me to tear it from Thy throne, And wor-ship on-ly Thee.
So pur-er light shall mark the road That leads me to the Lamb. A-MEN.

27 Alas! And Did My Savior Bleed?

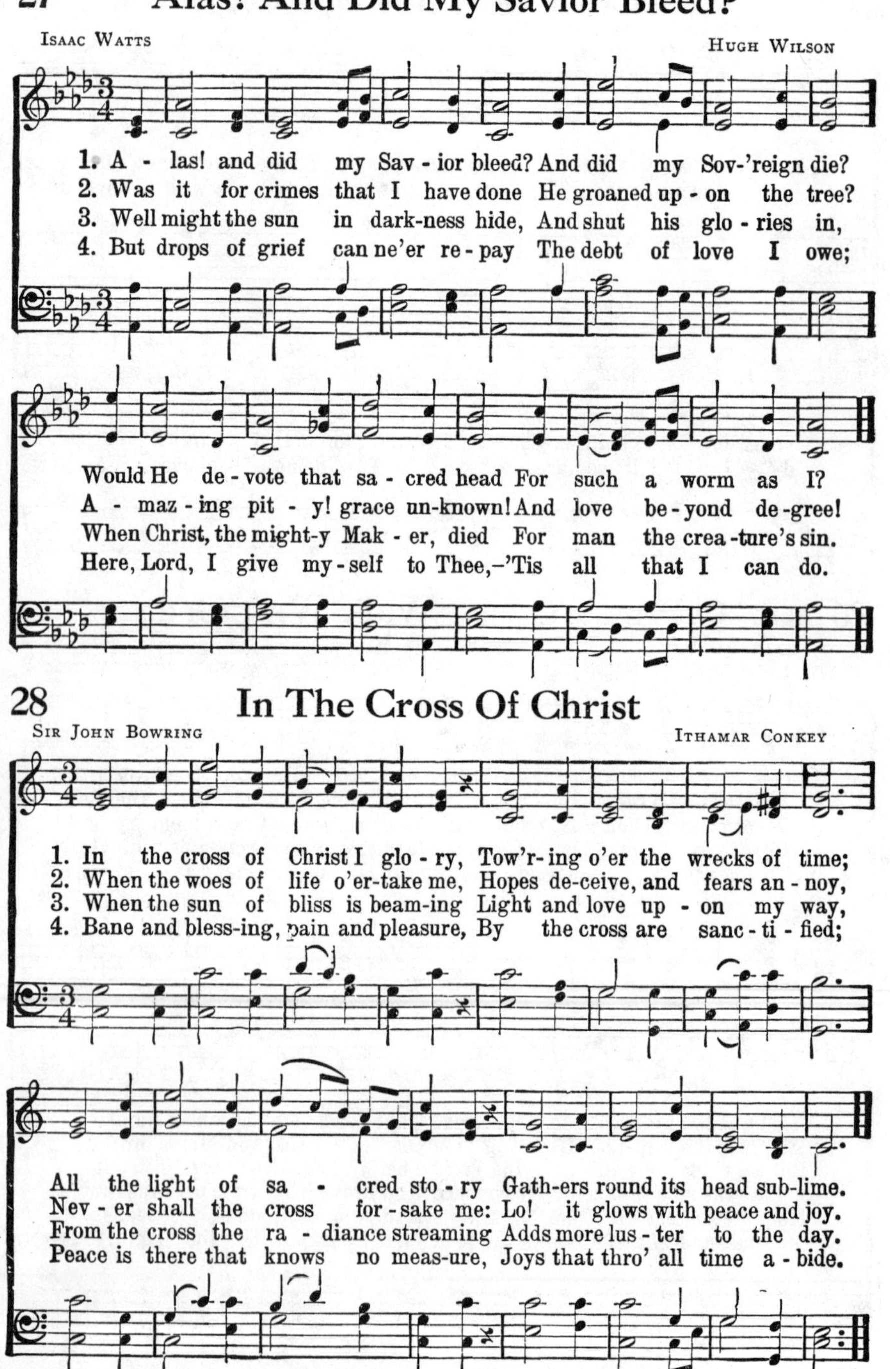
Isaac Watts
Hugh Wilson
1. A - las! and did my Sav - ior bleed? And did my Sov-'reign die?
2. Was it for crimes that I have done He groaned up - on the tree?
3. Well might the sun in dark-ness hide, And shut his glo - ries in,
4. But drops of grief can ne'er re - pay The debt of love I owe;
Would He de - vote that sa - cred head For such a worm as I?
A - maz - ing pit - y! grace un-known! And love be - yond de - gree!
When Christ, the might-y Mak - er, died For man the crea - ture's sin.
Here, Lord, I give my - self to Thee,–'Tis all that I can do.
28 In The Cross Of Christ
Sir John Bowring
Ithamar Conkey
1. In the cross of Christ I glo - ry, Tow'r-ing o'er the wrecks of time;
2. When the woes of life o'er-take me, Hopes de-ceive, and fears an - noy,
3. When the sun of bliss is beam-ing Light and love up - on my way,
4. Bane and bless-ing, pain and pleasure, By the cross are sanc - ti - fied;
All the light of sa - cred sto - ry Gath-ers round its head sub-lime.
Nev - er shall the cross for - sake me: Lo! it glows with peace and joy.
From the cross the ra - diance streaming Adds more lus - ter to the day.
Peace is there that knows no meas-ure, Joys that thro' all time a - bide.

29

Beneath The Cross Of Jesus

Elizabeth C. Clephane — Frederick C. Maker

1. Be-neath the cross of Je - sus I fain would take my stand,
2. Up - on that cross of Je - sus Mine eye at times can see
3. I take, O cross, thy shad - ow For my a - bid - ing place;
The shad - ow of a might - y rock With - in a wea - ry land;
The ver - y dy - ing form of One Who suf - fered there for me;
I ask no oth - er sun-shine than The sun - shine of His face;
A home with - in the wil - der - ness, A rest up - on the way.
And from my smit - ten heart with tears Two won - ders I con - fess,—
Con - tent to let the world go by, To know no gain or loss.
From the burning of the noon-tide heat, And the bur-den of the day.
The won - ders of His glo-rious love And my un-wor - thi - ness.
My sin - ful self my on - ly shame, My glo - ry all the cross.

30

The Old Rugged Cross

Geo. Bennard
Geo. Bennard
1. On a hill far a-way stood an old rug-ged cross, The em-blem of
2. Oh, that old rug-ged cross so de-spised by the world, Has a wondrous at-
3. In the old rug-ged cross, stained with blood so di-vine, A won-drous
4. To the old rug-ged cross I will ev-er be true, Its shame and re-
suf-f'ring and shame; And I love that old cross where the dear-est and best
trac-tion for me; For the dear Lamb of God left His glo-ry a-bove,
beau-ty I see; For 'twas on that old cross Je-sus suf-fered and died,
proach gladly bear; Then He'll call me some day to my home far a-way,
For a world of lost sin-ners was slain.
To bear it to dark Cal-va-ry.
To par-don and sanc-ti-fy me.
Where His glo-ry for-ev-er I'll share.
Chorus
So I'll cher-ish the old rug-ged cross, the
cross, ... Till my tro-phies at last I lay down; I will cling to the
old rugged cross,
old rug-ged cross, ... And ex-change it some day for a crown.
cross, the old rug-ged cross,

31 The Christ Of The Cross

F. C. H. FRANK C. HUSTON

Slowly, tenderly
1. On Cal - va-ry's brow there was plant-ed a cross, Which lift - ed a
2. They knew not their deeds of that one might-y hour, "O Fa - ther, for-
3. Let oth - ers, who will, praise the cross of the Christ, The Christ of the
Inst.
man up to shame; But He on the cross was the dear Son of God,
give them," He cried; They knew not the cross, long the em - blem of shame,
cross, is my theme; For tho' we must cher-ish the old rug-ged cross,
Who died a lost world to re - claim.
Was there by the Christ glo-ri - fied.
'Tis on - ly the Christ can re - deem.
CHORUS f
The Christ of the cross is the
ff
f
theme of my song, The won-der-ful Christ of the cross. He a-tone-ment has
ff
dim. rall.
made; He my ran-som has paid, So I'll praise Him, {The My} Christ of the cross.

32 When I Survey The Wondrous Cross

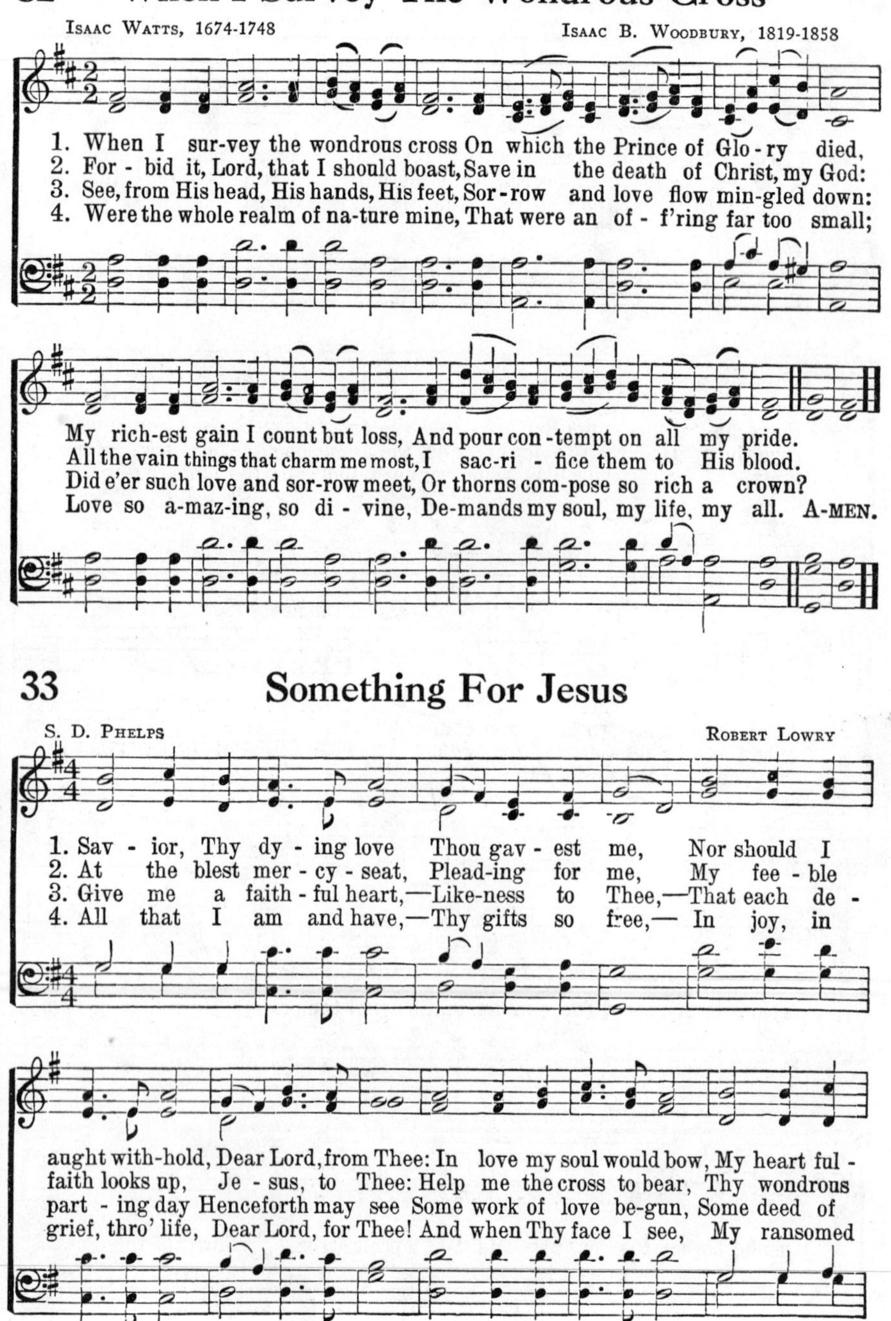
ISAAC WATTS, 1674-1748
ISAAC B. WOODBURY, 1819-1858
1. When I sur-vey the wondrous cross On which the Prince of Glo-ry died,
2. For - bid it, Lord, that I should boast, Save in the death of Christ, my God:
3. See, from His head, His hands, His feet, Sor-row and love flow min-gled down:
4. Were the whole realm of na-ture mine, That were an of - f'ring far too small;
My rich-est gain I count but loss, And pour con-tempt on all my pride.
All the vain things that charm me most, I sac-ri - fice them to His blood.
Did e'er such love and sor-row meet, Or thorns com-pose so rich a crown?
Love so a-maz-ing, so di - vine, De-mands my soul, my life, my all. A-MEN.
33 Something For Jesus
S. D. PHELPS
ROBERT LOWRY
1. Sav - ior, Thy dy - ing love Thou gav - est me, Nor should I
2. At the blest mer - cy - seat, Plead-ing for me, My fee - ble
3. Give me a faith - ful heart,—Like-ness to Thee,—That each de -
4. All that I am and have,—Thy gifts so free,— In joy, in
aught with-hold, Dear Lord, from Thee: In love my soul would bow, My heart ful -
faith looks up, Je - sus, to Thee: Help me the cross to bear, Thy wondrous
part - ing day Henceforth may see Some work of love be-gun, Some deed of
grief, thro' life, Dear Lord, for Thee! And when Thy face I see, My ransomed

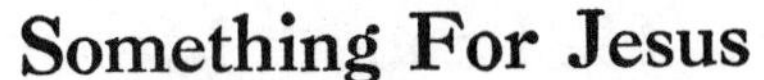

Something For Jesus

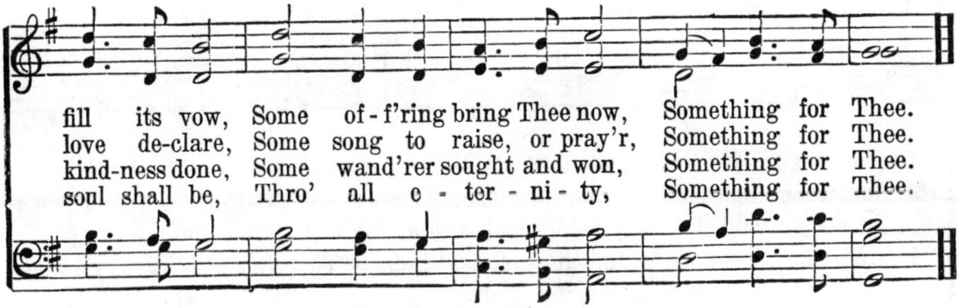

fill its vow, Some of-f'ring bring Thee now, Something for Thee.
love de-clare, Some song to raise, or pray'r, Something for Thee.
kind-ness done, Some wand'rer sought and won, Something for Thee.
soul shall be, Thro' all e-ter-ni-ty, Something for Thee.

34 Near The Cross

FANNY J. CROSBY | W. H. DOANE

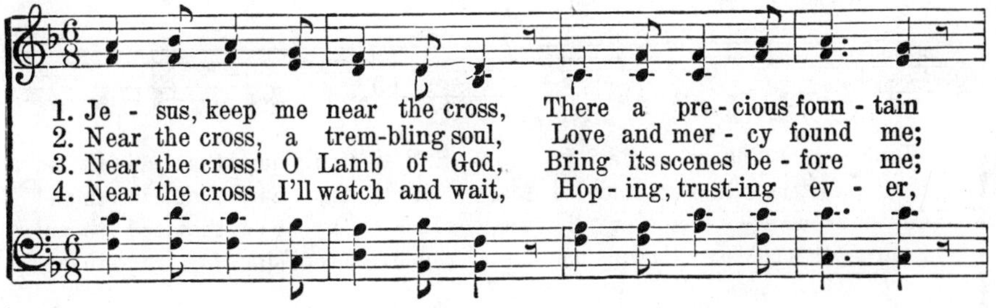

1. Je-sus, keep me near the cross, There a pre-cious foun-tain
2. Near the cross, a trem-bling soul, Love and mer-cy found me;
3. Near the cross! O Lamb of God, Bring its scenes be-fore me;
4. Near the cross I'll watch and wait, Hop-ing, trust-ing ev-er,

Free to all— a heal-ing stream, Flows from Cal-v'ry's moun-tain.
There the Bright and Morn-ing Star Sheds its beams a-round me.
Help me walk from day to day, With its shad-ows o'er me.
Till I reach the gold-en strand, Just be-yond the riv-er.

CHORUS

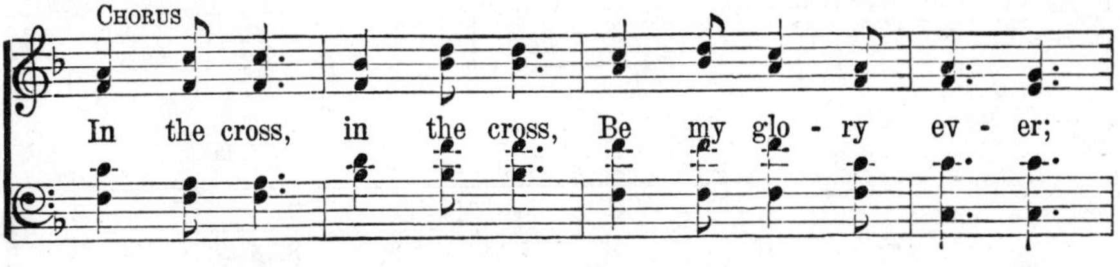

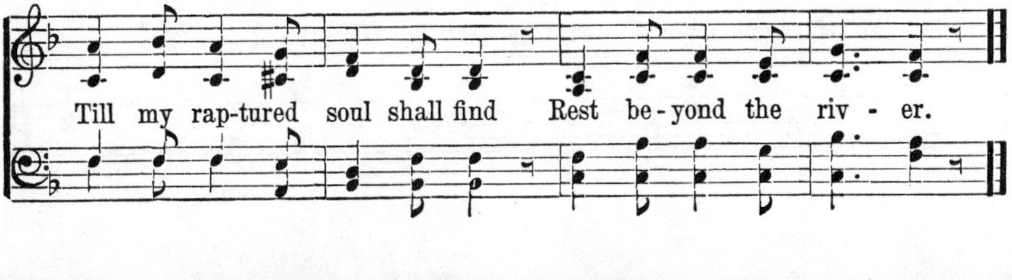

In the cross, in the cross, Be my glo-ry ev-er;
Till my rap-tured soul shall find Rest be-yond the riv-er.

35 He Leadeth Me

JOSEPH H. GILMORE — WILLIAM B. BRADBURY

1. He lead-eth me! O bless-ed tho't! O words with heav'nly comfort fraught!
2. Sometimes 'mid scenes of deepest gloom, Some-times where E-den's bowers bloom.
3. Lord, I would clasp Thy hand in mine, Nor ev - er mur - mur nor re-pine,
4. And when my task on earth is done, When, by Thy grace, the vic-t'ry's won,
What-e'er I do, wher-e'er I be, Still 'tis God's hand that lead-eth me.
By wa - ters still, o'er troub-led sea,— Still 'tis His hand that lead-eth me!
Con - tent, what-ev - er lot I see, Since 'tis my God that lead-eth me!
E'en death's cold wave I will not flee, Since God thro' Jor - dan lead-eth me.
REFRAIN
He lead - eth me, He lead - eth me, By His own hand He lead - eth me:
His faith-ful fol - lower I would be, For by His hand He lead-eth me.

36 Holy Quietness

M. P. Ferguson
Arr. from W. S. Marshall
1. Joys are flow-ing like a riv - er, Since the Com-fort - er has come;
2. Spring-ing in - to life and gladness, All a-round this glorious Guest,
3. Like a rain that falls from heav-en, Like the sun-light from the sky,
4. What a won-der - ful sal - va - tion, Where we al - ways see His face!
He a - bides with us for - ev - er, Makes the trust-ing heart His home.
Ban-ished un - be - lief and sad-ness, And we just o - bey and trust.
So the Ho - ly Ghost is giv - en, Com - ing on us from on high.
What a peaceful hab - i - ta - tion, What a qui - et rest-ing place.
Chorus
Blessed qui - et-ness, ho - ly qui-et-ness, What as - sur - ance in my soul;
On the storm-y sea, Speaking peace to me, How the bil-lows cease to roll.

37 O For A Thousand Tongues

AZMON
Charles Wesley
Carl G. Glaser
Arr. by Lowell Mason
1. O for a thou-sand tongues to sing My great Re-deem-er's praise, The glo-ries of my God and King, The triumphs of His grace.
2. My gracious Mas-ter and my God, As-sist me to pro-claim, To spread thro' all the earth a-broad The hon-ors of Thy name.
3. Je-sus! the name that charms our fears, That bids our sor-rows cease; 'Tis mu-sic in the sin-ner's ears, 'Tis life, and health, and peace.
4. He breaks the pow'r of canceled sin, He sets the pris-'nor free; His blood can make the foul-est clean; His blood a-vailed for me.
5. Hear Him, ye deaf; His praise, ye dumb, Your loosened tongues em-ploy; Ye blind, be-hold your Sav-ior come; And leap, ye lame, for joy.
38 Take The Name Of Jesus With You
Mrs. Lydia Baxter
W. H. Doane
1. Take the name of Je-sus with you, Child of sor-row and of woe; It will joy and com-fort give you, Take it, then, where'er you go.
2. Take the name of Je-sus ev-er, As a shield from ev-'ry snare; If temp-ta-tions 'round you gath-er, Breathe that ho-ly name in pray'r.
3. O the precious name of Je-sus! How it thrills our souls with joy, When His lov-ing arms re-ceive us, And His songs our tongues employ!
4. At the name of Je-sus bow-ing, Fall-ing pros-trate at His feet, King of kings in heav'n we'll crown Him, When our jour-ney is com-plete.

Take The Name Of Jesus With You

CHORUS
Precious name, O how sweet! Hope of earth and joy of heav'n;
Precious name, O how sweet!
Precious name, O how sweet!. . . Hope of earth and joy of heav'n.
Precious name, O how sweet, how sweet!

39 In The Hour Of Trial

PENITENCE. 6, 5, 6, 5. D

JAMES MONTGOMERY, 1834 | SPENCER LANE, 1879

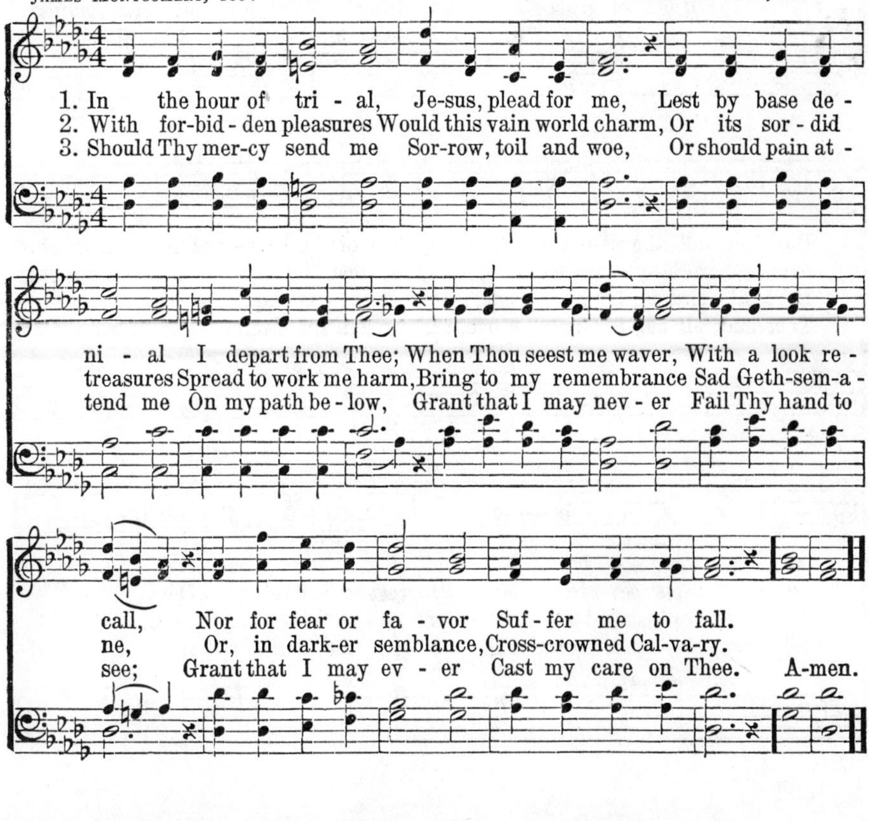

1. In the hour of tri - al, Je-sus, plead for me, Lest by base de - ni - al I depart from Thee; When Thou seest me waver, With a look re - call, Nor for fear or fa - vor Suf - fer me to fall.

2. With for-bid - den pleasures Would this vain world charm, Or its sor - did treasures Spread to work me harm, Bring to my remembrance Sad Geth-sem-a - ne, Or, in dark-er semblance, Cross-crowned Cal-va-ry.

3. Should Thy mer-cy send me Sor-row, toil and woe, Or should pain at - tend me On my path be - low, Grant that I may nev - er Fail Thy hand to see; Grant that I may ev - er Cast my care on Thee. A-men.

Safely Through Another Week

JOHN NEWTON

LOWELL MASON

1. Safe - ly through an - oth - er week God has brought us on our way;
2. While we pray for par-d'ning grace, Thro' the dear Re-deem-er's name,
3. Here we come Thy name to praise, Let us feel Thy pres-ence near;
4. May Thy gos - pel's joy - ful sound Con - quer sin - ners, com-fort saints;

Let us now a bless - ing seek, Wait - ing in His courts to - day;
Show Thy rec - on - cil - ed face; Take a - way our sin and shame:
May Thy glo - ry meet our eyes, While we in Thy house ap - pear:
Make the fruits of grace a - bound, Bring re - lief for all com - plaints:

Day of all the week the best, Em-blem of e - ter - nal rest: Day of
From our world-ly cares set free, May we rest this day in Thee: From our
Here af - ford us, Lord, a taste Of our ev - er - last - ing feast: Here af-
Thus may all our Sab-baths prove, Till we join the Church a - bove: Thus may

all the week the best, Em - blem of e - ter - nal rest.
world-ly cares set free, May we rest this day in Thee.
ford us, Lord, a taste Of our ev - er - last - ing feast.
all our Sab-baths prove, Till we join the Church a - bove. A - MEN.

41 We Gather Together

KREMSER. Irregular

Anonymous
Tr. by Theodore Baker
Netherland Folk Song, 1625
Arr. by Edward Kremser, 1838-1914
1. We gath - er to - geth - er to ask the Lord's bless - ing;
2. Be - side us to guide us, our God with us join - ing,
3. We all do ex - tol Thee, Thou Lead - er tri - um - phant,
He chas - tens and has - tens His will to make known;
Or - dain - ing, main - tain - ing His king - dom di - vine;
And pray that Thou still our De - fend - er wilt be.
The wick - ed op - press - ing now cease from dis - tress - ing,
So from the be - gin - ning the fight we were win - ning:
Let Thy con - gre - ga - tion es - cape trib - u - la - tion:
Sing prais - es to His Name: He for - gets not His own.
Thou, Lord, wast at our side, all glo - ry be Thine!
Thy Name be ev - er praised! O Lord, make us free! A - MEN.

Stanzas one and two in unison; stanza three in harmony

42 Father, I Stretch My Hands To Thee

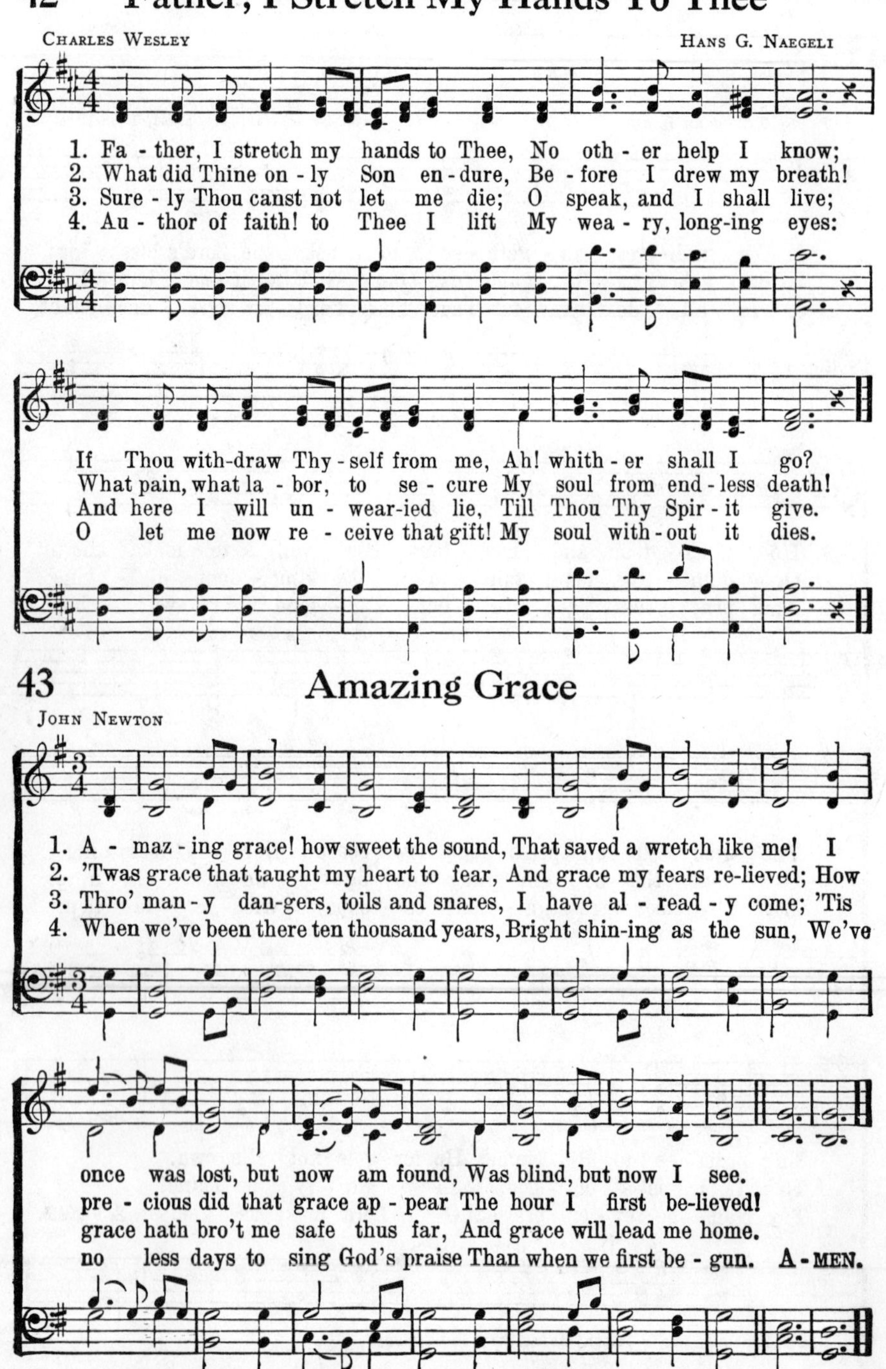

Charles Wesley
Hans G. Naegeli
1. Fa - ther, I stretch my hands to Thee, No oth - er help I know;
2. What did Thine on - ly Son en - dure, Be - fore I drew my breath!
3. Sure - ly Thou canst not let me die; O speak, and I shall live;
4. Au - thor of faith! to Thee I lift My wea - ry, long-ing eyes:
If Thou with-draw Thy - self from me, Ah! whith - er shall I go?
What pain, what la - bor, to se - cure My soul from end - less death!
And here I will un - wear-ied lie, Till Thou Thy Spir - it give.
O let me now re - ceive that gift! My soul with - out it dies.
43 Amazing Grace
John Newton
1. A - maz - ing grace! how sweet the sound, That saved a wretch like me! I
2. 'Twas grace that taught my heart to fear, And grace my fears re-lieved; How
3. Thro' man - y dan-gers, toils and snares, I have al - read - y come; 'Tis
4. When we've been there ten thousand years, Bright shin-ing as the sun, We've
once was lost, but now am found, Was blind, but now I see.
pre - cious did that grace ap - pear The hour I first be-lieved!
grace hath bro't me safe thus far, And grace will lead me home.
no less days to sing God's praise Than when we first be - gun. A - MEN.

44 Guide Me, O Thou Great Jehovah

WILLIAM WILLIAMS — THOMAS HASTINGS

1. Guide me, O Thou great Je - ho - vah, Pil - grim thro' this bar - ren
2. O - pen now the crys - tal fount - ain Whence the heal - ing wa - ters
3. When I tread the verge of Jor - dan, Bid my anx - ious fears sub -
land; I am weak, but Thou art might - y, Hold me with Thy pow'r-ful
flow; Let the fi - ery, cloud - y pil - lar Lead me all my jour - ney
side; Bear me thro' the swell - ing cur - rent, Land me safe on Ca-naan's
hand; Bread of heav - en, Feed me till I want no more;
thro'; Strong De - liv - 'rer, Be Thou still my Strength and Shield;
side: Songs of prais - es I will ev - er give to Thee;
Bread of heav - en, Feed me till I want no more.
Strong De - liv - 'rer, Be Thou still my Strength and Shield.
Songs of prais - es I will ev - er give to Thee.

45 Jesus Took My Burden

Rev. Johnson Oatman, Jr. — Bertha Mae Lillenas

1. When I, a poor, lost sin-ner, Be-fore the Lord did fall, And in the name of
2. Oft-times the way is drear-y, And rugged seems the road, Oft-times I'm weak and
3. When I was crushed with sorrow I bowed in deep de-spair, My load of grief and
4. I'll trust Him for the fu-ture, He know-eth all the way, For with His eye He'll
Je - sus For par-don loud did call; He heard my sup-pli-ca-tion, And
wea - ry, When bent beneath some load; But when I cry in weak-ness, "How
heart-ache Seemed more than I could bear; 'Twas then I heard a whis-per, "You
guide me A - long life's pil-grim way; And I will tell in heav-en, While
soon the weak was strong, For Je - sus took my bur-den, And left me with a song.
long, O Lord, how long?" Then Je-sus takes the bur-den, And leaves me with a song.
to the Lord be - long," Then Je-sus took my bur-den, And left me with a song.
a - ges roll a - long, How Je-sus took my bur-den, And left me with a song.
Chorus
Yes, Je - sus took my bur-den I could no lon - ger bear, Yes, Je-sus took my
bur-den In an - swer to my prayer; My anx-ious fears sub-sid-ed, My

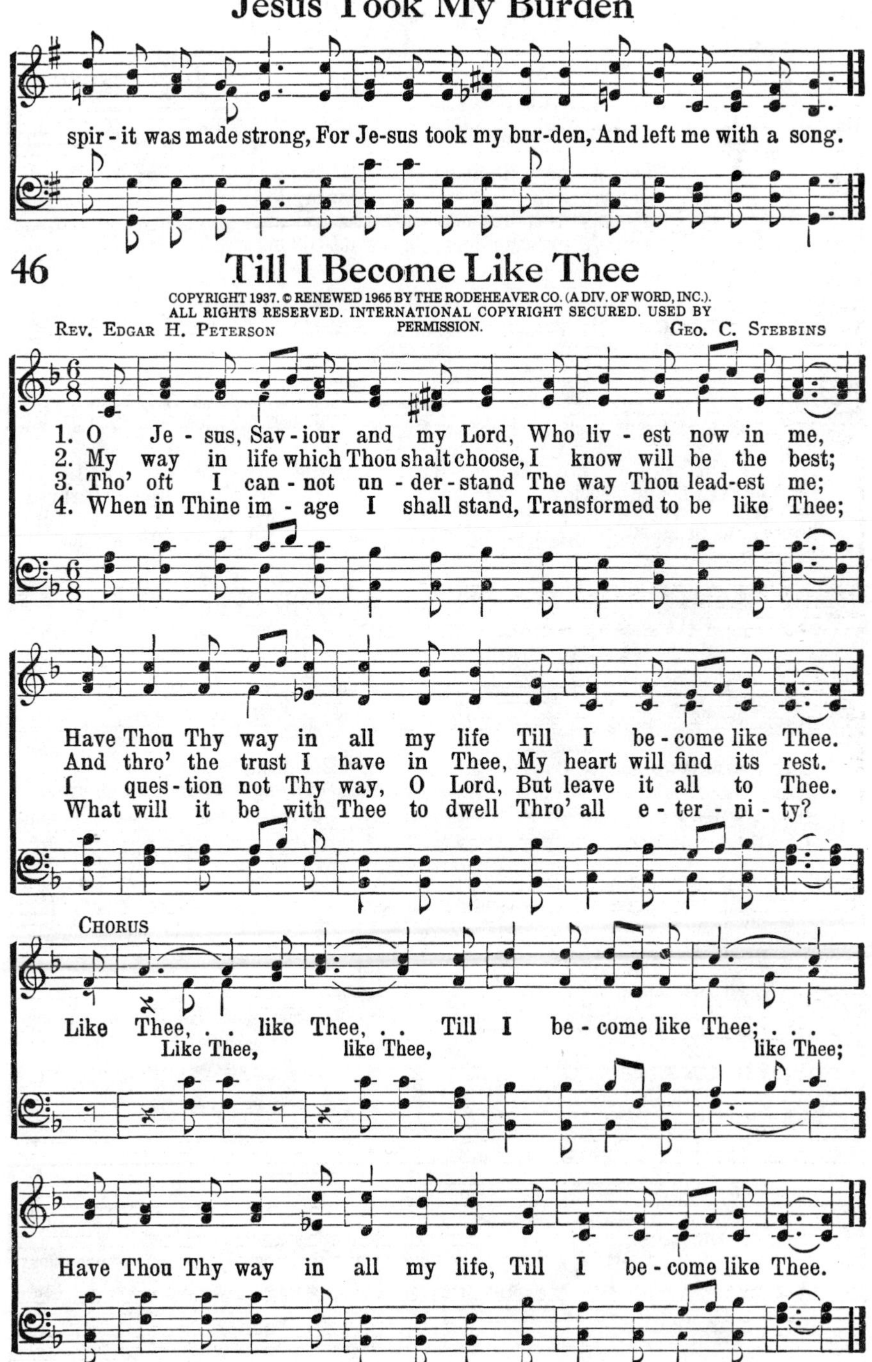
Jesus Took My Burden
spir - it was made strong, For Je-sus took my bur-den, And left me with a song.
46
Till I Become Like Thee
COPYRIGHT 1937. © RENEWED 1965 BY THE RODEHEAVER CO. (A DIV. OF WORD, INC.).
ALL RIGHTS RESERVED. INTERNATIONAL COPYRIGHT SECURED. USED BY PERMISSION.
Rev. Edgar H. Peterson
Geo. C. Stebbins
1. O Je - sus, Sav - iour and my Lord, Who liv - est now in me,
2. My way in life which Thou shalt choose, I know will be the best;
3. Tho' oft I can - not un - der - stand The way Thou lead-est me;
4. When in Thine im - age I shall stand, Transformed to be like Thee;
Have Thou Thy way in all my life Till I be - come like Thee.
And thro' the trust I have in Thee, My heart will find its rest.
I ques - tion not Thy way, O Lord, But leave it all to Thee.
What will it be with Thee to dwell Thro' all e - ter - ni - ty?
Chorus
Like Thee, . . like Thee, . . Till I be - come like Thee; . . .
Like Thee, like Thee, like Thee;
Have Thou Thy way in all my life, Till I be - come like Thee.

47 My Redeemer

P. P. Bliss
James McGranahan
1. I will sing of my Re-deem-er, And His won-drous love to me;
2. I will tell the won-drous sto-ry, How my lost es-tate to save,
3. I will praise my dear Re-deem-er, His tri-um-phant pow'r I'll tell,
4. I will sing of my Re-deem-er, And His heav'n-ly love to me;
On the cru-el cross He suf-fered, From the curse to set me free.
In His bound-less love and mer-cy, He the ran-som free-ly gave.
How the vic-to-ry He giv-eth O-ver sin, and death, and hell.
He from death to life hath bro't me, Son of God with Him to be.
Chorus
Sing, oh, sing . . . . of my Re-deem-er,
of my Re-deem-er, Sing, oh, sing of my Re-deem-er,
With His blood . . . . He pur-chased me, ...
He pur-chased me, With His blood He pur-chased me,
On the cross . . . . He sealed my par-don,
He sealed my par-don, On the cross He sealed my par-don,

My Redeemer

Paid the debt, ... and made me free. . . . . .
and made me free, and made me free.

48 How Firm A Foundation

George Keith

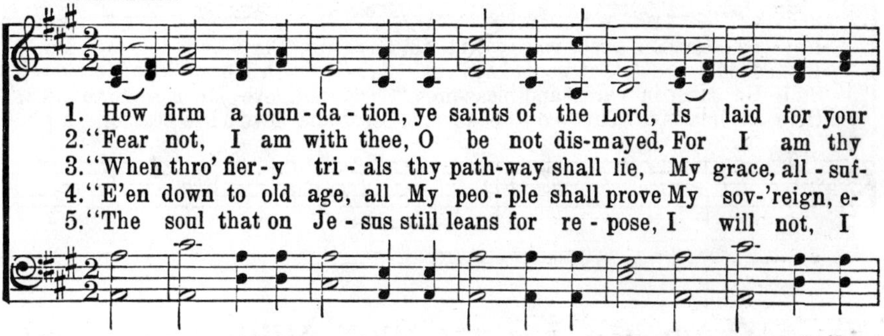

1. How firm a foun-da-tion, ye saints of the Lord, Is laid for your
2. "Fear not, I am with thee, O be not dis-mayed, For I am thy
3. "When thro' fier-y tri-als thy path-way shall lie, My grace, all-suf-
4. "E'en down to old age, all My peo-ple shall prove My sov-'reign, e-
5. "The soul that on Je-sus still leans for re-pose, I will not, I

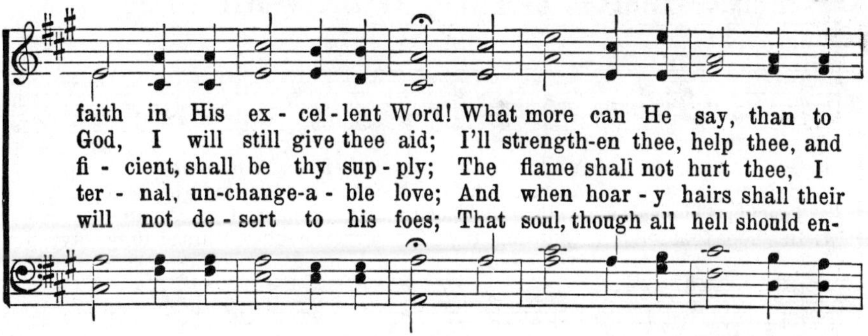

faith in His ex-cel-lent Word! What more can He say, than to
God, I will still give thee aid; I'll strength-en thee, help thee, and
fi-cient, shall be thy sup-ply; The flame shall not hurt thee, I
ter-nal, un-change-a-ble love; And when hoar-y hairs shall their
will not de-sert to his foes; That soul, though all hell should en-

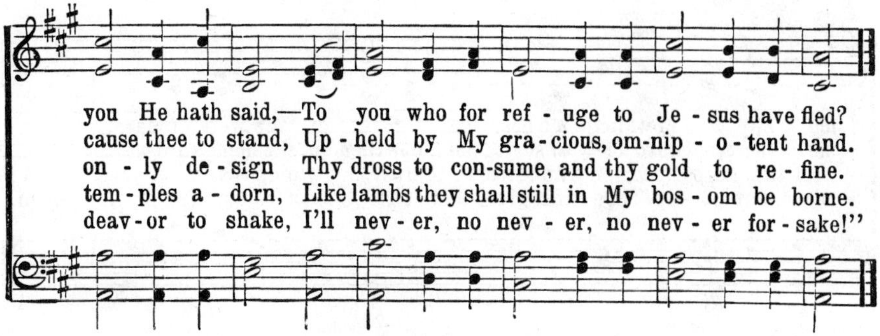

you He hath said,—To you who for ref-uge to Je-sus have fled?
cause thee to stand, Up-held by My gra-cious, om-nip-o-tent hand.
on-ly de-sign Thy dross to con-sume, and thy gold to re-fine.
tem-ples a-dorn, Like lambs they shall still in My bos-om be borne.
deav-or to shake, I'll nev-er, no nev-er, no nev-er for-sake!"

49 Jesus Calls Us

Mrs. Cecil F. Alexander — William H. Jude

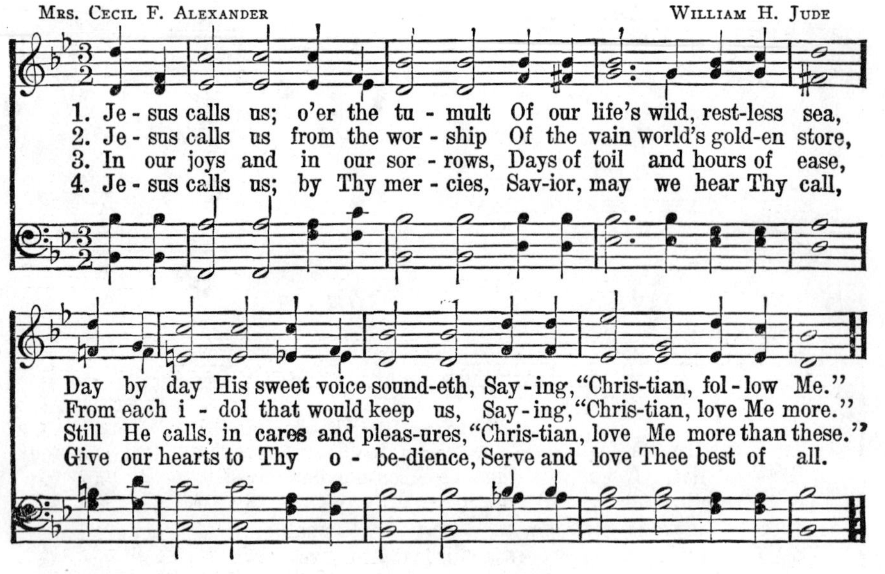
1. Je - sus calls us; o'er the tu - mult Of our life's wild, rest-less sea,
2. Je - sus calls us from the wor - ship Of the vain world's gold-en store,
3. In our joys and in our sor - rows, Days of toil and hours of ease,
4. Je - sus calls us; by Thy mer - cies, Sav-ior, may we hear Thy call,
Day by day His sweet voice sound-eth, Say - ing, "Chris-tian, fol - low Me."
From each i - dol that would keep us, Say - ing, "Chris-tian, love Me more."
Still He calls, in cares and pleas-ures, "Chris-tian, love Me more than these."
Give our hearts to Thy o - be-dience, Serve and love Thee best of all.

50 O Master, Let Me Walk With Thee

Washington Gladden — CANONBURY. L. M. — Robert Schumann

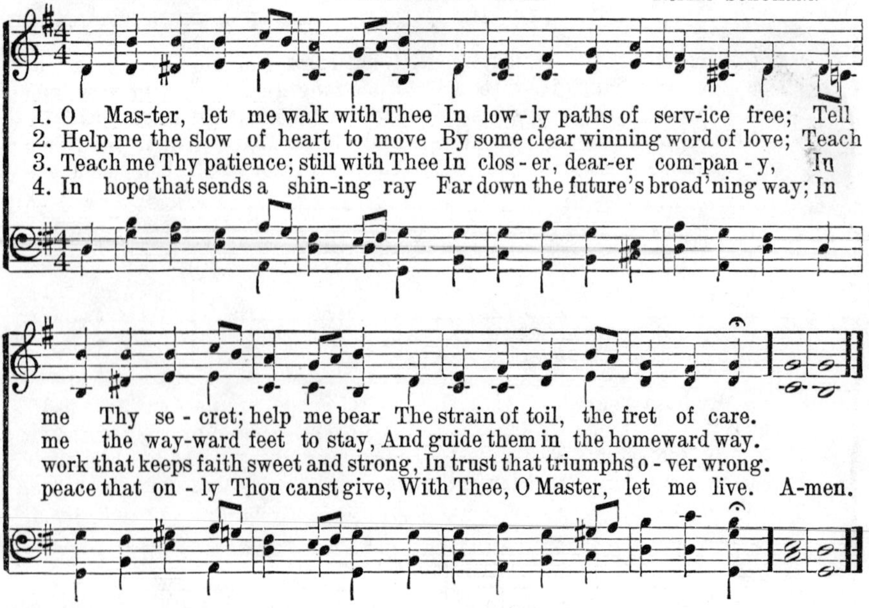

1. O Mas-ter, let me walk with Thee In low - ly paths of serv-ice free; Tell
2. Help me the slow of heart to move By some clear winning word of love; Teach
3. Teach me Thy patience; still with Thee In clos - er, dear-er com-pan - y, In
4. In hope that sends a shin-ing ray Far down the future's broad'ning way; In

me Thy se - cret; help me bear The strain of toil, the fret of care.
me the way-ward feet to stay, And guide them in the homeward way.
work that keeps faith sweet and strong, In trust that triumphs o - ver wrong.
peace that on - ly Thou canst give, With Thee, O Master, let me live. A-men.

51 Moment By Moment

D. W. Whittle
May Whittle Moody
1. Dy - ing with Je - sus, by death reckoned mine: Liv-ing with Je - sus, a
2. Nev - er a tri - al that He is not there, Nev-er a bur-den that
3. Nev - er a heartache, and nev - er a groan, Nev-er a teardrop and
4. Nev - er a weak-ness that He doth not feel, Nev-er a sickness that
new life di - vine; Looking to Je - sus till glo - ry doth shine, Mo-ment by
He doth not bear, Nev - er a sor-row that He doth not share, Mo-ment by
nev - er a moan; Nev - er a dan-ger but there on the throne, Mo-ment by
He can-not heal; Mo-ment by moment, in woe or in weal, Je - sus, my
mo-ment, O Lord, I am Thine.
mo-ment, I'm un - der His care.
mo-ment He thinks of His own.
Sav-ior, a-bides with me still.
Chorus
Mo-ment by mo-ment I'm kept in His love;
Mo-ment by moment I've life from a - bove; Looking to Je - sus till
glo - ry doth shine; Mo - ment by mo - ment, O Lord, I am Thine.

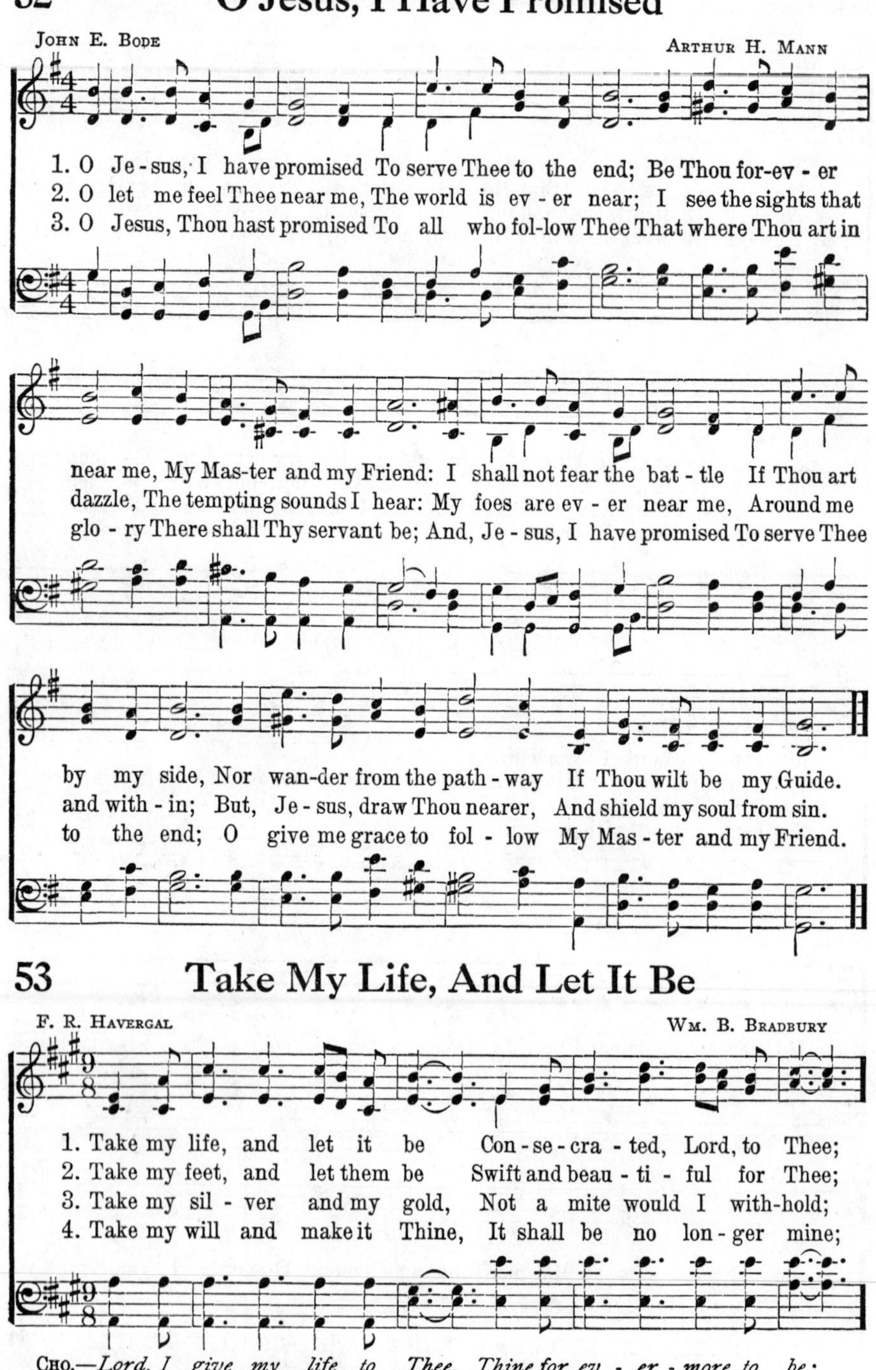
52 O Jesus, I Have Promised
John E. Bode
Arthur H. Mann
1. O Je-sus, I have promised To serve Thee to the end; Be Thou for-ev-er
2. O let me feel Thee near me, The world is ev-er near; I see the sights that
3. O Jesus, Thou hast promised To all who fol-low Thee That where Thou art in
near me, My Mas-ter and my Friend: I shall not fear the bat-tle If Thou art
dazzle, The tempting sounds I hear: My foes are ev-er near me, Around me
glo-ry There shall Thy servant be; And, Je-sus, I have promised To serve Thee
by my side, Nor wan-der from the path-way If Thou wilt be my Guide.
and with-in; But, Je-sus, draw Thou nearer, And shield my soul from sin.
to the end; O give me grace to fol-low My Mas-ter and my Friend.
53 Take My Life, And Let It Be
F. R. Havergal
Wm. B. Bradbury
1. Take my life, and let it be Con-se-cra-ted, Lord, to Thee;
2. Take my feet, and let them be Swift and beau-ti-ful for Thee;
3. Take my sil-ver and my gold, Not a mite would I with-hold;
4. Take my will and make it Thine, It shall be no lon-ger mine;
Cho.—Lord, I give my life to Thee, Thine for ev-er-more to be;

Take My Life, And Let It Be
D. C.
Take my hands, and let them move At the im-pulse of Thy love.
Take my voice, and let me sing Always, on - ly for my King.
Take my mo-ments and my days, Let them flow in ceaseless praise.
Take my heart, it is Thine own, It shall be Thy roy - al throne. A-men.
Lord, I give my life to Thee, Thine for ev - er-more to be.
54
I Need Thee Every Hour
Mrs. Annie S. Hawks
Rev. Robert Lowry
1. I need Thee ev - 'ry hour, Most gra - cious Lord; No ten - der voice like
2. I need Thee ev - 'ry hour, Stay Thou near by; Temp-ta-tions lose their
3. I need Thee ev - 'ry hour, In joy or pain; Come quick-ly and a-
4. I need Thee ev - 'ry hour, Most Ho - ly One; O make me Thine in-
Chorus
Thine Can peace af - ford.
pow'r When Thou art nigh. I need Thee, O I need Thee; Ev - 'ry hour I
bide, Or life is vain.
deed, Thou bless-ed Son!
need Thee! O bless me now, my Sav - ior, I come to Thee!

55 Savior, More Than Life

Fanny J. Crosby
W. H. Doane
1. Sav - ior, more than life to me, I am cling-ing, cling-ing close to Thee;
2. Thro' this chang-ing world be-low, Lead me gen - tly, gen - tly as I go;
3. Let me love Thee more and more, Till this fleet-ing, fleet-ing life is o'er;
Fine
Let Thy pre-cious blood ap - plied, Keep me ev - er, ev - er near Thy side.
Trusting Thee, I can-not stray, I can nev - er, nev - er lose my way.
Till my soul is lost in love, In a bright-er, bright-er world a - bove.
D. S.—May Thy ten - der love to me Bind me clo - ser, clo - ser, Lord, to Thee.
Refrain
D. S.
Ev - 'ry day, ev - 'ry hour, Let me feel Thy cleans-ing pow'r;
Ev - 'ry day and hour, ev - 'ry day and hour,
56 Must Jesus Bear The Cross Alone?
Thos. Shepherd
Geo. N. Allen
1. Must Je - sus bear the cross a - lone, And all the world go free?
2. How hap - py are the saints a - bove, Who once went sor-rowing here!
3. The con - se - cra - ted cross I'll bear, Till death shall set me free;
4. Up - on the crys - tal pave-ment, down, At Je - sus' pierc - ed feet,

Must Jesus Bear The Cross Alone?
No, there's a cross for ev - 'ry one, And there's a cross for me.
But now they taste un - min - gled love, And joy with-out a tear.
And then go home my crown to wear, For there's a crown for me.
Joy - ful, I'll cast my gold - en crown, And His dear name re - peat.
57
Take Time To Be Holy
W. D. Longstaff
Geo. C. Stebbins
1. Take time to be ho - ly, Speak oft with thy Lord; A - bide in Him al - ways, And feed on His Word. Make friends of God's chil - dren; Help those who are weak; For - get-ting in noth-ing His bless-ing to seek.
2. Take time to be ho - ly, The world rush-es on; . . Spend much time in se - cret With Je - sus a - lone— By look - ing to Je - sus, Like Him thou shalt be; . . Thy friends in thy con-duct His likeness shall see. .
3. Take time to be ho - ly, Let Him be thy Guide, And run not be-fore Him, What - ev - er be - tide; . . In joy or in sor - row, Still fol - low thy Lord, And, look-ing to Je - sus, Still trust in His Word.
4. Take time to be ho - ly, Be calm in thy soul; . Each tho't and each mo - tive Be - neath His con - trol; . . Thus led by His Spir - it To foun-tains of love, Thou soon shalt be fit - ted For serv- ice a - bove.

58 O Master Workman Of The Race

ST. MICHEL'S. C. M. D.

USED BY PERMISSION OF THE PILGRIM PRESS.

JAY T. STOCKING, 1870- FROM W. GAWLER'S HYMNS AND PSALMS, 1789

1. O Mas - ter Work-man of the race, Thou Man of Gal - i - lee,
2. O Car - pen - ter of Naz - a - reth, Build - er of life di - vine,
3. O Thou who dost the vi - sion send And giv - est each his task,
Who with the eyes of ear - ly youth E - ter - nal things did see:
Who shap - est man to God's own law, Thy - self the fair de - sign:
And with the task suf - fi - cient strength: Show us Thy will, we ask;
We thank Thee for Thy boy - hood faith That shone Thy whole life through;
Build us a tower of Christ-like height, That we the land may view,
Give us a con-science bold and good; Give us a pur - pose true,
"Did ye not know it is my work My Fa - ther's work to do?"
And see, like Thee, our no - blest work Our Fa - ther's work to do.
That it may be our high - est joy, Our Fa - ther's work to do. A-MEN.

59 I Walk With The King

COPYRIGHT 1915 BY HOMER A. RODEHEAVER. © RENEWED, 1943, THE RODEHEAVER CO. (A DIV. OF WORD, INC.). ALL RIGHTS RESERVED. INTERNATIONAL COPYRIGHT SECURED. USED BY PERMISSION.
JAMES ROWE
B. D. ACKLEY
1. In sor-row I wan-dered, my spir-it op-prest, But now I am hap-py—se-cure-ly I rest; From morn-ing till eve-ning glad car-ols I sing, And this is the rea-son—I walk with the King.
2. For years in the fet-ters of sin I was bound, The world could not help me—no com-fort I found; But now like the birds and the sunbeams of spring, I'm free and re-joic-ing—I walk with the King.
3. O soul near de-spair in the low-lands of strife, Look up and let Je-sus come in-to your life; The joy of sal-va-tion to you He would bring—Come in-to the sun-light and walk with the King.
CHORUS
I walk with the King, hal-le-lu-jah! I walk with the King, praise His name! No lon-ger I roam, my soul fa-ces home, I walk and I talk with the King.

60 More Like The Master

C. H. G.
Chas. H. Gabriel
1. More like the Mas-ter I would ev - er be, More of His meek-ness,
2. More like the Mas-ter is my dai - ly prayer; More strength to car-ry
3. More like the Mas-ter I would live and grow; More of His love to
more hu - mil - i - ty; More zeal to la - bor, more cour-age to be true,
cross - es I must bear; More ear-nest ef - fort to bring His kingdom in;
oth - ers I would show; More self-de - ni - al, like His in Gal - i - lee,
rit.
Chorus.
More con - se - cra - tion for work He bids me do. . . . . . Take Thou my
More of His Spir - it, the wan-der - er to win. . . . .
More like the Mas - ter I long to ev - er be. . . . . Take my heart, O
heart, . . I would be Thine a - lone; . . Take Thou my heart . . and
take my heart, I would be Thine a-lone; Take my heart, O take my heart and
make it all Thine own; . . Purge me from sin, . . . O Lord, I now im-
make it all Thine own; Purge Thou me from ev'ry sin, O Lord, I

More Like The Master

plore, ... Wash me and keep . . . . me Thine for-ev - er - more.
now im-plore, Wash and keep, O wash and keep me Thine for-ev - er - more.

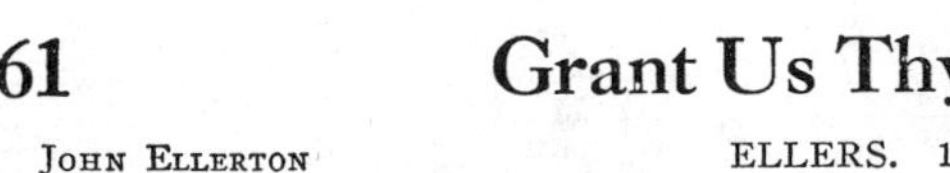

61 Grant Us Thy Peace

JOHN ELLERTON — ELLERS. 10s — EDWARD J. HOPKINS

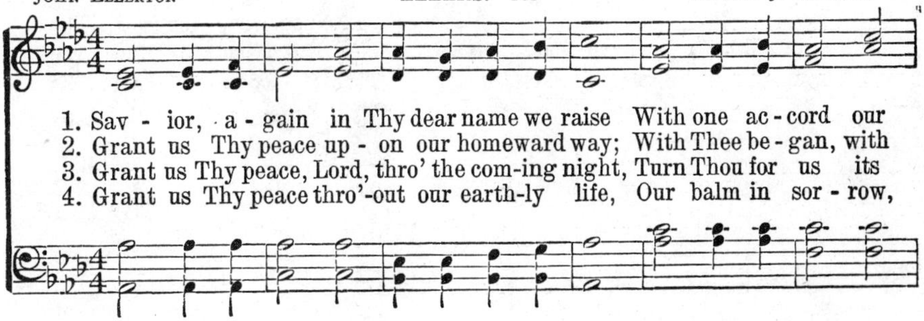

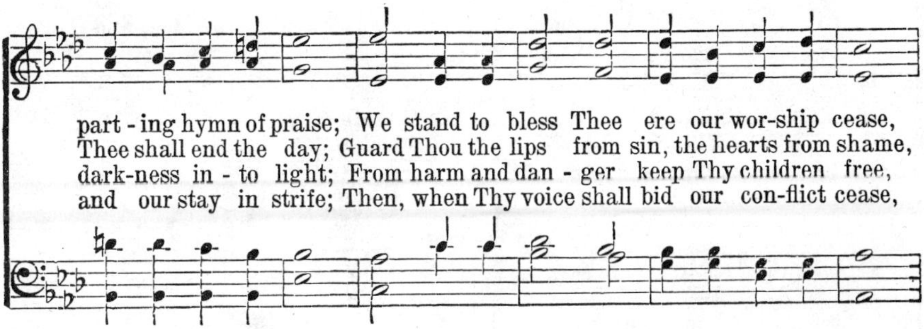

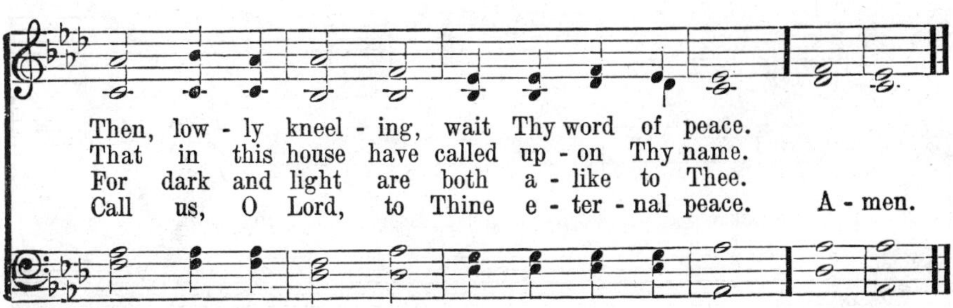

1. Sav - ior, a - gain in Thy dear name we raise With one ac - cord our part - ing hymn of praise; We stand to bless Thee ere our wor-ship cease, Then, low - ly kneel - ing, wait Thy word of peace.

2. Grant us Thy peace up - on our homeward way; With Thee be - gan, with Thee shall end the day; Guard Thou the lips from sin, the hearts from shame, That in this house have called up - on Thy name.

3. Grant us Thy peace, Lord, thro' the com-ing night, Turn Thou for us its dark-ness in - to light; From harm and dan - ger keep Thy children free, For dark and light are both a - like to Thee.

4. Grant us Thy peace thro'-out our earth-ly life, Our balm in sor - row, and our stay in strife; Then, when Thy voice shall bid our con-flict cease, Call us, O Lord, to Thine e - ter - nal peace. A - men.

62 In The Garden

C. A. M. — C. Austin Miles

1. I come to the gar - den a - lone, While the dew is still on the
2. He speaks, and the sound of His voice Is so sweet the birds hush their
3. I'd stay in the gar - den with Him Tho' the night a - round me be
ros - es, And the voice I hear, Fall - ing on my ear, The
sing - ing, And the mel - o - dy That He gave to me, With-
fall - ing, But He bids me go; Thro' the voice of woe His
Son of God dis - clos - es.
in my heart is ring - ing.
voice to me is call - ing.
CHORUS
And He walks with me, and He
talks with me, And He tells me I am His own; And the
joy we share as we tar - ry there, None oth - er has ev - er known.

63 When The Whole World Lives For Him

W. C. Poole B. D. Ackley

1. When the whole world lives for Je - sus, When the whole world owns Him King, There will be a day of bless - ing That o- be - di - ence will bring.
2. When the whole world lives for Je - sus, And o - beys His ev - 'ry call, There will be a day of glad - ness When we crown Him Lord of all.
3. When the whole world lives for Je - sus, Let us work and haste that day, When each tribe and land and na - tion Glad - ly owns His rule and sway.
CHORUS
When the whole world lives for Him,
When the whole wide world shall live for Him,
When the whole world lives for Je - sus; Sin will flee a- way, bring the per - fect day, When the whole world lives for Him.

Blessed Assurance

FANNY J. CROSBY MRS. J. F. KNAPP

CHORUS
1. Bless-ed as-sur-ance, Je-sus is mine! Oh, what a fore-taste of glo-ry di-vine! Heir of sal-va-tion, pur-chase of God, Born of His Spir-it, washed in His blood.
2. Per-fect sub-mis-sion, per-fect de-light, Vi-sions of rap-ture now burst on my sight; An-gels de-scend-ing, bring from a-bove Ech-oes of mer-cy, whis-pers of love.
3. Per-fect sub-mis-sion, all is at rest, I in my Sav-ior am hap-py and blest; Watching and wait-ing, look-ing a-bove, Filled with His goodness, lost in His love.
This is my sto-ry, this is my song, Prais-ing my Sav-ior all the day long; This is my sto-ry, this is my song, Prais-ing my Sav-ior all the day long.

65 I Love To Tell The Story

KATHERINE HANKEY
WILLIAM G. FISCHER
1. I love to tell the story Of unseen things a - bove, Of Je - sus
2. I love to tell the sto - ry; More won-der - ful it seems Than all the
3. I love to tell the sto - ry; 'Tis pleas-ant to re - peat What seems each
4. I love to tell the sto - ry; For those who know it best Seem hun - ger -
and His glo - ry, Of Je - sus and His love, I love to tell the sto - ry,
gold - en fan-cies Of all my golden dreams. I love to tell the sto - ry,
time I tell it, More won-der-ful - ly sweet. I love to tell the sto - ry;
ing and thirsting To hear it like the rest. And when, in scenes of glo - ry,
Because I know 'tis true, It sat - is-fies my longings, As nothing else can do.
It did so much for me; And that is just the rea-son I tell it now to thee
For some have never heard The message of salvation From God's own holy word.
I sing the new, new song, 'Twill be the old, old story, That I have loved so long.
CHORUS
I love to tell the sto - ry! 'Twill be my theme in glo - ry
To tell the old, old sto - ry Of Je - sus and His love.

66 True-Hearted, Whole-Hearted

Frances R. Havergal
Geo. C. Stebbins
1. True-hearted, whole-hearted, faith-ful and loy - al, King of our lives, by Thy
2. True-hearted, whole-hearted, full - est al - le-giance Yielding henceforth to our
3. True-hearted, whole-hearted, Sav - ior all - glo-rious! Take Thy great pow-er and
grace we will be; Un-der the standard ex - alt - ed and roy - al, Strong in Thy
glo - ri - ous King; Val-iant en-deav-or and lov - ing o-be-dience, Free - ly and
reign there a - lone, O - ver our wills and af-fec-tions vic-to-rious, Free - ly sur-
Chorus
strength we will bat-tle for Thee.
joy - ous - ly now would we bring.
ren-dered and whol-ly Thine own.
Peal out the watch-word! si - lence it nev-er!
Peal out the watch-word! si - lence it nev-er!
Song of our spir-its, re - joic - ing and free; Peal out the watch-word!
Song of our spir - its, re - joic-ing and free; Peal out the watch-word!
loy - al for - ev - er, King of our lives, by Thy grace we will be.
loy - al for - ev - er, King of our lives, by Thy grace we will be.

67 Help Somebody To-day

Mrs. Frank A. Breck
Chas. H. Gabriel
1. Look all a-round you, find some one in need, Help some-bod-y to - day!
2. Man - y are wait-ing a kind, lov-ing word, Help some-bod-y to - day!
3. Man - y have bur-dens too heav - y to bear, Help some-bod-y to - day!
4. Some are dis-cour-aged and wear-y in heart, Help some-bod-y to - day!
Tho' it be lit - tle—a neigh-bor - ly deed—Help some-bod - y to - day!
Thou hast a mes-sage, O let it be heard, Help some-bod - y to - day!
Grief is the por - tion of some ev - 'ry-where, Help some-bod - y to - day!
Some one the jour-ney to Heaven should start, Help some-bod - y to - day!
Chorus.
Help some-bod - y to - day, . . Some-bod - y a - long life's way; . . Let
to-day,
home-ward way;
sorrow be ended, The friendless befriended, Oh, help somebody to-day! A - men.

Be Still, My Soul

FINLANDIA. 10. 10. 10. 10. 10. 10.

KATHARINA VON SCHLEGEL, 1697-?
Tr. by JANE L. BORTHWICK, 1813-1897

JEAN SIBELIUS, 1865-?
Arr. for THE HYMNAL, 1933

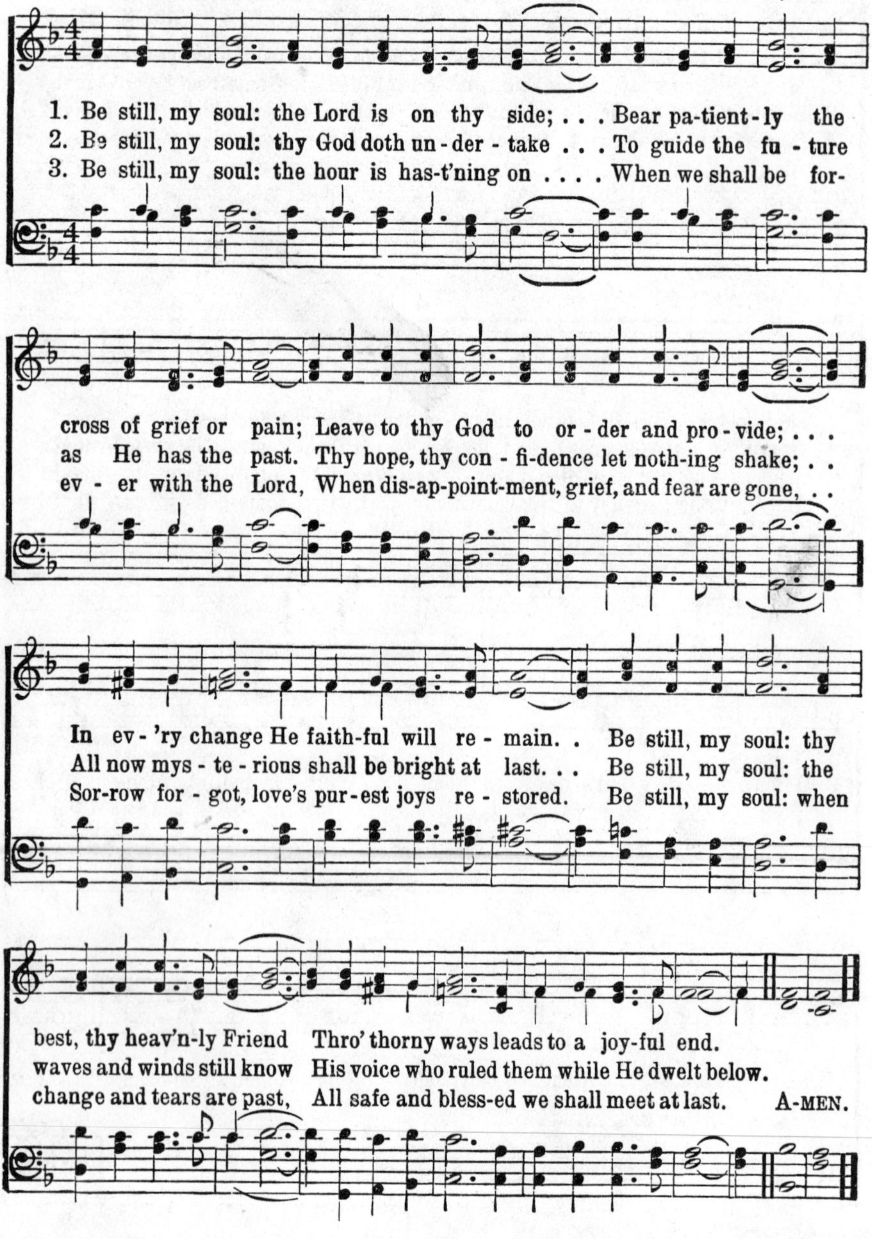

1. Be still, my soul: the Lord is on thy side; . . . Bear pa-tient-ly the
2. Be still, my soul: thy God doth un-der-take . . . To guide the fu-ture
3. Be still, my soul: the hour is has-t'ning on . . . . When we shall be for-

cross of grief or pain; Leave to thy God to or-der and pro-vide; . . .
as He has the past. Thy hope, thy con-fi-dence let noth-ing shake; . .
ev-er with the Lord, When dis-ap-point-ment, grief, and fear are gone, . .

In ev-'ry change He faith-ful will re-main. . Be still, my soul: thy
All now mys-te-rious shall be bright at last. . . Be still, my soul: the
Sor-row for-got, love's pur-est joys re-stored. Be still, my soul: when

best, thy heav'n-ly Friend Thro' thorny ways leads to a joy-ful end.
waves and winds still know His voice who ruled them while He dwelt below.
change and tears are past, All safe and bless-ed we shall meet at last. A-MEN.

69 Savior, Like A Shepherd Lead Us

DOROTHY ANN THRUPP
WILLIAM B. BRADBURY
1. Sav - ior, like a shep-herd lead us, Much we need Thy ten- der care;
2. We are Thine; do Thou be - friend us, Be the Guardian of our way;
3. Thou hast promised to re - ceive us, Poor and sin- ful though we be;
4. Ear - ly let us seek Thy fa - vor; Ear - ly let us do Thy will;
In Thy pleas-ant pas-tures feed us, For our use Thy folds pre-pare:
Keep Thy flock, from sin de - fend us, Seek us when we go a - stray:
Thou hast mer - cy to re - lieve us, Grace to cleanse, and pow'r to free:
Bless - ed Lord, and on - ly Sav - ior, With Thy love our bos- oms fill:
Bless-ed Je - sus, Bless-ed Je - sus, Thou hast bought us, Thine we are;
Bless-ed Je - sus, Bless-ed Je - sus, Hear Thy chil- dren when they pray;
Bless-ed Je - sus, Bless-ed Je - sus, Ear - ly let us turn to Thee;
Bless-ed Je - sus, Bless-ed Je - sus, Thou hast loved us, love us still;
Bless-ed Je - sus, Bless-ed Je - sus, Thou hast bought us, Thine we are.
Bless-ed Je - sus, Bless-ed Je - sus, Hear Thy chil-dren when they pray.
Bless-ed Je - sus, Bless-ed Je - sus, Ear - ly let us turn to Thee.
Bless-ed Je - sus, Bless-ed Je - sus, Thou hast loved us, love us still.

70 We May Not Climb The Heavenly Steeps

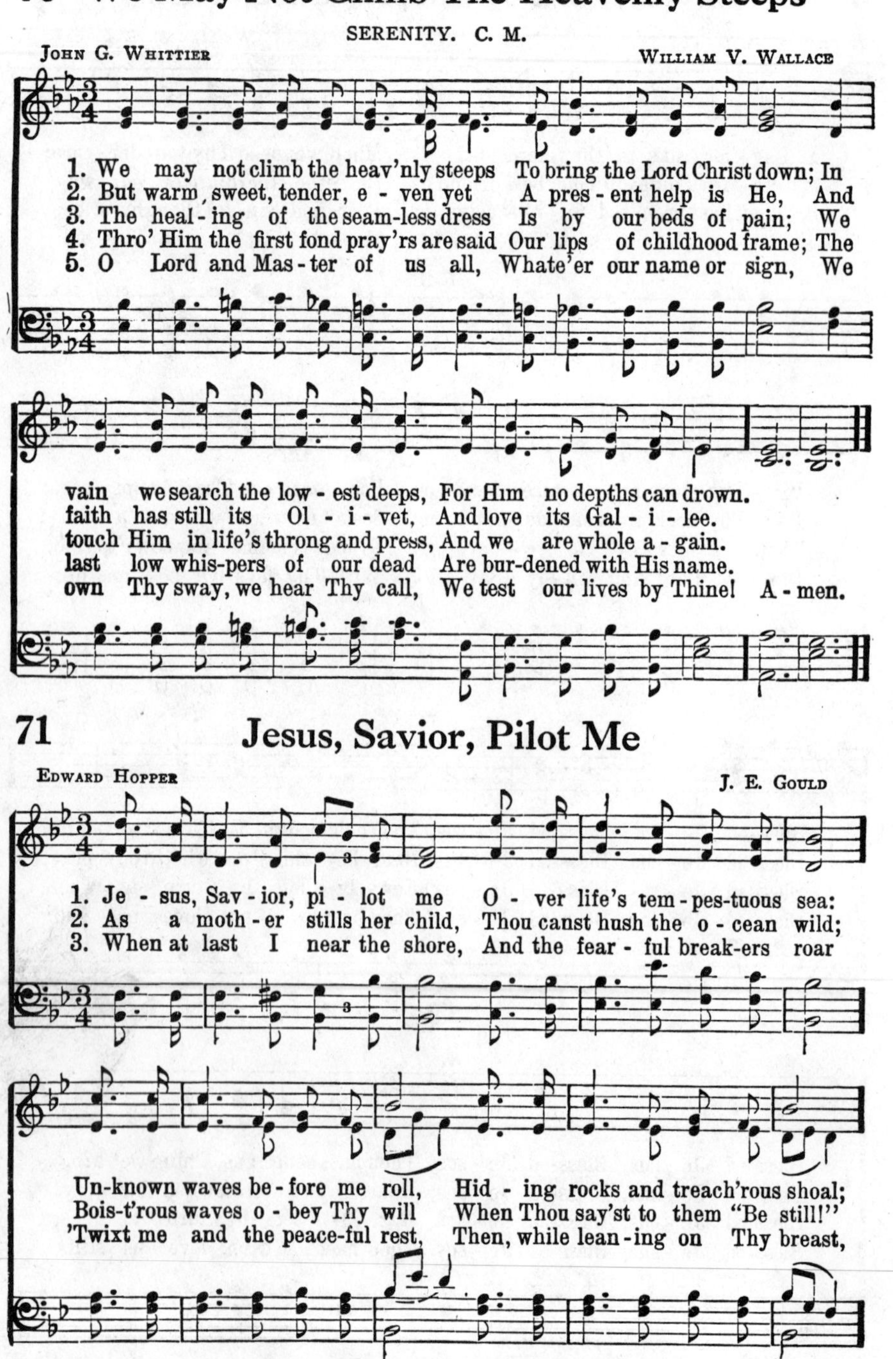
SERENITY. C. M.
John G. Whittier
William V. Wallace
1. We may not climb the heav'nly steeps To bring the Lord Christ down; In vain we search the low - est deeps, For Him no depths can drown.
2. But warm, sweet, tender, e - ven yet A pres - ent help is He, And faith has still its Ol - i - vet, And love its Gal - i - lee.
3. The heal - ing of the seam-less dress Is by our beds of pain; We touch Him in life's throng and press, And we are whole a - gain.
4. Thro' Him the first fond pray'rs are said Our lips of childhood frame; The last low whis-pers of our dead Are bur-dened with His name.
5. O Lord and Mas - ter of us all, Whate'er our name or sign, We own Thy sway, we hear Thy call, We test our lives by Thine! A - men.
71
Jesus, Savior, Pilot Me
Edward Hopper
J. E. Gould
1. Je - sus, Sav - ior, pi - lot me O - ver life's tem - pes-tuous sea: Un-known waves be - fore me roll, Hid - ing rocks and treach'rous shoal;
2. As a moth - er stills her child, Thou canst hush the o - cean wild; Bois-t'rous waves o - bey Thy will When Thou say'st to them "Be still!"
3. When at last I near the shore, And the fear - ful break-ers roar 'Twixt me and the peace-ful rest, Then, while lean - ing on Thy breast,

Jesus, Savior, Pilot Me

Chart and com - pass come from Thee, Je - sus, Sav - ior, pi - lot me.
Won - drous Sov-'reign of the sea, Je - sus, Sav - ior, pi - lot me.
May I hear Thee say to me, "Fear not, I will pi - lot thee."

72 Have Thine Own Way, Lord

A. A. P. — Geo. C. Stebbins

Slowly

1. Have Thine own way, Lord! Have Thine own way!.. Thou art the
2. Have Thine own way, Lord! Have Thine own way!.. Search me and
3. Have Thine own way, Lord! Have Thine own way!.. Wound-ed and
4. Have Thine own way, Lord! Have Thine own way!.. Hold o'er my

Pot - ter; I am the clay... Mould me and make me Aft - er Thy
try me, Mas-ter, to - day!... Whit - er than snow, Lord, Wash me just
wea - ry, Help me, I pray!. Pow - er—all pow - er—Sure - ly is
be - ing Ab - so - lute sway!. Fill with Thy Spir - it Till all shall

will,... While I am wait - ing, Yield - ed and still...
now,... As in Thy pres - ence Hum - bly I bow...
Thine! Touch me and heal me, Sav - ior di - vine!..
see.... Christ on - ly, al - ways, Liv - ing in me!....

73 Prayer Is The Soul's Sincere Desire

CAMPMEETING. C. M.

JAMES MONTGOMERY, 1771-1854 — *Early American Melody*

1. Prayer is the soul's sin - cere de - sire, Un - ut - tered or ex - pressed;
2. Prayer is the bur - den of a sigh, The fall - ing of a tear,
3. Prayer is the sim - plest form of speech That in - fant lips can try;
4. Prayer is the con - trite sin - ner's voice, Re - turn - ing from his ways;
5. Prayer is the Chris - tian's vi - tal breath, The Chris - tian's na - tive air,
6. O Thou, by whom we come to God, The Life, the Truth, the Way;

The mo - tion of a hid - den fire That trem - bles in the breast.
The up - ward glanc - ing of an eye, When none but God is near.
Prayer the sub - lim - est strains that reach The Ma - jes - ty on high.
While an - gels in their songs re - joice And cry, "Be - hold, he prays!"
His watch - word at the gates of death; He en - ters heav'n with prayer.
The path of prayer Thy - self hast trod: Lord, teach us how to pray! A - MEN.

74 A Charge To Keep

CHARLES WESLEY — LOWELL MASON

1. A charge to keep I have, A God to glo - ri - fy;
2. To serve the pres - ent age, My call - ing to ful - fill;
3. Arm me with jeal - ous care, As in Thy sight to live,
4. Help me to watch and pray, And on Thy - self re - ly,

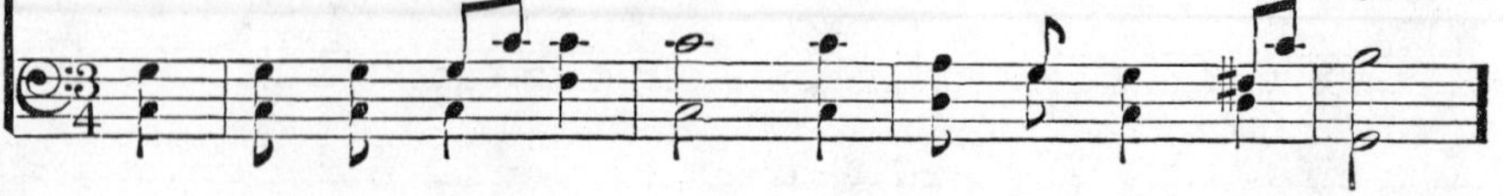

A nev - er - dy - ing soul to save, And fit it for the sky.
O may it all my pow'rs en - gage, To do my Mas - ter's will!
And O, Thy serv - ant, Lord, pre - pare, A strict ac - count to give!
As - sured, if I my trust be - tray, I shall for - ev - er die.

75 We're Marching To Zion

Isaac Watts
Robert Lowry
Spirited
1. Come, we that love the Lord, And let our joys be known, Join
2. Let those re - fuse to sing Who nev - er knew our God; But
3. The hill of Zi - on yields A thou - sand sa - cred sweets Be-
4. Then let our songs a - bound, And ev - 'ry tear be dry; We're
in a song with sweet ac - cord, Join in a song with sweet ac-cord, And
chil-dren of the heav'n-ly King, But chil-dren of the heav'n-ly King, May
fore we reach the heav'n-ly fields, Be - fore we reach the heav'n-ly fields, Or
marching thro' Immanuel's ground, We're marching thro' Immanuel's ground, To
thus sur - - round the throne, And thus sur-round the throne.
speak their joys a - broad, May speak their joys a - broad.
walk the gold - en streets, Or walk the gold - en streets.
fair - - er worlds on high, To fair - er worlds on high.
thus sur-round the throne, And thus sur - round the throne.
Chorus
We're march - ing to Zi - on, Beau-ti - ful, beau-ti - ful Zi - on; We're
We're march-ing on to Zi - on,
march-ing up-ward to Zi - on, The beau-ti - ful cit - y of God.
Zi - on, Zi - on,

76 Rock Of Ages

Augustus M. Toplady — Thomas Hastings

1. Rock of A - ges, cleft for me, Let me hide my - self in Thee;
2. Could my tears for - ev - er flow, Could my zeal no lan - guor know,
3. While I draw this fleet - ing breath, When my eyes shall close in death,
Let the wa - ter and the blood, From Thy wound - ed side which flowed,
These for sin could not a - tone; Thou must save, and Thou a - lone:
When I rise to worlds un - known, And be - hold Thee on Thy throne,
Be of sin the doub - le cure, Save from wrath and make me pure.
In my hand no price I bring, Sim - ply to Thy cross I cling.
Rock of A - ges, cleft for me, Let me hide my - self in Thee.

77 Nearer, My God, To Thee

Sarah F. Adams — Arr. by Lowell Mason

1. Near - er, my God, to Thee, Near - er to Thee! E'en though it
2. Though like the wan - der - er, The sun gone down, Dark - ness be
3. There let the way ap - pear, Steps un - to Heav'n: All that Thou
4. Then, with my wak - ing tho'ts Bright with Thy praise, Out of my
5. Or if on joy - ful wing, Cleav - ing the sky, Sun, moon, and

Nearer, My God, To Thee
be a cross That rais-eth me; Still all my song shall be,
o-ver me, My rest a stone; Yet in my dreams I'd be
send-est me, In mer-cy giv'n: An-gels to beck-on me,
sto-ny griefs Beth-el I'll raise; So by my woes to be
stars for-got, Up-wards I'll fly, Still all my song shall be,
Near-er, my God, to Thee, Near-er, my God, to Thee, Near-er to Thee!
78
Jesus, Lover Of My Soul
Charles Wesley
S. B. Marsh
Fine
1. Je-sus, Lov-er of my soul, Let me to Thy bos-om fly,
While the near-er wa-ters roll, While the tem-pest still is high!
2. Oth-er ref-uge have I none; Hangs my help-less soul on Thee:
Leave, ah, leave me not a-lone, Still sup-port and com-fort me!
3. Thou, O Christ, art all I want; More than all in Thee I find;
Raise the fall-en, cheer the faint, Heal the sick, and lead the blind.
4. Plenteous grace with Thee is found, Grace to cov-er all my sin;
Let the heal-ing streams a-bound, Make and keep me pure with-in.
D.C.—Safe in-to the ha-ven guide, O re-ceive my soul at last!
D.C.—Cov-er my de-fense-less head With the shad-ow of Thy wing.
D.C.—False and full of sin I am, Thou art full of truth and grace.
D.C.—Spring Thou up with-in my heart, Rise to all e-ter-ni-ty.
D.C.
Hide me, O my Sav-ior, hide, Till the storm of life is past;
All my trust on Thee is stayed, All my help from Thee I bring;
Just and ho-ly is Thy name, I am all un-right-eous-ness;
Thou of life the foun-tain art; Free-ly let me take of Thee;

79 Dear Lord And Father Of Mankind

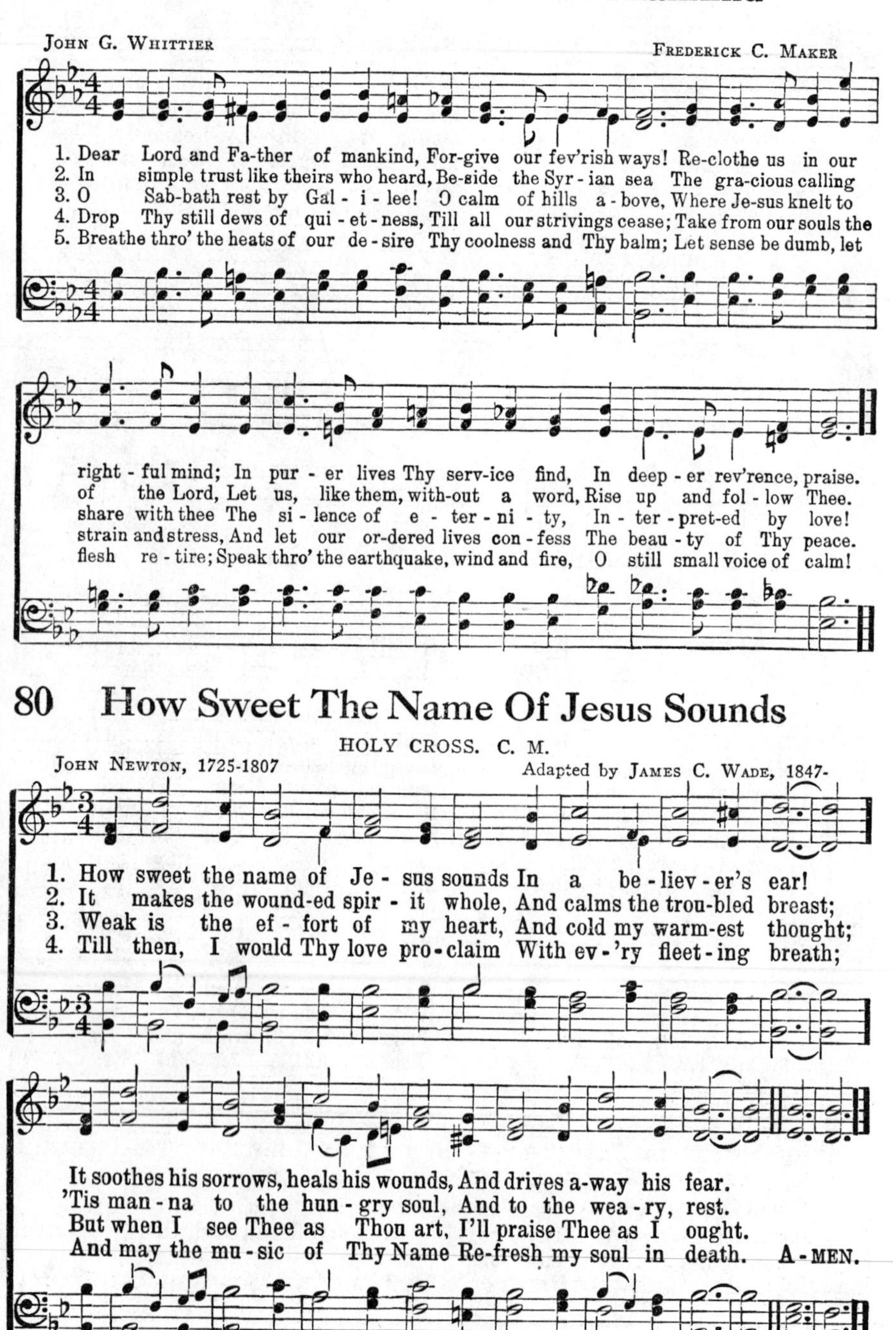
John G. Whittier
Frederick C. Maker
1. Dear Lord and Fa-ther of mankind, For-give our fev'rish ways! Re-clothe us in our
2. In simple trust like theirs who heard, Be-side the Syr - ian sea The gra-cious calling
3. O Sab-bath rest by Gal - i - lee! O calm of hills a - bove, Where Je-sus knelt to
4. Drop Thy still dews of qui - et - ness, Till all our strivings cease; Take from our souls the
5. Breathe thro' the heats of our de - sire Thy coolness and Thy balm; Let sense be dumb, let
right - ful mind; In pur - er lives Thy serv-ice find, In deep - er rev'rence, praise.
of the Lord, Let us, like them, with-out a word, Rise up and fol - low Thee.
share with thee The si - lence of e - ter - ni - ty, In - ter - pret-ed by love!
strain and stress, And let our or-dered lives con - fess The beau - ty of Thy peace.
flesh re - tire; Speak thro' the earthquake, wind and fire, O still small voice of calm!
80 How Sweet The Name Of Jesus Sounds
HOLY CROSS. C. M.
John Newton, 1725-1807
Adapted by James C. Wade, 1847-
1. How sweet the name of Je - sus sounds In a be - liev - er's ear!
2. It makes the wound-ed spir - it whole, And calms the trou-bled breast;
3. Weak is the ef - fort of my heart, And cold my warm-est thought;
4. Till then, I would Thy love pro-claim With ev - 'ry fleet - ing breath;
It soothes his sorrows, heals his wounds, And drives a-way his fear.
'Tis man - na to the hun - gry soul, And to the wea - ry, rest.
But when I see Thee as Thou art, I'll praise Thee as I ought.
And may the mu - sic of Thy Name Re-fresh my soul in death. A - men.

81 The Church's One Foundation

Samuel J. Stone
Samuel S. Wesley
1. The Church-'s one foun - da - tion Is Je - sus Christ her Lord;
2. E - lect from ev - 'ry na - tion, Yet one o'er all the earth,
3. 'Mid toil and trib - u - la - tion, And tu - mult of her war,
4. Yet she on earth hath un - ion With God the Three in One,
She is His new cre - a - tion By wa - ter and the word:
Her char - ter of sal - va - tion, One Lord, one faith, one birth;
She waits the con - sum - ma - tion Of peace for ev - er - more;
And mys - tic sweet com - mun - ion With those whose rest is won:
From heav'n He came and sought her To be His ho - ly bride; With
One ho - ly name she bless - es, Par-takes one ho - ly food, And
Till, with the vis - ion glo - rious, Her long - ing eyes are blest, And
O hap - py ones and ho - ly! Lord, give us grace that we, Like
His own blood He bought her, And for her life He died.
to one hope she press - es, With ev - 'ry grace en - dued.
the great church vic - to - rious Shall be the church at rest.
them, the meek and low - ly, On high may dwell with Thee. A - men.

82 A Mighty Fortress Is Our God

Martin Luther
Tr. by Frederick H. Hedge
EIN' FESTE BURG P. M.
Martin Luther
1. A might-y fortress is our God, A bul-wark nev - er fail - ing:
2. Did we in our own strength confide, Our striving would be los - ing;
3. And tho' this world with dev-ils filled, Should threaten to un - do us;
4. That word a - bove all earthly pow'rs, No thanks to them—a - bid - eth;
Our help - er He, a - mid the flood Of mor - tal ills pre - vail - ing.
Were not the right Man on our side, The man of God's own choos - ing.
We will not fear, for God hath willed His truth to tri - umph thro' us.
The Spir - it and the gifts are ours, Thro' Him who with us sid - eth.
For still our ancient foe Doth seek to work us woe; His craft and pow'r are great,
Dost ask who that may be? Christ Jesus, it is He; Lord Sabaoth is His name,
The Prince of darkness grim, We tremble not for him; His rage we can en - dure,
Let goods and kindred go, This mortal life al - so: The bod - y they may kill:
And, armed with cru-el hate, On earth is not his e - qual.
From age to age the same, And He must win the bat - tle.
For lo! his doom is sure, One lit - tle word shall fell him.
God's truth a - bid-eth still, His kingdom is for - ev - er. A - men.

83 Spirit Of Faith, Come Down

BEALOTH. S. M. D.

Charles Wesley, 1707-1788 — From Mason's Sacred Harp, 1843

1. Spir - it of faith, come down, Re - veal the things of God;
2. No man can tru - ly say That Je - sus is the Lord,
3. O that the world might know The all - a - ton - ing Lamb!
And make to us the God-head known, And wit - ness with the blood.
Un - less Thou take the veil a - way, And breathe the Liv - ing Word.
Spir - it of faith, de-scend and show The vir - tue of His Name.
'Tis Thine the blood to ap - ply And give us eyes to see,
Then, on - ly then, we feel Our in - terest in His blood,
The grace which all may find, The sav - ing pow'r, im - part;
Who did for ev - 'ry sin - ner die, Hath sure - ly died for me.
And cry, with joy un-speak - a - ble, "Thou art my Lord, my God!"
And tes - ti - fy to all man-kind, And speak in ev - 'ry heart. A - men.

84 Since Jesus Came Into My Heart

R. H. McDaniel — Chas. H. Gabriel

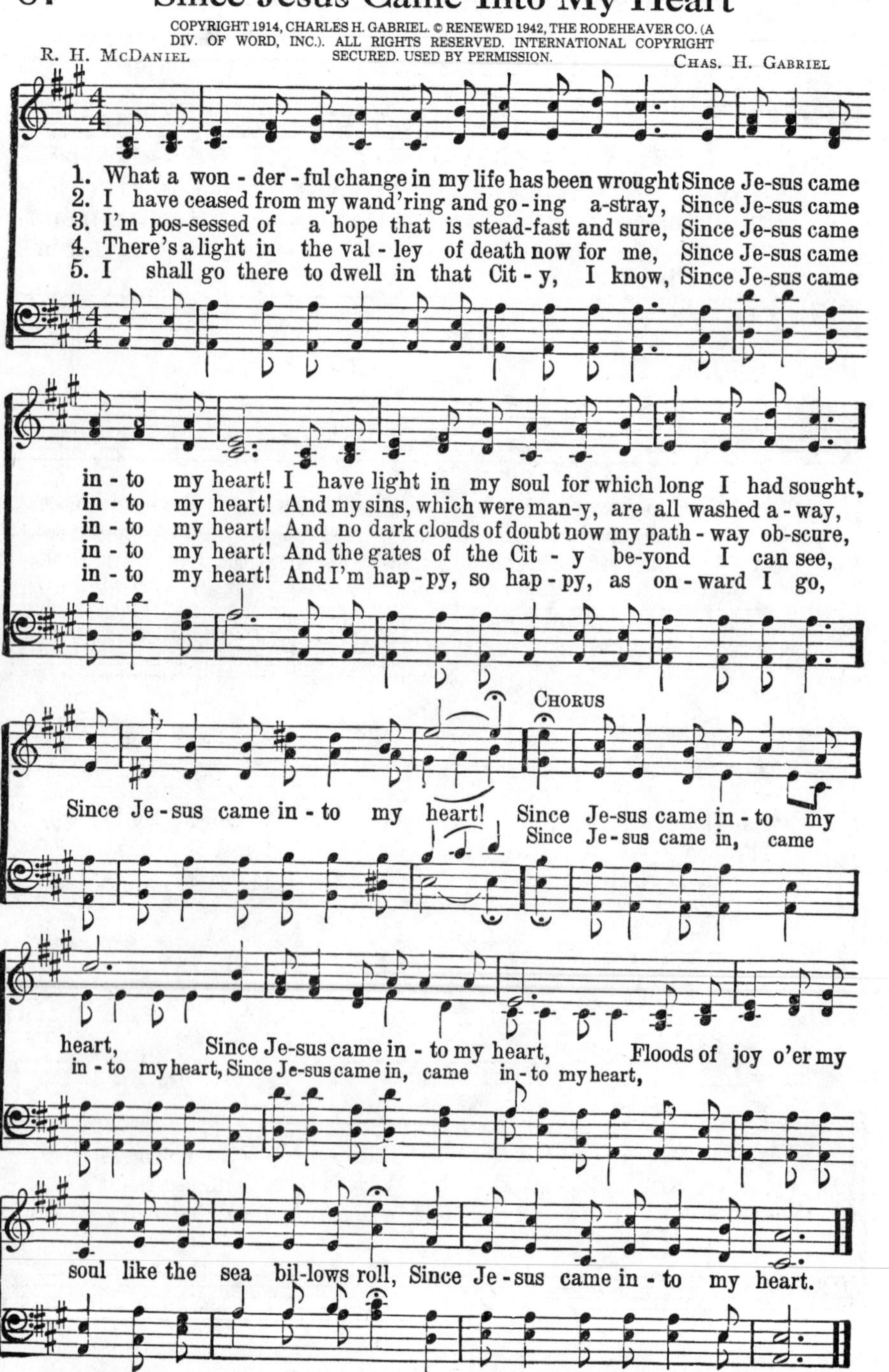
1. What a won - der - ful change in my life has been wrought Since Je-sus came
2. I have ceased from my wand'ring and go - ing a-stray, Since Je-sus came
3. I'm pos-sessed of a hope that is stead-fast and sure, Since Je-sus came
4. There's a light in the val - ley of death now for me, Since Je-sus came
5. I shall go there to dwell in that Cit - y, I know, Since Je-sus came
in - to my heart! I have light in my soul for which long I had sought,
in - to my heart! And my sins, which were man-y, are all washed a - way,
in - to my heart! And no dark clouds of doubt now my path - way ob-scure,
in - to my heart! And the gates of the Cit - y be-yond I can see,
in - to my heart! And I'm hap - py, so hap - py, as on - ward I go,
Since Je - sus came in - to my heart!
Chorus
Since Je-sus came in - to my heart,
Since Je - sus came in, came in - to my heart,
Since Je-sus came in - to my heart,
Since Je-sus came in, came in - to my heart,
Floods of joy o'er my soul like the sea bil-lows roll, Since Je - sus came in - to my heart.

85 Onward, Christian Soldiers

SABINE BARING-GOULD

ARTHUR SULLIVAN

1. On-ward, Christian soldiers, Marching as to war, With the cross of Je - sus
2. At the sign of tri-umph Satan's host doth flee; On, then, Christian sol-diers,
3. Like a might-y ar - my Moves the Church of God; Brothers, we are treading
4. Onward, then, ye peo - ple, Join our happy throng, Blend with ours your voices
Go - ing on be - fore! Christ, the roy-al Mas - ter, Leads a-gainst the foe;
On to vic - to - ry! Hell's foun-da-tions quiv - er At the shout of praise;
Where the saints have trod; We are not di - vid - ed; All one bod - y we,
In the tri-umph song; Glo - ry, laud, and hon - or, Un - to Christ the King:
REFRAIN
For-ward in - to bat - tle, See His ban-ner go!
Brothers, lift your voi - ces, Loud your anthems raise! Onward, Christian sol-diers,
One in hope and doc - trine, One in char - i - ty.
This thro' countless a - ges Men and an-gels sing.
March-ing as to war, With the cross of Je - sus Go-ing on be - fore!

86 Faith Of Our Fathers

Frederick W. Faber
H. F. Hemy
1. Faith of our fa - thers! liv - ing still In spite of dun-geon, fire and sword:
2. Our fa-thers, chained in prisons dark, Were still in heart and conscience free:
3. Faith of our fa - thers! we will love Both friend and foe in all our strife:
O how our hearts beat high with joy Whene'er we hear that glo-rious word!
How sweet would be their children's fate, If they, like them, could die for thee!
And preach thee, too, as love knows how, By kind-ly words and vir-tuous life:
Faith of our fa-thers! ho - ly faith! We will be true to thee till death!
Faith of our fa-thers! ho - ly faith! We will be true to thee till death!
Faith of our fa-thers! ho - ly faith! We will be true to thee till death!
87
Blest Be The Tie
John Fawcett
Hans G. Naegeli
1. Blest be the tie that binds Our hearts in Chris-tian love; The
2. Be - fore our Fa-ther's throne, We pour our ar - dent prayers; Our
3. We share our mu - tual woes, Our mu - tual bur-dens bear; And
4. When we a - sun - der part, It gives us in - ward pain; But

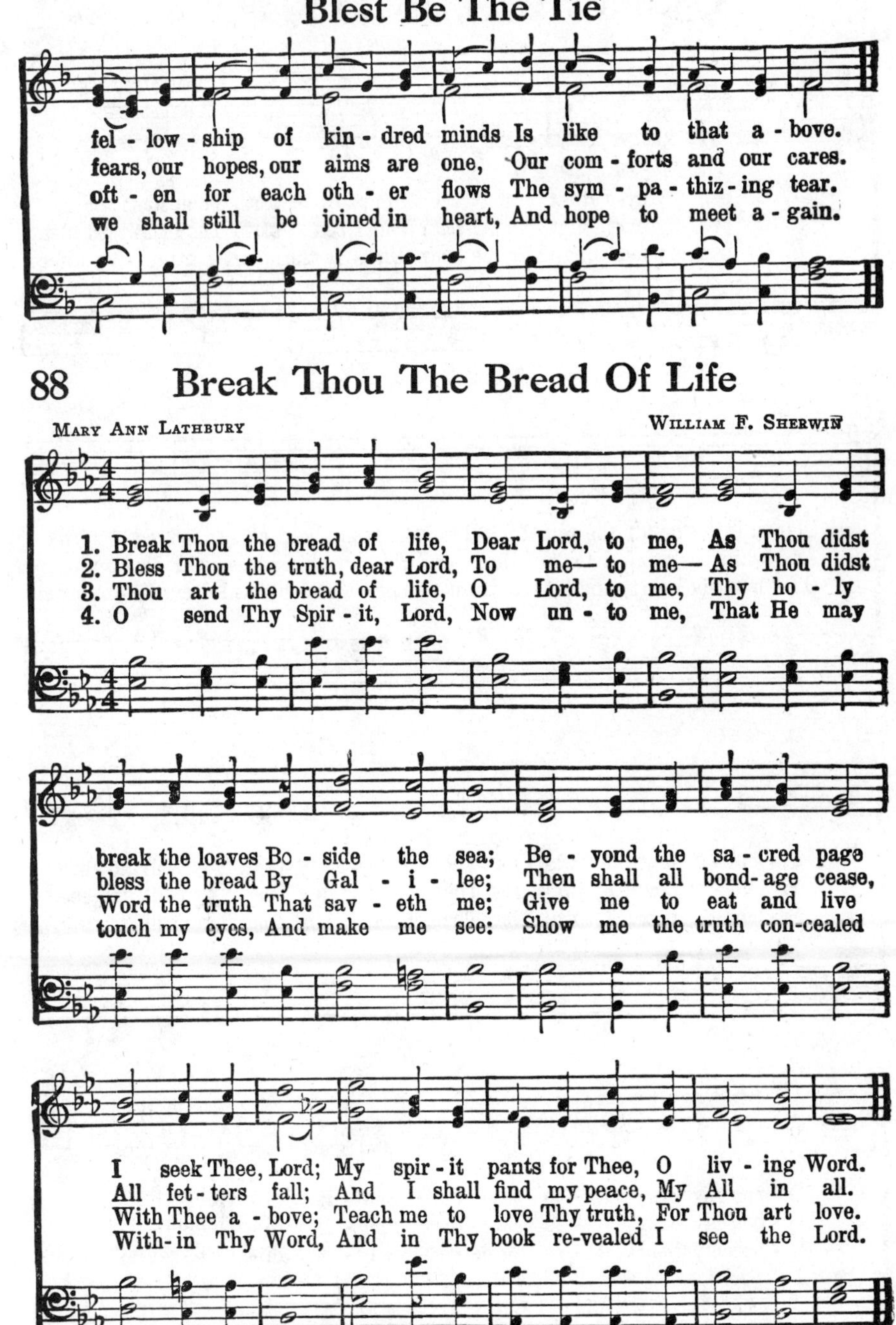
Blest Be The Tie
fel - low - ship of kin - dred minds Is like to that a - bove.
fears, our hopes, our aims are one, Our com - forts and our cares.
oft - en for each oth - er flows The sym - pa - thiz - ing tear.
we shall still be joined in heart, And hope to meet a - gain.
88 Break Thou The Bread Of Life
Mary Ann Lathbury
William F. Sherwin
1. Break Thou the bread of life, Dear Lord, to me, As Thou didst
2. Bless Thou the truth, dear Lord, To me— to me— As Thou didst
3. Thou art the bread of life, O Lord, to me, Thy ho - ly
4. O send Thy Spir - it, Lord, Now un - to me, That He may
break the loaves Be - side the sea; Be - yond the sa - cred page
bless the bread By Gal - i - lee; Then shall all bond - age cease,
Word the truth That sav - eth me; Give me to eat and live
touch my eyes, And make me see: Show me the truth con-cealed
I seek Thee, Lord; My spir - it pants for Thee, O liv - ing Word.
All fet - ters fall; And I shall find my peace, My All in all.
With Thee a - bove; Teach me to love Thy truth, For Thou art love.
With-in Thy Word, And in Thy book re-vealed I see the Lord.

89 Open My Eyes, That I May See

C. H. S. CHARLES H. SCOTT

1. O - pen my eyes, that I may see Glimps-es of truth Thou hast for me;
2. O - pen my ears, that I may hear Voi - ces of truth Thou send-est clear;
3. O - pen my mouth, and let me bear Glad - ly the warm truth ev-'ry-where;
Place in my hands the won-der-ful key That shall un-clasp, and set me free.
And while the wave-notes fall on my ear, Ev - 'ry-thing false will dis - ap-pear.
O - pen my heart, and let me pre-pare Love with Thy chil-dren thus to share.
Si-lent-ly now I wait for Thee, Read-y, my God, Thy will to see;
Si-lent-ly now I wait for Thee, Read-y, my God, Thy will to see;
Si-lent-ly now I wait for Thee, Read-y, my God, Thy will to see;
O - pen my eyes, il - lu - mine me, Spir - it di - vine!
O - pen my ears, il - lu - mine me, Spir - it di - vine!
O - pen my heart, il - lu - mine me, Spir - it di - vine! A - MEN.

90 Tell Me The Story Of Jesus

Fanny J. Crosby — Jno. R. Sweney

1. Tell me the sto - ry of Je - sus, Write on my heart ev - 'ry word;
2. Fast-ing a - lone in the des - ert, Tell of the days that are past,
3. Tell of the cross where they nailed Him, Writh-ing in an-guish and pain;

Cho.—*Tell me the sto - ry of Je - sus, Write on my heart ev - 'ry word;*

Fine

Tell me the sto - ry most pre - cious, Sweet-est that ev - er was heard.
How for our sins He was tempt - ed, Yet was tri - um-phant at last.
Tell of the grave where they laid Him, Tell how He liv - eth a - gain.

Tell me the sto - ry most pre - cious, Sweet - est that ev - er was heard.

Tell how the an - gels, in cho - rus, Sang as they welcomed His birth,
Tell of the years of His la - bor, Tell of the sor - row He bore,
Love in that sto - ry so ten - der, Clear - er than ev - er I see:

D. C. for Chorus

"Glo - ry to God in the high - est! Peace and good ti - dings to earth."
He was de-spised and af - flict - ed, Home-less, de - ject - ed and poor.
Stay, let me weep while you whis - per, Love paid the ran - som for me.

91 I Will Sing The Wondrous Story

F. H. Rowley
Peter P. Bilhorn
1. I will sing the won-drous sto - ry Of the Christ who died for me,
2. I was lost, but Je - sus found me, Found the sheep that went a - stray,
3. I was bruised, but Je - sus healed me; Faint was I from man-y a fall;
4. Days of dark-ness still come o'er me, Sor-row's paths I oft - en tread,
5. He will keep me till the riv - er Rolls its wa - ters at my feet;
How He left His home in glo - ry For the cross of Cal - va - ry.
Threw His lov - ing arms a - round me, Drew me back in - to His way.
Sight was gone, and fears pos-sessed me, But He freed me from them all.
But the Sav - iour still is with me; By His hand I'm safe - ly led.
Then He'll bear me safe - ly o - ver, Where the loved ones I shall meet.
Chorus
Yes, I'll sing . . . . . the won-drous sto - ry Of the
Yes, I'll sing
the won-drous sto - ry
Christ . . . . who died for me, ... Sing it with . . . . the saints in
Of the Christ
who died for me,
Sing it with
glo - ry, Gath-ered by . . . . . . the crys-tal sea . . . .
the saints in glo - ry,
Gath-ered by
the crystal sea.

Tell It To Jesus

J. E. Rankin, D.D. — E. S. Lorenz

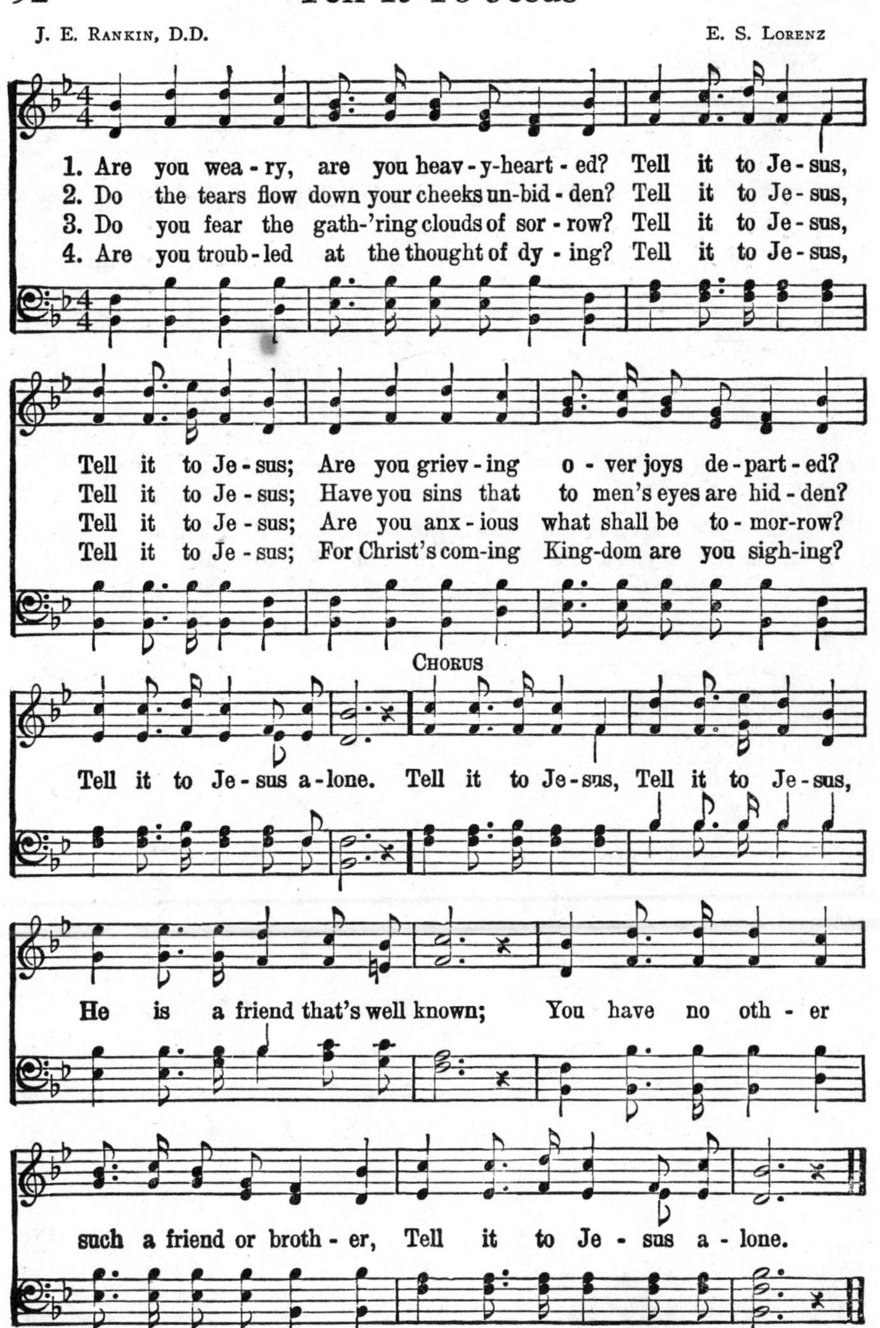
1. Are you wea - ry, are you heav - y-heart - ed? Tell it to Je - sus,
2. Do the tears flow down your cheeks un-bid - den? Tell it to Je - sus,
3. Do you fear the gath-'ring clouds of sor - row? Tell it to Je - sus,
4. Are you troub - led at the thought of dy - ing? Tell it to Je - sus,
Tell it to Je - sus; Are you griev - ing o - ver joys de - part - ed?
Tell it to Je - sus; Have you sins that to men's eyes are hid - den?
Tell it to Je - sus; Are you anx - ious what shall be to - mor-row?
Tell it to Je - sus; For Christ's com-ing King-dom are you sigh-ing?
Chorus
Tell it to Je - sus a - lone. Tell it to Je - sus, Tell it to Je - sus,
He is a friend that's well known; You have no oth - er
such a friend or broth - er, Tell it to Je - sus a - lone.

93

I've Found A Friend

FRIEND. 8. 7. 8. 7. D.

JAMES G. SMALL, 1817-1888
GEORGE C. STEBBINS, 1846-
1. I've found a Friend, O such a Friend! He loved me ere I knew Him;
2. I've found a Friend, O such a Friend! He bled, He died to save me;
3. I've found a Friend, O such a Friend! So kind, and true, and ten - der,
He drew me with the cords of love, And thus He bound me to Him.
And not a - lone the gift of life, But His own self He gave me.
So wise a Coun - sel - or and Guide, So might - y a De-fend - er!
And 'round my heart still close- ly twine Those ties which naught can sev-er,
Naught that I have my own I call, I hold it for the Giv - er;
From Him who loves me now so well, What pow'r my soul can sev - er?
For I am His, and He is mine, For-ev - er and for-ev - er.
My heart, my strength, my life, my all Are His, and His for-ev - er.
Shall life or death, or earth or hell? No! I am His for-ev - er. A-MEN.

94 God Will Take Care Of You

C. D. Martin
W. S. Martin
1. Be not dis - mayed what-e'er be - tide, God will take care of you;
2. Thro' days of toil when heart doth fail, God will take care of you;
3. All you may need He will pro - vide, God will take care of you;
4. No mat - ter what may be the test, God will take care of you;
Be - neath His wings of love a - bide, God will take care of you.
When dan-gers fierce your path as - sail, God will take care of you.
Noth - ing you ask will be de - nied, God will take care of you.
Lean, wear - y one, up - on His breast, God will take care of you.
Chorus
God will take care of you, Thro' ev - 'ry day, O'er all the way;
He will take care of you, God will take care of you. . .
take care of you.

95 Dwelling In Beulah Land

C. A. M. — C. Austin Miles

1. Far a-way the noise of strife up-on my ear is fall-ing, Then I know the
2. Far be-low the storm of doubt up-on the world is beat-ing, Sons of men in
3. Let the storm-y breez-es blow, their cry can-not a-larm me; I am safe-ly
4. Viewing here the works of God, I sink in con-tem-pla-tion, Hearing now His

sins of earth be-set on ev-'ry hand: Doubt and fear and things of earth in
bat-tle long the en-e-my with-stand: Safe am I with-in the cas-tle
sheltered here, pro-tect-ed by God's hand: Here the sun is al-ways shin-ing,
bless-ed voice, I see the way He planned: Dwell-ing in the Spir-it, here I

vain to me are call-ing, None of these shall move me from Beu-lah Land.
of God's word re-treat-ing, Nothing then can reach me—'tis Beu-lah Land.
here there's naught can harm me, I am safe for-ev-er in Beu-lah Land.
learn of full sal-va-tion, Glad-ly will I tar-ry in Beu-lah Land.

Chorus

I'm liv-ing on the moun-tain, un-der-neath a cloud-less sky, I'm
Praise God!

drink-ing at the foun-tain that never shall run dry; O yes! I'm feasting on the

Dwelling In Beulah Land

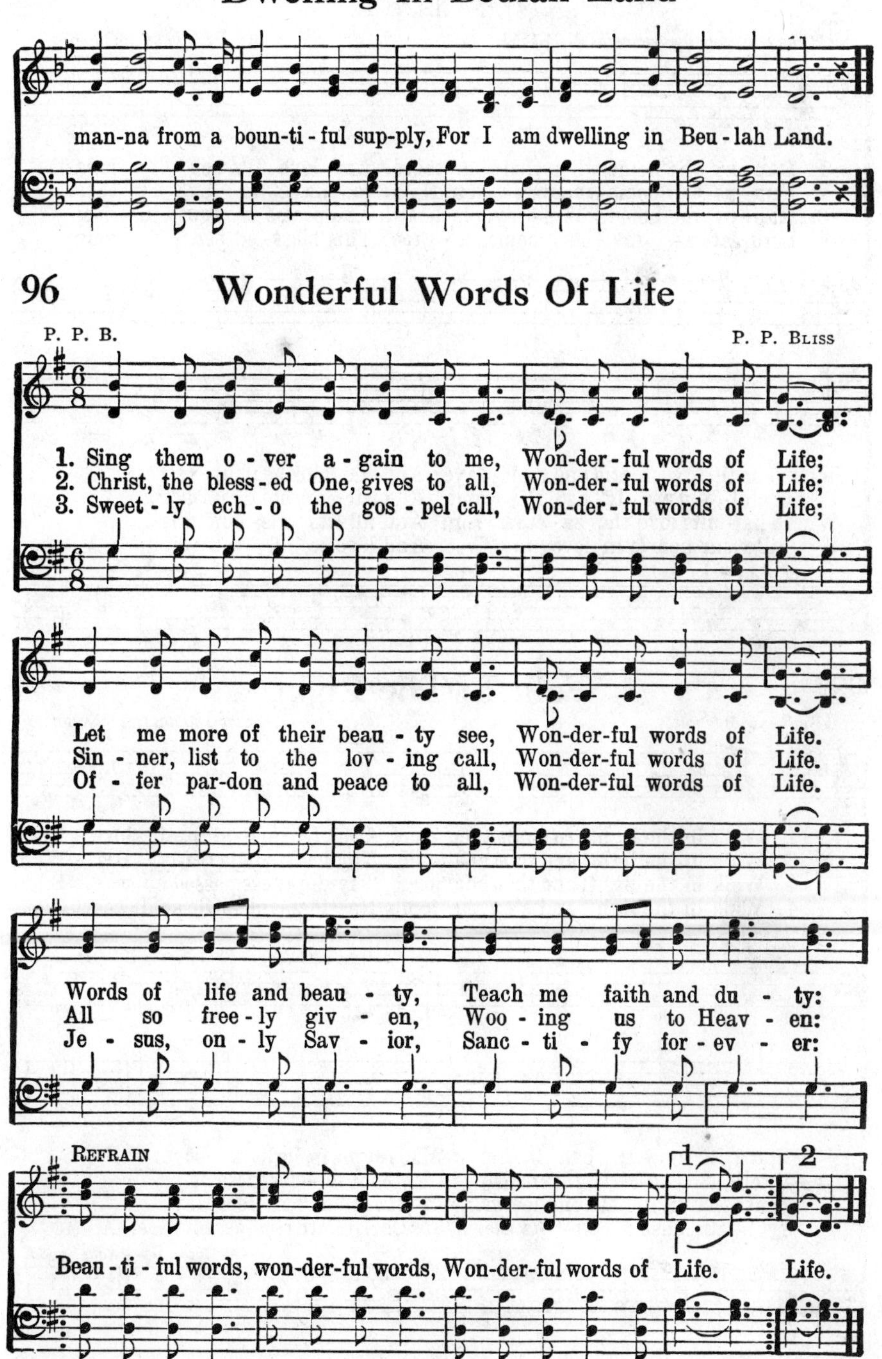

man-na from a boun-ti-ful sup-ply, For I am dwelling in Beu-lah Land.
96 Wonderful Words Of Life
P. P. B.
P. P. Bliss
1. Sing them o-ver a-gain to me, Won-der-ful words of Life;
2. Christ, the bless-ed One, gives to all, Won-der-ful words of Life;
3. Sweet-ly ech-o the gos-pel call, Won-der-ful words of Life;
Let me more of their beau-ty see, Won-der-ful words of Life.
Sin-ner, list to the lov-ing call, Won-der-ful words of Life.
Of-fer par-don and peace to all, Won-der-ful words of Life.
Words of life and beau-ty, Teach me faith and du-ty:
All so free-ly giv-en, Woo-ing us to Heav-en:
Je-sus, on-ly Sav-ior, Sanc-ti-fy for-ev-er:
Refrain
Beau-ti-ful words, won-der-ful words, Won-der-ful words of Life.
1
2
Life.

97 Happy The Home

ST. AGNES. C. M.
HENRY WARE, the younger, 1794-1843
JOHN B. DYKES, 1823-1876
1. Hap-py the home when God is there, And love fills ev-'ry breast;
2. Hap-py the home where Je-sus' Name Is sweet to ev-'ry ear;
3. Hap-py the home where prayer is heard, And praise is wont to rise;
4. Lord, let us in our homes a-gree This bless-ed peace to gain;
When one their wish, and one their prayer, And one their heav'nly rest.
Where chil-dren ear-ly lisp His fame, And par-ents hold Him dear.
Where par-ents love the sa-cred Word And all its wis-dom prize.
U-nite our hearts in love to Thee, And love to all will reign.
A-MEN.
98
Walk In The Light
BERNARD BARTON
From FRANCIS J. HAYDN
1. Walk in the light! so shalt thou know That fel-low-ship of love His
2. Walk in the light! and thou shalt find Thy heart made tru-ly His Who
3. Walk in the light! and thou shalt own Thy darkness passed a-way, Be-
4. Walk in the light! and e'en the tomb No fear-ful shade shall wear; Glo-
Spir-it on-ly can be-stow Who reigns in light a-bove.
dwells in cloud-less light enshrined, In whom no dark-ness is.
cause that light hath on thee shone In which is per-fect day.
ry shall chase a-way its gloom, For Christ hath conquered there.
A-MEN.

99 His Way With Thee

C. S. N.
Cyrus S. Nusbaum
1. Would you live for Je - sus, and be al-ways pure and good? Would you walk with
2. Would you have Him make you free, and fol-low at His call? Would you know the
3. Would you in His king-dom find a place of con-stant rest? Would you prove Him
Him with - in the nar-row road? Would you have Him bear your burden, car - ry
peace that comes by giv - ing all? Would you have Him save you, so that you need
true in prov - i - den-tial test? Would you in His serv - ice la - bor al-ways
all your load? Let Him have His way with thee.
nev - er fall? Let Him have His way with thee. His pow'r can make you what you
at your best? Let Him have His way with thee.
Chorus.
ought to be; His blood can cleanse your heart and make you free; His love can fill your
soul, and you will see 'Twas best for Him to have His way with thee. A - men.
rit.

100 Let The Lower Lights Be Burning

P. P. B. P. P. Bliss

1. Bright-ly beams our Fa-ther's mer-cy From His lighthouse ev - er - more;
2. Dark the night of sin has set-tled, Loud the an - gry bil-lows roar;
3. Trim your fee - ble lamp, my brother! Some poor sea - man, tempest-tossed,
But to us He gives the keep-ing Of the lights a - long the shore.
Ea - ger eyes are watching, long-ing, For the lights a - long the shore.
Try - ing now to make the har-bor, In the dark-ness may be lost.
Chorus
Let the low - er lights be burning! Send a gleam a-cross the wave!
Some poor fainting, struggling sea-man You may res - cue, you may save.

101 Return, O Wanderer, Return

WOODWORTH. L. M.

William B. Collyer, 1782-1854 William B. Bradbury, 1816-1868

1. Re-turn, O wan-der-er, re-turn, And seek an in - jured Fa-ther's face;
2. Re-turn, O wan-der-er, re-turn, And seek a Fa - ther's melt-ing heart;
3. Re-turn, O wan-der-er, re-turn; Thy Sav - iour bids thy spir - it live;
4. Re-turn, O wan-der-er, re-turn, And wipe a - way the fall - ing tear;

Return, O Wanderer, Return

Those warm desires that in thee burn Were kindled by re-claim-ing grace.
His pity-ing eyes thy grief dis-cern, His hand shall heal thine inward smart.
Go to His bleeding feet, and learn How freely Je - sus can for - give.
'Tis God who says, "No longer mourn;" 'Tis mercy's voice invites thee near. A-MEN.
102
Just For Today
E. R. Wilberforce
H. R. Palmer
1. Lord, for to-mor-row and its needs I do not pray; Keep me, my God, from stain of sin Just for to - day. Help me to la - bor ear - nest - ly, And du - ly pray; Let me be kind in word and deed, Fa - ther, to - day.
2. Let me no wrong or i - dle word Un-think-ing say; Set Thou a seal up-on my lips Thru all to - day. Let me in sea - son, Lord, be grave, In sea - son gay; Let me be faith-ful to Thy grace, Dear Lord, to-day.
3. And if, to - day, this life of mine Should ebb a - way, Give me Thy sac-ra-ment di - vine, Fa - ther, to - day. So for to - mor-row and its needs I do not pray; Still keep me, guide me, love me, Lord, Thru each to - day.
cres.
ff
rall.

103 Jesus Spreads His Banner O'er Us
Roswell Park
AUTUMN. 8s. 7s. D.
Louis von Esch
1. Je-sus spreads His ban-ner o'er us, Cheers our fam-ished souls with food;
2. In Thy ho - ly in - car - na - tion, When the an - gels sang Thy birth;
He the ban-quet spreads be-fore us, Of His mys - tic flesh and blood.
In Thy fast - ing and temp-ta - tion, In Thy la - bors on the earth.
Precious ban-quet, bread of heav - en, Wine of gladness, flowing free;
In Thy tri - al and re - jec - tion, In Thy suff'rings on the tree,
May we taste it, kind-ly giv - en, In remembrance, Lord, of Thee.
In Thy glorious res - ur - rec - tion, May we, Lord, remember Thee. A - men.
104 I'll Live For Him
R. E. Hudson
C. R. Dunbar
1. My life, my love I give to Thee, Thou Lamb of God who died for me;
2. I now be-lieve Thou dost re-ceive, For Thou hast died that I might live;
3. O Thou who died on Cal - va - ry, To save my soul and make me free,
Cho.—I'll live for Him who died for me, How hap-py then my life shall be!

I'll Live For Him
D. C. Chorus
Oh, may I ev - er faith - ful be, My Sav - ior and my God!
And now henceforth I'll trust in Thee, My Sav - ior and my God!
I'll con - se - crate my life to Thee, My Sav - ior and my God!
I'll live for Him who died for me, My Sav - ior and my God!
105 For The Beauty Of The Earth
Folliott S. Pierpont
Conrad Kocher
1. For the beau - ty of the earth, For the beau - ty of the skies,
2. For the beau - ty of each hour Of the day and of the night,
3. For the joy of ear and eye; For the heart and mind's de - light;
4. For the joy of hu - man love, Broth-er, sis - ter, par - ent, child,
5. For Thy church that ev - er - more Lift - eth ho - ly hands a - bove,
6. For Thy-self, best Gift Di - vine! To our race so free - ly giv'n;
For the love which from our birth O - ver and a - round us lies,—
Hill and vale, and tree and flow'r, Sun and moon, and stars of light,—
For the mys - tic har - mo - ny Link-ing sense to sound and sight,—
Friends on earth, and friends a - bove; For all gen - tle thot's and mild,—
Of - f'ring up on ev - 'ry shore Its pure sac - ri - fice of love,—
For that great, great love of Thine, Peace on earth, and joy in heav'n, —
1–6. Christ our God, to Thee we raise This our hymn of grate - ful praise.

106 This Is My Father's World

Traditional English Melody
Arranged by S. F. L.
Maltbie D. Babcock
1. This is my Fa-ther's world, And to my list-'ning ears, All
2. This is my Fa-ther's world, The birds their car-ols raise, The
3. This is my Fa-ther's world, O let me ne'er for-get That
na-ture sings, and round me rings The mu-sic of the spheres.
morn-ing light, the lil-y white, De-clare their Ma-ker's praise.
though the wrong seems oft so strong, God is the Ru-ler yet.
This is my Fa-ther's world, I rest me in the thought Of
This is my Fa-ther's world, He shines in all that's fair; In the
This is my Fa-ther's world, The bat-tle is not done, Je-
rocks and trees, of skies and seas—His hand the won-ders wrought.
rus-tling grass I hear Him pass, He speaks to me ev-'ry-where,
sus who died shall be sat-is-fied, And earth and heav'n be one. A-men.

107 The Beautiful Garden Of Prayer

Eleanor Allen Schroll

J. H. Fillmore

1. There's a garden where Jesus is waiting,
There's a place that is wondrously fair;
For it glows with the light of His presence,
'Tis the beautiful garden of pray'r.

2. There's a garden where Jesus is waiting,
And I go with my burden and care,
Just to learn from His lips words of comfort,
In the beautiful garden of pray'r.

3. There's a garden where Jesus is waiting,
And He bids you to come meet Him there;
Just to bow and receive a new blessing,
In the beautiful garden of pray'r.

Refrain

O the beautiful garden, the garden of pray'r,
O the beautiful garden of pray'r;
There my Savior awaits, and He opens the gates
To the beautiful garden of pray'r.

108 Sunrise

W. C. Poole B. D. Ackley

Solo
1. When I shall come to the end of my way, When I shall rest at the
2. When in His beau-ty I see the great King, Join with the ran-somed His
3. When life is o - ver and day-light is passed, In heav-en's har-bor my
close of life's day, When "Wel-come home" I shall hear Je - sus say, O
prais - es to sing, When I shall join them my trib - utes to bring, O
an - chor is cast, When I see Je - sus my Sav - ior at last, O
that will be sun-rise for me. . . . .
Chorus
Sun-rise to-mor-row, sun-rise to-
mor-row, Sun-rise in glo - ry is wait-ing for me; Sun-rise to-mor - row,
sun-rise to - mor - row, Sun - rise with Je - sus for e - ter - ni - ty.

109 When They Ring The Golden Bells

Dion De Marbelle

1. There's a land beyond the riv - er, That we call the sweet for-ev-er, And we
2. We shall know no sin or sor-row, In that ha-ven of tomorrow, When our
3. When our days shall know their number, When in death we sweetly slumber, When the
on - ly reach that shore by faith's decree; One by one we'll gain the portals, There to
barque shall sail beyond the sil-ver sea; We shall on - ly know the blessing Of our
King commands the spirit to be free; Nev-er-more with anguish laden, We shall
Fine.
dwell with the immortals, When they ring the golden bells for you and me.
Father's sweet caressing, When they ring the golden bells for you and me.
reach that love-ly Aiden, When they ring the golden bells for you and me.
you and me.
D.S.–yond the shin-ing riv-er, When they ring the gold-en bells for you and me.
Chorus
Don't you hear the bells now ringing, Don't you hear the angels singing? 'Tis the
D. S.
glory hal-le - lu-jah Ju-bi-lee. (Ju-bi-lee.) In that far-off sweet forever, Just be -

110 He Keeps Me Singing

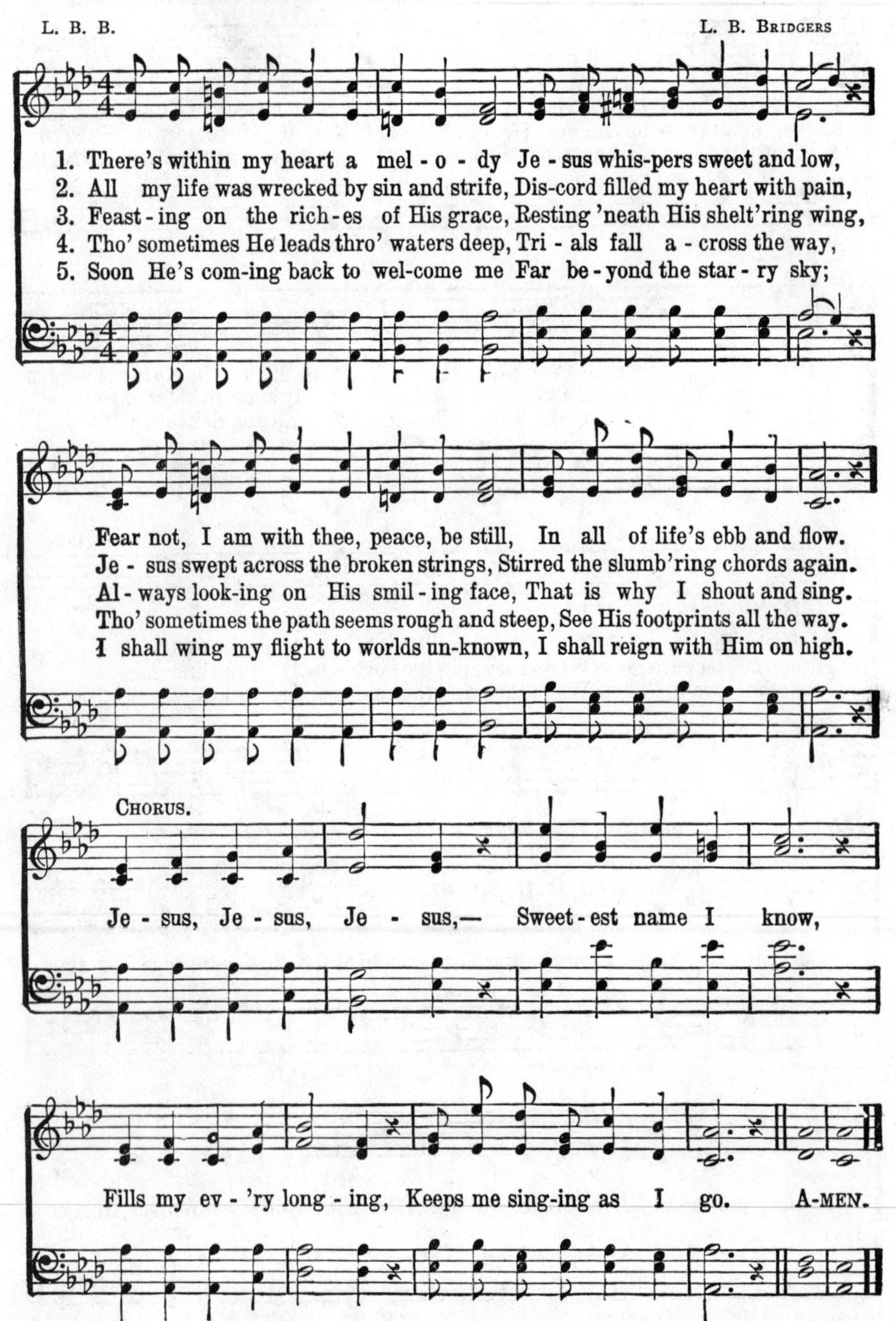

L. B. B.
L. B. Bridgers
1. There's within my heart a mel - o - dy Je - sus whis-pers sweet and low,
2. All my life was wrecked by sin and strife, Dis-cord filled my heart with pain,
3. Feast - ing on the rich - es of His grace, Resting 'neath His shelt'ring wing,
4. Tho' sometimes He leads thro' waters deep, Tri - als fall a - cross the way,
5. Soon He's com-ing back to wel-come me Far be - yond the star - ry sky;
Fear not, I am with thee, peace, be still, In all of life's ebb and flow.
Je - sus swept across the broken strings, Stirred the slumb'ring chords again.
Al - ways look-ing on His smil - ing face, That is why I shout and sing.
Tho' sometimes the path seems rough and steep, See His footprints all the way.
I shall wing my flight to worlds un-known, I shall reign with Him on high.
Chorus.
Je - sus, Je - sus, Je - sus,— Sweet - est name I know,
Fills my ev - 'ry long - ing, Keeps me sing-ing as I go. A-men.

111 Jesus Is All The World To Me

W. L. T.
Will L. Thompson
1. Je - sus is all the world to me, My life, my joy, my all;
2. Je - sus is all the world to me, My Friend in tri - als sore;
3. Je - sus is all the world to me, And true to Him I'll be;
4. Je - sus is all the world to me, I want no bet - ter friend;
He is my strength from day to day, With - out Him I would fall.
I go to Him for bless-ings, and He gives them o'er and o'er.
Oh, how could I this Friend de - ny, When He's so true to me?
I trust Him now, I'll trust Him when Life's fleet - ing days shall end.
When I am sad, to Him I go, No oth - er one can
He sends the sun - shine and the rain, He sends the har - vest's
Fol - low - ing Him I know I'm right, He watch - es o'er me
Beau - ti - ful life with such a Friend; Beau - ti - ful life that
f
pp
cheer me so; When I am sad He makes me glad, He's my Friend.
gold - en grain; Sun-shine and rain, har - vest of grain, He's my Friend.
day and night; Fol - low - ing Him, by day and night, He's my Friend.
has no end; E - ter - nal life, e - ter - nal joy, He's my Friend.

112 It Is Morning In My Heart

A. H. A. — Rev. A. H. Ackley

1. All the dark-ness of the night has passed a-way, It is morn-ing in my heart; I am liv-ing in the sun-light of the day, It is morn-ing in my heart.
2. I can hear the songbirds sing-ing their re-frain, It is morn-ing in my heart; And I know that life for me be-gins a-gain, It is morn-ing in my heart.
3. Christ has made the world a par-a-dise to me, It is morn-ing in my heart; Ev-'ry du-ty in the light of love I see, It is morn-ing in my heart.
4. Joy has come to dwell with me for-ev-er-more, It is morn-ing in my heart, I shall sing it when I reach the oth-er shore, It is morn-ing in my heart.

Refrain

It is morning, it is morning in my heart, . . . (in my heart,)
Je-sus made the gloomy shadows all de-part; . . . . . (made all de-part;)
Songs of gladness now I sing, for since Je-sus is my King
It is morning, it is morn-ing in my heart.

113 Welcome, Happy Morning

HERMAS. 6. 5. 6. 5. D. with Refrain
Venantius Fortunatus, c. 530-609
Tr. by John Ellerton, 1826-1893
Frances R. Havergal, 1836-1879
1. "Wel-come, happy morn-ing;" Age to age shall say; "Hell to-day is vanquished, Heav'n is won to - day." Lo, the dead is liv - ing, God for - ev - er - more: Him, their true Cre-a - tor, All His works a - dore.
2. Earth with joy con-fess - es, Clothing her for spring, All good gifts returned with Her re - turn-ing King. Bloom in ev - 'ry mead - ow, Leaves on ev-'ry bough, Speak His sorrows end - ed; Hail His tri-umph now.
3. Come then, true and faith-ful, Now ful-fill Thy Word, 'Tis Thine own third morning, Rise, O bur - ied Lord! Show Thy face in brightness, Bid the na-tions see, Bring a-gain our day-light; Day re-turns with Thee!
Refrain
"Welcome, happy morn-ing," Age to age shall say: "Hell to-day is vanquished, Heav'n is won to-day." A - men.

114 Still, Still With Thee

CONSOLATION. 11. 10. 11. 10.

HARRIET B. STOWE, 1812-1896 Arr. from FELIX MENDELSSOHN-BARTHOLDY, 1809-1847

1. Still, still with Thee, when pur - ple morn - ing break - eth,
2. A - lone with Thee, a - mid the mys - tic shad - ows,
3. Still, still with Thee! As to each new - born morn - ing
4. When sinks the soul, sub - dued by toil, to slum - ber,
5. So shall it be at last in that bright morn - ing,
When the bird wak - eth, and the shad - ows flee;
The sol - emn hush of na - ture new - ly born;
A fresh and sol - emn splen - dor still is giv'n,
Its clos - ing eyes look up to Thee in prayer;
When the soul wak - eth, and the shad - ows flee;
Fair - er than morn - ing, love - li - er than day - light,
A - lone with Thee in breath - less ad - o - ra - tion,
So does this bless - ed con - scious - ness, a - wak - ing,
Sweet the re - pose be - neath Thy wings o'er - shad - ing,
O in that hour, fair - er than day - light dawn - ing,
Dawns the sweet con - scious-ness, I am with Thee.
In the calm dew and fresh-ness of the morn.
Breathe each day near - ness un - to Thee and heav'n.
But sweet - er still, to wake and find Thee there.
Shall rise the glo - rious thought, I am with Thee. A - MEN.

115 God, That Madest Earth and Heaven

AR HYD Y NOS 8. 4. 8. 4. 8. 8. 8. 4.

Reginald Heber
Richard Whately

Welsh Melody

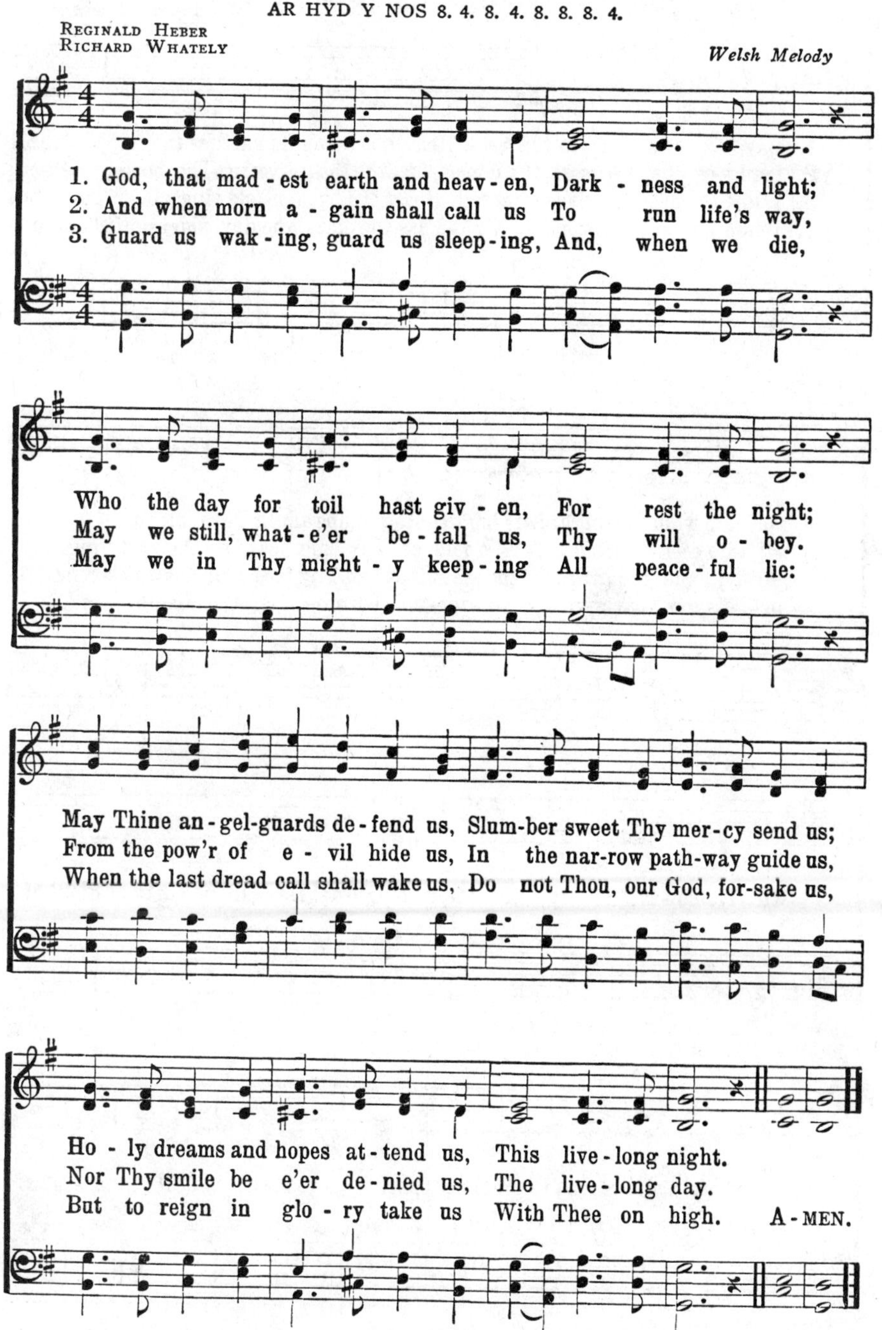

1. God, that mad - est earth and heav - en, Dark - ness and light;
2. And when morn a - gain shall call us To run life's way,
3. Guard us wak - ing, guard us sleep - ing, And, when we die,
Who the day for toil hast giv - en, For rest the night;
May we still, what - e'er be - fall us, Thy will o - bey.
May we in Thy might - y keep - ing All peace - ful lie:
May Thine an - gel-guards de - fend us, Slum-ber sweet Thy mer-cy send us;
From the pow'r of e - vil hide us, In the nar-row path-way guide us,
When the last dread call shall wake us, Do not Thou, our God, for-sake us,
Ho - ly dreams and hopes at - tend us, This live - long night.
Nor Thy smile be e'er de - nied us, The live - long day.
But to reign in glo - ry take us With Thee on high. A - MEN.

116 Day Is Dying In The West

Mary A. Lathbury | William F. Sherwin

1. Day is dy - ing in the west, Heav'n is touching earth with rest; Wait and wor-ship while the night Sets her evening lamps alight Thro' all the sky.
2. Lord of life, be-neath the dome Of the u - ni-verse, Thy home, Gath-er us, who seek Thy face, To the fold of Thy embrace, For Thou art nigh.
3. While the deep'ning shadows fall, Heart of Love, en-fold - ing all, Thro' the glo - ry and the grace Of the stars that veil Thy face, Our hearts as-cend.
4. When for - ev - er from our sight Pass the stars, the day, the night, Lord of an - gels, on our eyes Let e - ter - nal morning rise, And shad-ows end!
Refrain.
Ho - ly, ho - ly, ho - ly, Lord God of Hosts! Heav'n and earth are full of Thee! Heav'n and earth are praising Thee, O Lord most high! A - men.

117 Now The Day Is Over

SABINE BARING-GOULD — JOSEPH BARNBY

1. Now the day is o - ver, Night is draw - ing nigh, . .
2. Je - sus, give the wea - ry Calm and sweet re - pose; . .
3. Grant to lit - tle chil - dren Vi - sions bright of Thee; . .
4. Thro' the long night-watch - es May Thine an - gels spread . .
5. When the morn - ing wak - ens, Then may I a - rise

Shad - ows of the eve - ning Steal a - cross the sky.
With Thy ten-d'rest bless - ing May our eye - lids close.
Guard the sail - ors toss - ing On the deep blue sea.
Their white wings a - bove me, Watching 'round my bed.
Pure and fresh and sin - less In Thy ho - ly eyes. A-MEN.

eve - ning Steal a - cross the sky.

118 Saviour, Breathe An Evening Blessing

(EVENING PRAYER)

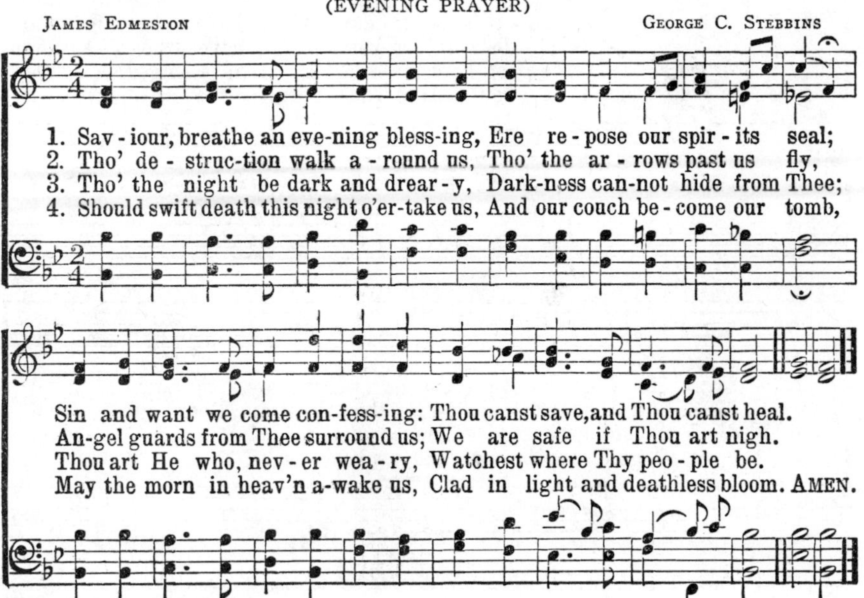
JAMES EDMESTON
GEORGE C. STEBBINS
1. Sav - iour, breathe an eve-ning bless-ing, Ere re - pose our spir - its seal;
2. Tho' de - struc-tion walk a - round us, Tho' the ar - rows past us fly,
3. Tho' the night be dark and drear - y, Dark-ness can-not hide from Thee;
4. Should swift death this night o'er-take us, And our couch be - come our tomb,
Sin and want we come con-fess-ing: Thou canst save, and Thou canst heal.
An-gel guards from Thee surround us; We are safe if Thou art nigh.
Thou art He who, nev - er wea - ry, Watchest where Thy peo - ple be.
May the morn in heav'n a-wake us, Clad in light and deathless bloom. AMEN.

119 Softly Now The Light Of Day

George W. Doane
Louis M. Gottschalk
1. Soft - ly now the light of day Fades up - on our sight a - way;
2. Thou whose all per - vad - ing eye Naught es - capes without, with-in,
3. Soon from us the light of day Shall for - ev - er pass a - way;
Free from care, from la - bor free, Lord, we would commune with Thee.
Par - don each in - firm - i - ty, O - pen fault, and se - cret sin.
Then, from sin and sor - row free, Take us, Lord, to dwell with Thee.
120 An Evening Prayer
COPYRIGHT 1911 BY CHARLES H. GABRIEL. © RENEWED 1939, THE RODEHEAVER CO. (A DIV. OF WORD, INC.). ALL RIGHTS RESERVED. INTERNATIONAL COPYRIGHT SECURED. USED BY PERMISSION.
C. M. Battersby. Arr. by C. H. G.
Chas. H. Gabriel
1. If I have wounded an - y soul to - day, If I have caused one foot to
2. If I have ut-tered i - dle words or vain, If I have turned a - side from
3. If I have been perverse or hard, or cold, If I have longed for shel-ter
4. Forgive the sins I have confessed to Thee; Forgive the se - cret sins I
go astray, If I have walked in my own will-ful way, Dear Lord, for - give!
want or pain, Lest I my-self shall suffer thro' the strain, Dear Lord, for-give!
in Thy fold, When Thou hast given me some fort to hold, Dear Lord, for - give!
do not see; O guide me, love me, and my keep - er be, A - men.

121 The Church In The Wildwood

W. S. P. — Dr. Wm. S. Pitts

1. There's a church in the val - ley by the wild-wood, No love - li - er
2. Oh, come to the church in the wild-wood, To the trees where the
3. How sweet on a clear Sab-bath morn-ing, To list to the
4. From the church in the val - ley by the wild-wood, When day fades a-

spot in the dale; No place is so dear to my child-hood As the
wild flow - ers bloom; Where the part-ing hymn will be chant-ed, We will
clear ring-ing bell; Its tones so sweet - ly are call - ing, Oh,
way in - to night, I would fain from this spot of my child-hood Wing my

D.S.—*No spot is so dear to my child-hood As the*

Fine Chorus

lit - tle brown church in the vale.
weep by the side of the tomb. Come to the
come to the church in the vale.
way to the man-sions of light. Oh, come, come, come, come, come, come,

lit-tle brown church in the vale.

D.S.

church in the wild - wood, Oh, come to the church in the vale;
come, come, come, come, come, come, come, come, come, come, come, come, come;

122 My Faith Looks Up To Thee
Ray Palmer
Lowell Mason
1. My faith looks up to Thee, Thou Lamb of Cal - va - ry, Sav - ior di - vine; Now hear me when I pray, Take all my sin a - way, O let me from this day Be whol - ly Thine!
2. May Thy rich grace impart Strength to my fainting heart, My zeal in-spire; As Thou hast died for me, O may my love to Thee, Pure, warm, and changeless be,—A liv - ing fire!
3. While life's dark maze I tread, And griefs around me spread, Be Thou my Guide; Bid darkness turn to day, Wipe sorrow's tears a - way, Nor let me ev - er stray From Thee a - side.
123 Revive Us Again
Wm. P. Mackay
John J. Husband
1. We praise Thee, O God! for the Son of Thy love, For Je - sus who died, and is now gone a - bove.
2. We praise Thee, O God! for Thy Spir - it of light, Who has shown us our Sav - ior, and scattered our night.
3. All glo - ry and praise to the Lamb that was slain, Who has borne all our sins, and has cleansed ev'ry stain.
4. Re - vive us a - gain; fill each heart with Thy love; May each soul be re - kin - dled with fire from a - bove.
Chorus
Hal - le - lu - jah! Thine the glo - ry, Hal - le-

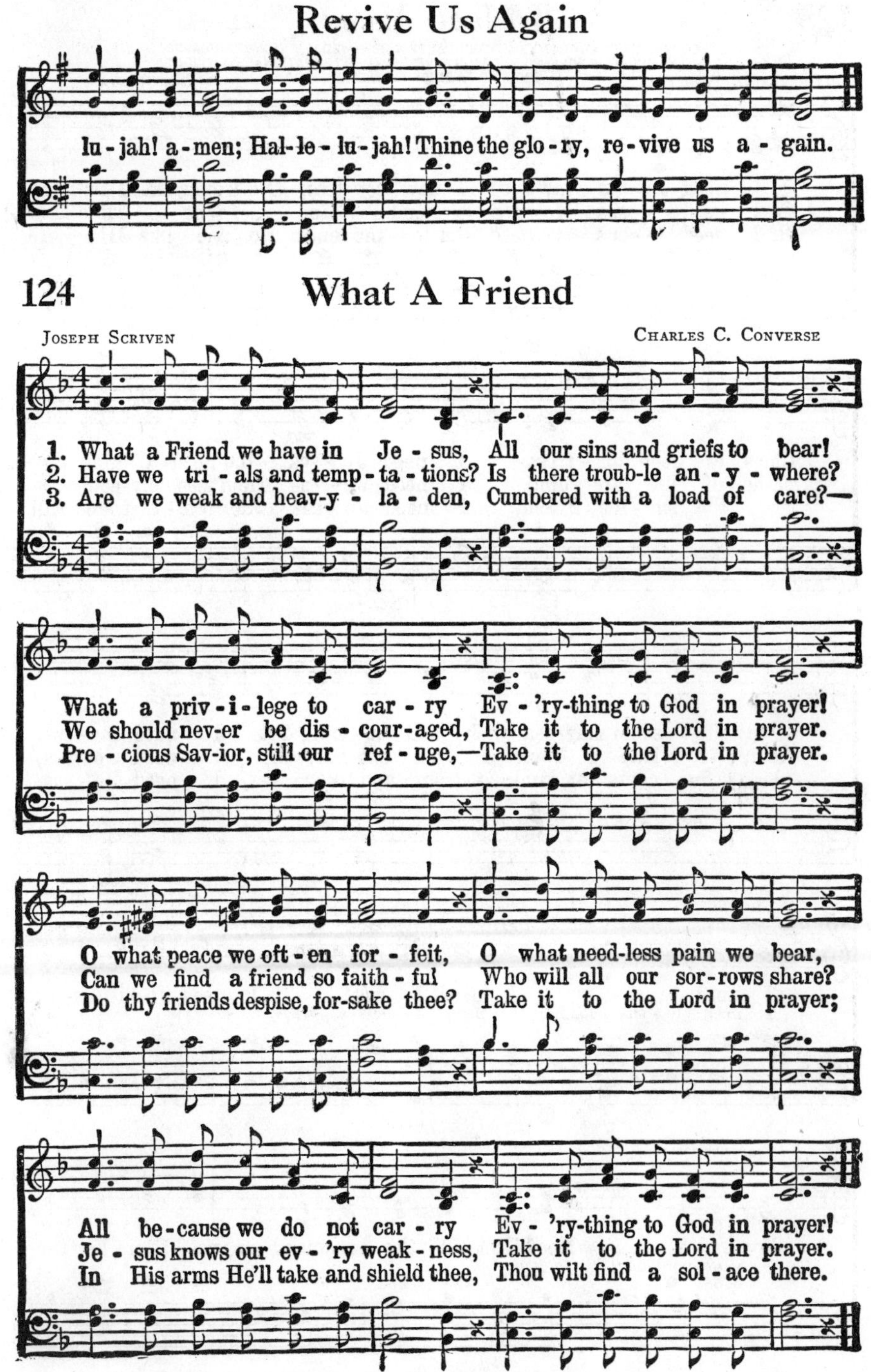
Revive Us Again
lu - jah! a - men; Hal - le - lu - jah! Thine the glo - ry, re - vive us a - gain.
124
What A Friend
Joseph Scriven
Charles C. Converse
1. What a Friend we have in Je - sus, All our sins and griefs to bear!
2. Have we tri - als and temp - ta - tions? Is there troub-le an - y - where?
3. Are we weak and heav-y - la - den, Cumbered with a load of care?—
What a priv - i - lege to car - ry Ev - 'ry-thing to God in prayer!
We should nev-er be dis - cour-aged, Take it to the Lord in prayer.
Pre - cious Sav-ior, still our ref - uge,—Take it to the Lord in prayer.
O what peace we oft - en for - feit, O what need-less pain we bear,
Can we find a friend so faith - ful Who will all our sor-rows share?
Do thy friends despise, for-sake thee? Take it to the Lord in prayer;
All be-cause we do not car - ry Ev - 'ry-thing to God in prayer!
Je - sus knows our ev - 'ry weak - ness, Take it to the Lord in prayer.
In His arms He'll take and shield thee, Thou wilt find a sol - ace there.

125 I Need Jesus

George O. Webster — Chas. H. Gabriel

1. I need Je-sus, my need I now con-fess; No friend like Him in times of deep dis-tress; I need Je-sus, the need I glad-ly own; Tho' some may bear their load a-lone, Yet I need Je-sus.
2. I need Je-sus, I need a friend like Him, A friend to guide when paths of life are dim; I need Je-sus when foes my soul as-sail; A-lone I know I can but fail,—So I need Je-sus,
3. I need Je-sus, I need Him to the end; No one like Him—He is the sin-ners Friend; I need Je-sus, no oth-er friend will do; So con-stant, kind, so strong, and true,—Yes, I need Je-sus,
Chorus
I need Je-sus, I need Je-sus, I need Je-sus ev-'ry day; . . . .
I need Je-sus with me I need Je-sus al-ways, ev-'ry day;
Need Him in the sunshine hour, need Him when the

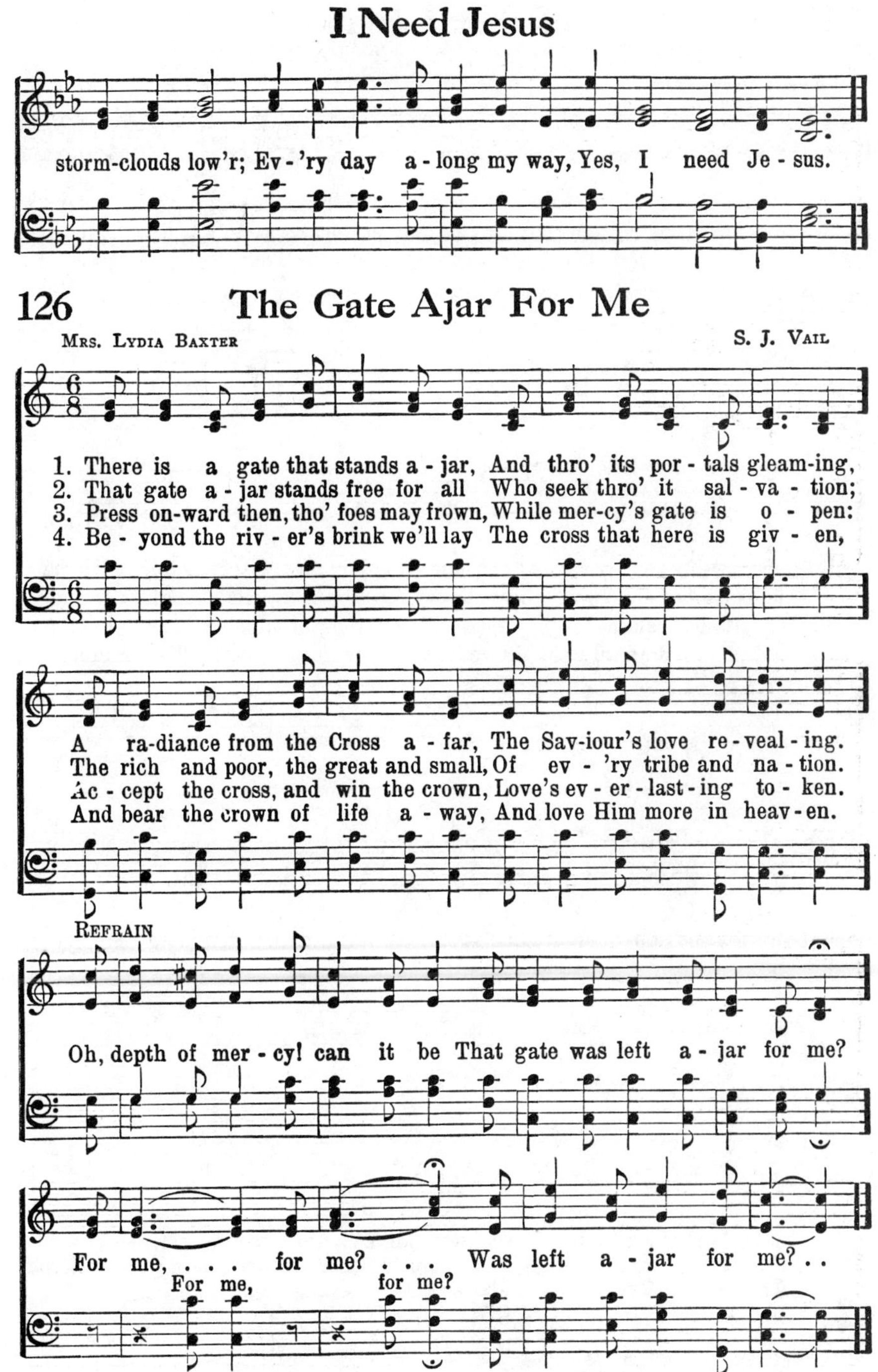
I Need Jesus
storm-clouds low'r; Ev-'ry day a-long my way, Yes, I need Je-sus.
126 The Gate Ajar For Me
Mrs. Lydia Baxter
S. J. Vail
1. There is a gate that stands a-jar, And thro' its por-tals gleam-ing,
2. That gate a-jar stands free for all Who seek thro' it sal-va-tion;
3. Press on-ward then, tho' foes may frown, While mer-cy's gate is o-pen:
4. Be-yond the riv-er's brink we'll lay The cross that here is giv-en,
A ra-diance from the Cross a-far, The Sav-iour's love re-veal-ing.
The rich and poor, the great and small, Of ev-'ry tribe and na-tion.
Ac-cept the cross, and win the crown, Love's ev-er-last-ing to-ken.
And bear the crown of life a-way, And love Him more in heav-en.
Refrain
Oh, depth of mer-cy! can it be That gate was left a-jar for me?
For me, . . . for me? . . . Was left a-jar for me? . .
For me, for me?

127 Higher Ground

Johnson Oatman, Jr. — Chas. H. Gabriel

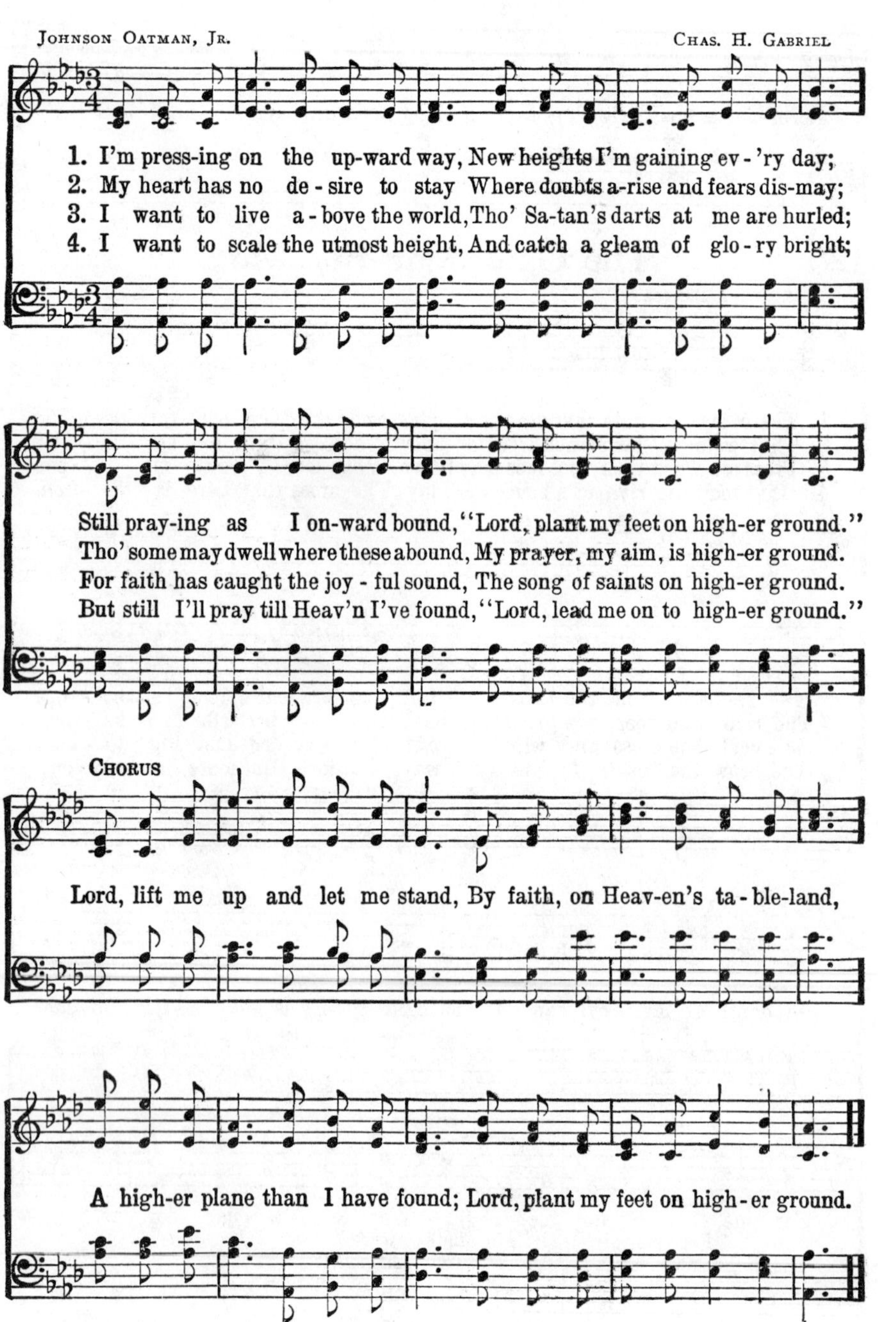
1. I'm press-ing on the up-ward way, New heights I'm gaining ev - 'ry day;
2. My heart has no de - sire to stay Where doubts a-rise and fears dis-may;
3. I want to live a - bove the world, Tho' Sa-tan's darts at me are hurled;
4. I want to scale the utmost height, And catch a gleam of glo - ry bright;
Still pray-ing as I on-ward bound, "Lord, plant my feet on high-er ground."
Tho' some may dwell where these abound, My prayer, my aim, is high-er ground.
For faith has caught the joy - ful sound, The song of saints on high-er ground.
But still I'll pray till Heav'n I've found, "Lord, lead me on to high-er ground."
Chorus
Lord, lift me up and let me stand, By faith, on Heav-en's ta - ble-land,
A high-er plane than I have found; Lord, plant my feet on high - er ground.

Jesus Is Calling

Fanny J. Crosby

Geo. C. Stebbins

1. Je-sus is ten-der-ly call-ing thee home—Call-ing to-day, call-ing to-day; Why from the sun-shine of love wilt thou roam Far-ther and far-ther a-way?
2. Je-sus is call-ing the wea-ry to rest— Call-ing to-day, call-ing to-day; Bring Him thy bur-den and thou shalt be blest: He will not turn thee a-way.
3. Je-sus is wait-ing; O come to Him now— Wait-ing to-day, wait-ing to-day; Come with thy sins; at His feet low-ly bow; Come, and no lon-ger de-lay.
4. Je-sus is plead-ing; O list to His voice: Hear Him to-day, hear Him to-day; They who be-lieve on His name shall re-joice; Quick-ly a-rise and a-way.
Refrain
Call - - ing to-day, ... Call - - ing to-day, ... Je - - - - sus is call - - - - ing, is ten-der-ly call-ing to-day.
Call-ing, call-ing to-day, to-day, Call-ing, call-ing to-day, to-day, Je-sus is ten-der-ly call-ing to-day,

129 Give Me Thy Heart

E. E. Hewitt
Annie F. Bourne
1. "Give me thy heart," says the Fa - ther a - bove, No gift so pre-cious to
2. "Give me thy heart," says the Sav - ior of men, Call - ing in mer - cy a-
3. "Give me thy heart," says the Spir - it di - vine, "All that thou hast, to my
Him as our love, Soft - ly He whis-pers wher - ev - er thou art,
gain and a - gain; "Turn now from sin, and from e - vil de - part,
keep - ing re - sign; Grace more a - bound-ing is mine to im - part,
Chorus
"Grate - ful - ly trust me, and give me thy heart."
Have I not died for thee? give me thy heart." "Give me thy heart,
Make full sur - ren - der and give me thy heart."
p
Give me thy heart," Hear the soft whisper, wher-ev - er thou art; From this dark
rit.
world He would draw thee a-part, Speak-ing so ten-der-ly, "Give me thy heart."

130 O That Will Be Glory

C. H. G.
Chas. H. Gabriel
1. When all my la-bors and tri-als are o'er, And I am safe on that
2. When, by the gift of His in-fi-nite grace, I am ac-cord-ed in
3. Friends will be there I have loved long a-go; Joy like a riv-er a-
beau-ti-ful shore, Just to be near the dear Lord I a-dore,
Heav-en a place, Just to be there and to look on His face,
round me will flow; Yet, just a smile from my Sav-ior, I know,
rit.
Chorus. Faster.
Will thro' the a-ges be glo-ry for me. . . .
O that will be
O . . . . . . that will
glo-ry for me, Glo-ry for me, glo-ry for me; When by His grace
be glo-ry for me, Glo-ry for me, glo-ry for me;. . . . . .
rit.
I shall look on His face, That will be glo-ry, be glo-ry for me. A-men.

131 Jesus Saves

Priscilla J. Owens — Wm. J. Kirkpatrick

1. We have heard the joy - ful sound: Je - sus saves! Je - sus saves!
2. Waft it on the roll - ing tide; Je - sus saves! Je - sus saves!
3. Sing a - bove the bat - tle strife, Je - sus saves! Je - sus saves!
4. Give the winds a might - y voice, Je - sus saves! Je - sus saves!
Spread the ti - dings all a - round: Je - sus saves! Je - sus saves!
Tell to sin - ners far and wide: Je - sus saves! Je - sus saves!
By His death and end - less life, Je - sus saves! Je - sus saves!
Let the na - tions now re - joice,— Je - sus saves! Je - sus saves!
Bear the news to ev - 'ry land, Climb the steeps and cross the waves;
Sing, ye is - lands of the sea; Ech - o back, ye o - cean caves;
Sing it soft - ly thro' the gloom, When the heart for mer - cy craves;
Shout sal - va - tion full and free; High - est hills and deep-est caves;
On - ward!—'tis our Lord's com - mand; Je - sus saves! Je - sus saves!
Earth shall keep her ju - bi - lee: Je - sus saves! Je - sus saves!
Sing in tri - umph o'er the tomb,— Je - sus saves! Je - sus saves!
This our song of vic - to - ry,— Je - sus saves! Je - sus saves!

132 O Jesus, Thou Art Standing

William W. How | Justin H. Knecht

1. O Je - sus, Thou art stand - ing Out - side the fast-closed door,
2. O Je - sus, Thou art knock - ing; And lo, that hand is scarred,
3. O Je - sus, Thou art plead - ing In ac - cents meek and low,
In low - ly pa-tience wait - ing To pass the thresh - old o'er:
And thorns Thy brow en - cir - cle, And tears Thy face have marred:
"I died for you, my chil - dren, And will you treat Me so?"
Shame on us, Chris-tian broth - ers, His name and sign who bear,
O love that pass - eth knowl - edge, So pa - tient - ly to wait!
O Lord, with shame and sor - row We o - pen now the door;
O shame, thrice shame up - on us, To keep Him stand - ing there!
O sin that hath no e - qual, So fast to bar the gate!
Dear Sav - ior, en - ter, en - ter, And leave us nev - er - more.

133 Where He Leads Me

E. W. Blandly — J. S. Norris

1. I can hear my Sav - iour call - ing, I can hear my Sav - iour call - ing,
2. I'll go with Him thro' the gar - den, I'll go with Him thro' the gar - den,
3. I'll go with Him thro' the judg-ment, I'll go with Him thro' the judg-ment,
4. He will give me grace and glo - ry, He will give me grace and glo - ry,
Ref.—Where He leads me I will fol - low, Where He leads me I will fol - low,
I can hear my Sav - iour call-ing, "Take thy cross and fol-low, fol - low Me."
I'll go with Him thro' the gar - den, I'll go with Him, with Him all the way.
I'll go with Him thro' the judg-ment, I'll go with Him, with Him all the way.
He will give me grace and glo - ry, And go with me, with me all the way.
Where He leads me I will fol - low, I'll go with Him, with Him all the way.

134 A Prayer For Peace

Lucy H. King Smith — Spencer Lane

1. God, Je - ho - vah, Fa - ther, Come we now to Thee; We have felt the
2. When the hour of bat - tle Held us with its pain, Guns with sul - len
3. Save the world from tri - al, Now we plead with Thee, Bought by self - de-
4. Glo-rious then the dawn-ing With Thy presence near, Beauteous wake the
bur - den Of war's en - mi - ty. Take a - way hate's an - guish, Our Geth-
rat - tle, Thousands there lay slain, Hid in dark-ness heav - en, Not a
ni - al Must the fu - ture be; Lift the hope of na - tions To in-
morn-ing, Peace bells chiming clear; Long lost voic-es sing - ing—O the

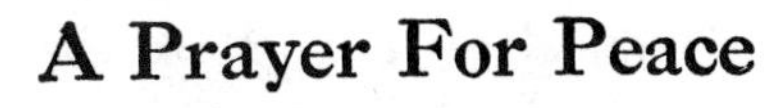

A Prayer For Peace

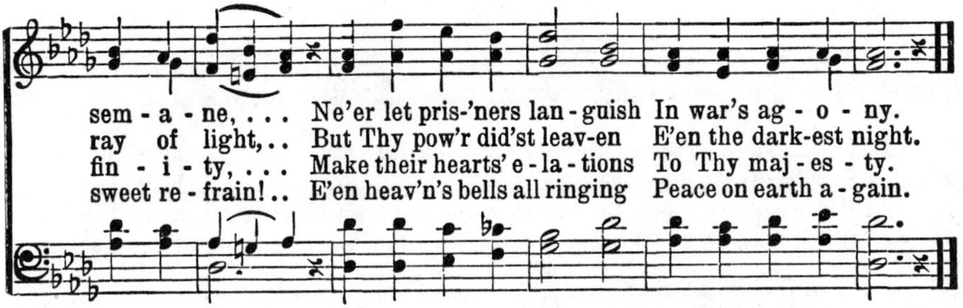

sem - a - ne, . . . Ne'er let pris-'ners lan - guish In war's ag - o - ny.
ray of light, . . But Thy pow'r did'st leav-en E'en the dark-est night.
fin - i - ty, . . . Make their hearts' e - la - tions To Thy maj - es - ty.
sweet re - frain! . . E'en heav'n's bells all ringing Peace on earth a - gain.

135 'Tis So Sweet To Trust In Jesus

Louisa M. R. Stead — Wm. J. Kirkpatrick

1. 'Tis so sweet to trust in Je - sus, Just to take Him at His Word;
2. O how sweet to trust in Je - sus, Just to trust His cleans-ing blood;
3. Yes, 'tis sweet to trust in Je - sus, Just from sin and self to cease;
4. I'm so glad I learned to trust Thee, Pre - cious Je - sus, Sav-iour, Friend;

Just to rest up - on His prom-ise; Just to know, "Thus saith the Lord."
Just in sim - ple faith to plunge me 'Neath the heal-ing, cleans-ing flood!
Just from Je - sus sim - ply tak - ing Life and rest, and joy and peace.
And I know that Thou art with me, Wilt be with me to the end.

Chorus

Je - sus, Je - sus, how I trust Him! How I've proved Him o'er and o'er!
p Je - sus, Je - sus, pre - cious Je - sus! O for grace to trust Him more!

136 I Am Praying For You

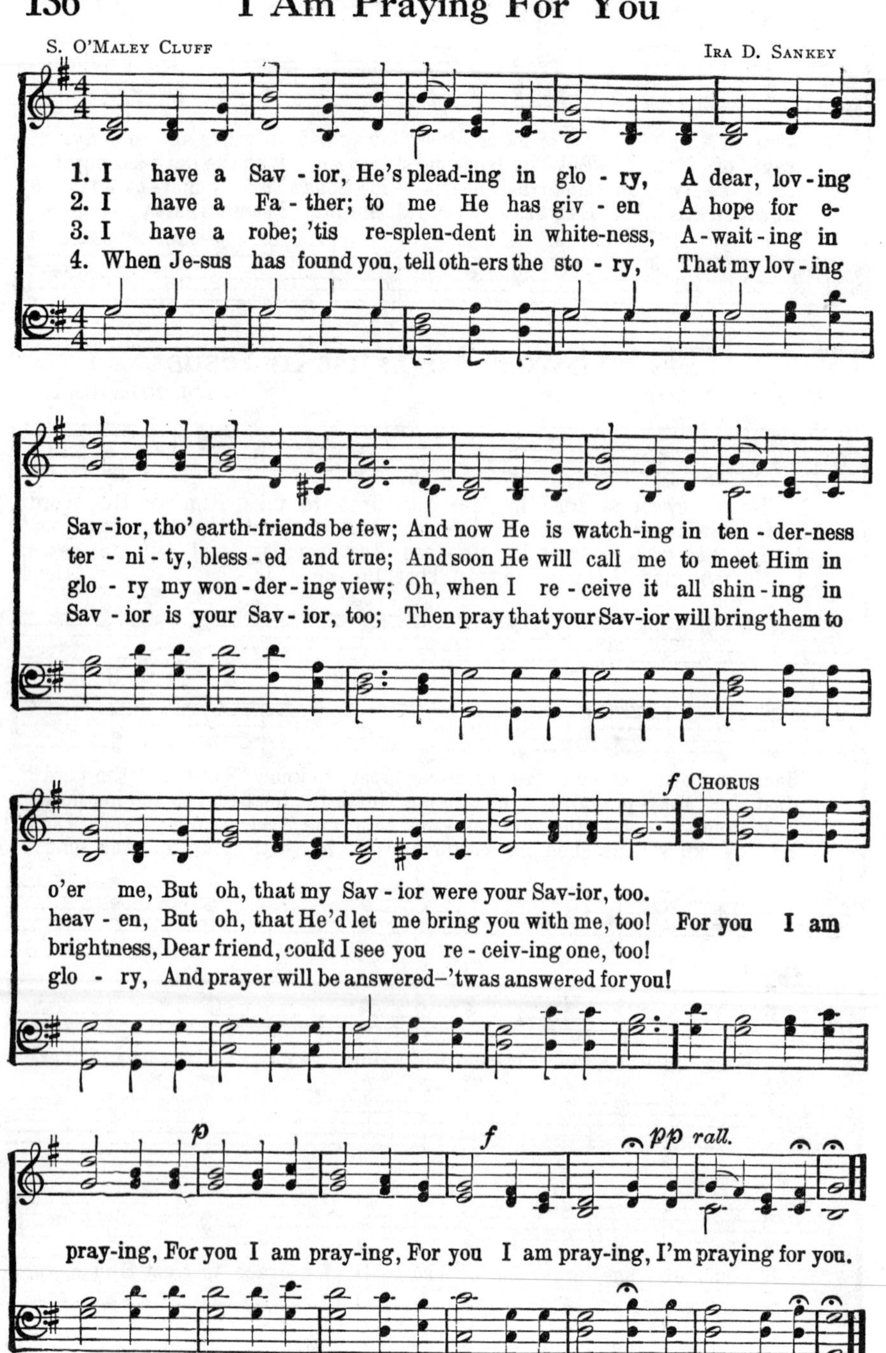
S. O'Maley Cluff
Ira D. Sankey
1. I have a Sav - ior, He's plead-ing in glo - ry, A dear, lov - ing
2. I have a Fa - ther; to me He has giv - en A hope for e-
3. I have a robe; 'tis re-splen-dent in white-ness, A - wait - ing in
4. When Je-sus has found you, tell oth-ers the sto - ry, That my lov - ing
Sav-ior, tho' earth-friends be few; And now He is watch-ing in ten - der-ness
ter - ni - ty, bless - ed and true; And soon He will call me to meet Him in
glo - ry my won - der - ing view; Oh, when I re - ceive it all shin - ing in
Sav - ior is your Sav - ior, too; Then pray that your Sav-ior will bring them to
o'er me, But oh, that my Sav - ior were your Sav-ior, too.
heav - en, But oh, that He'd let me bring you with me, too!
brightness, Dear friend, could I see you re - ceiv-ing one, too!
glo - ry, And prayer will be answered–'twas answered for you!
f CHORUS
For you I am
p
f
pp rall.
pray-ing, For you I am pray-ing, For you I am pray-ing, I'm praying for you.

137 Softly And Tenderly

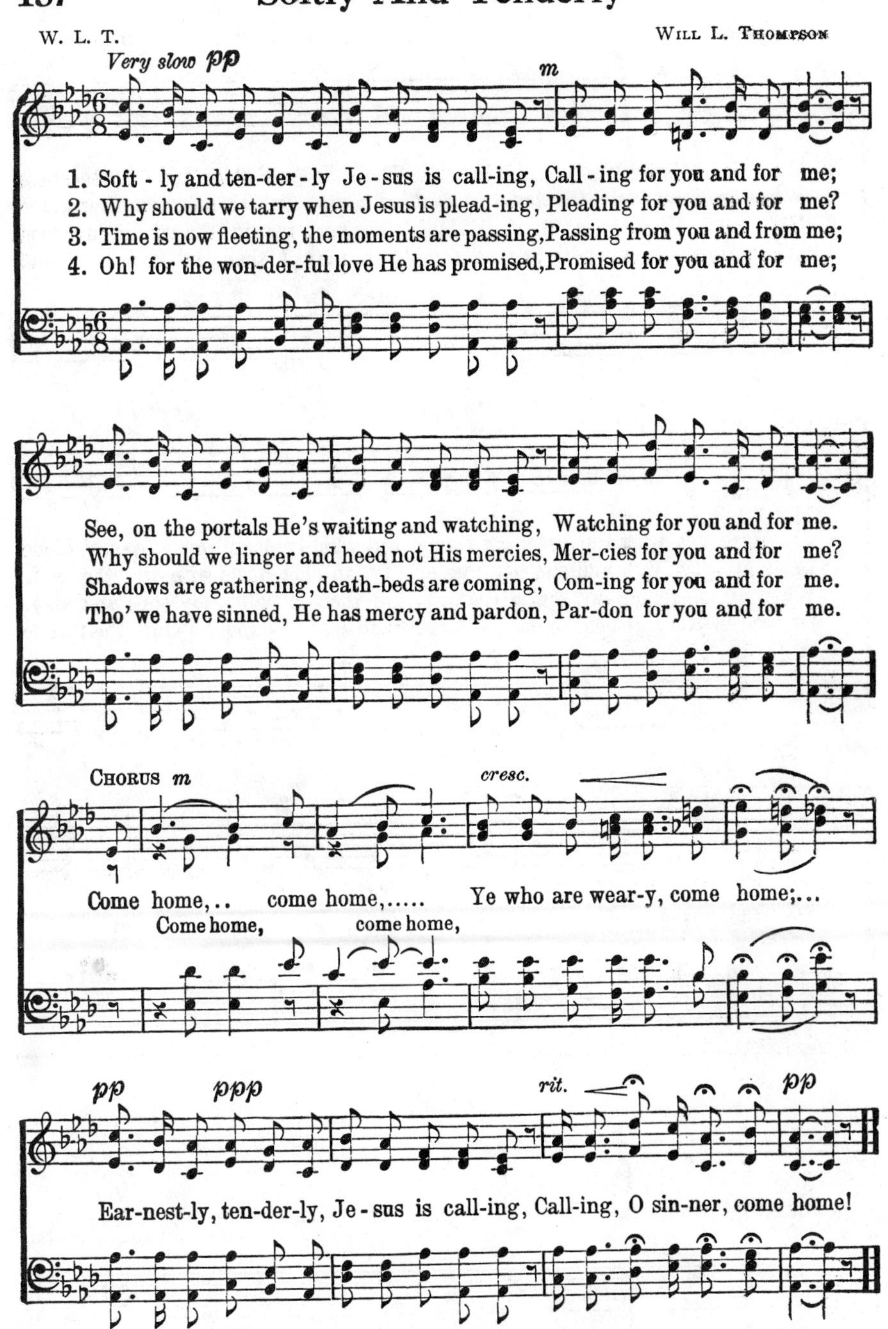
W. L. T.
Will L. Thompson
Very slow pp
m
1. Soft - ly and ten-der-ly Je-sus is call-ing, Call-ing for you and for me;
2. Why should we tarry when Jesus is plead-ing, Pleading for you and for me?
3. Time is now fleeting, the moments are passing, Passing from you and from me;
4. Oh! for the won-der-ful love He has promised, Promised for you and for me;
See, on the portals He's waiting and watching, Watching for you and for me.
Why should we linger and heed not His mercies, Mer-cies for you and for me?
Shadows are gathering, death-beds are coming, Com-ing for you and for me.
Tho' we have sinned, He has mercy and pardon, Par-don for you and for me.
Chorus m
cresc.
Come home,.. come home,..... Ye who are wear-y, come home;...
Come home, come home,
pp
ppp
rit.
pp
Ear-nest-ly, ten-der-ly, Je-sus is call-ing, Call-ing, O sin-ner, come home!

138 My Hope Is Built

Edward Mote — William B. Bradbury

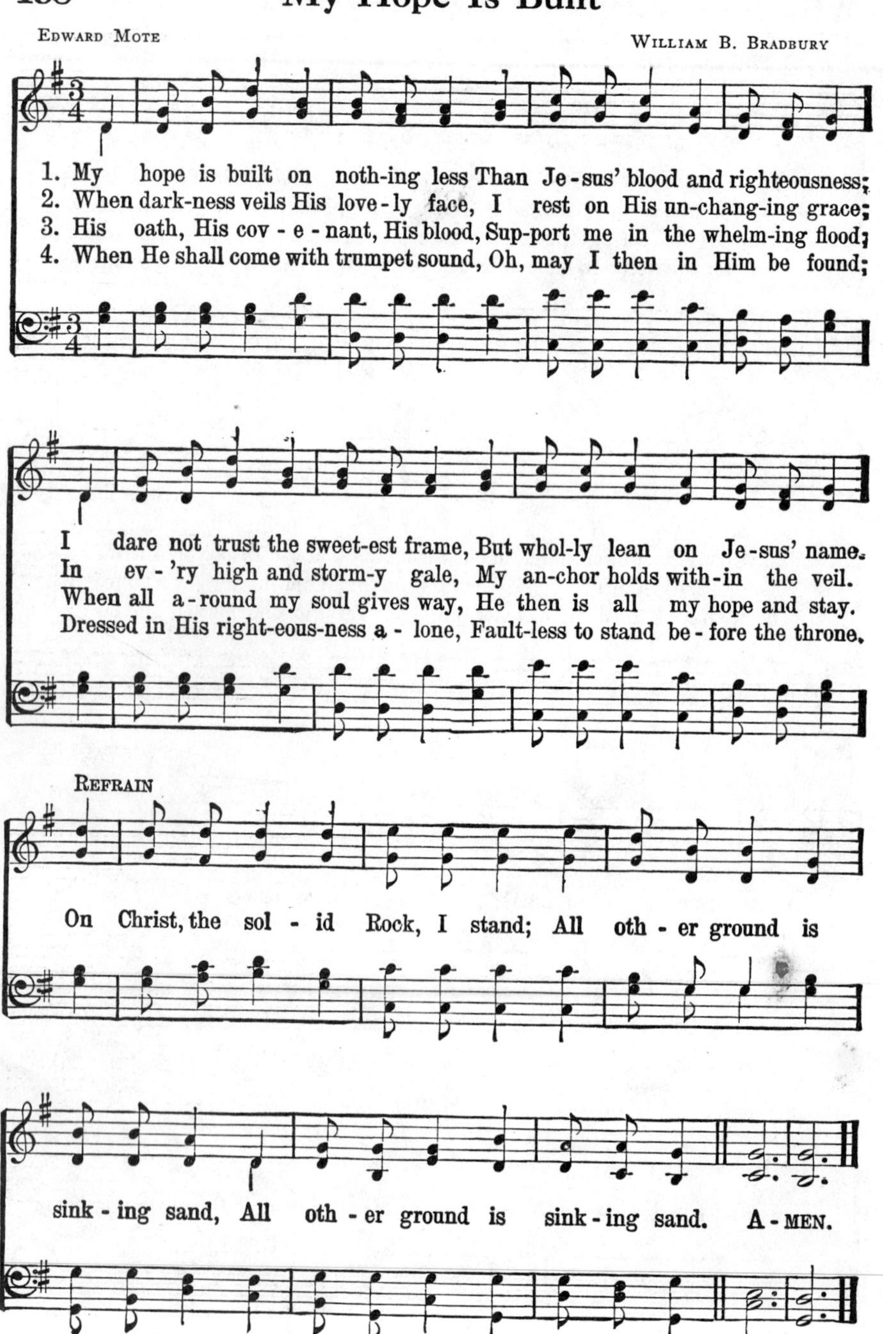
1. My hope is built on noth-ing less Than Je-sus' blood and righteousness;
2. When dark-ness veils His love-ly face, I rest on His un-chang-ing grace;
3. His oath, His cov-e-nant, His blood, Sup-port me in the whelm-ing flood;
4. When He shall come with trumpet sound, Oh, may I then in Him be found;
I dare not trust the sweet-est frame, But whol-ly lean on Je-sus' name.
In ev-'ry high and storm-y gale, My an-chor holds with-in the veil.
When all a-round my soul gives way, He then is all my hope and stay.
Dressed in His right-eous-ness a-lone, Fault-less to stand be-fore the throne.
Refrain
On Christ, the sol-id Rock, I stand; All oth-er ground is sink-ing sand, All oth-er ground is sink-ing sand. A-men.

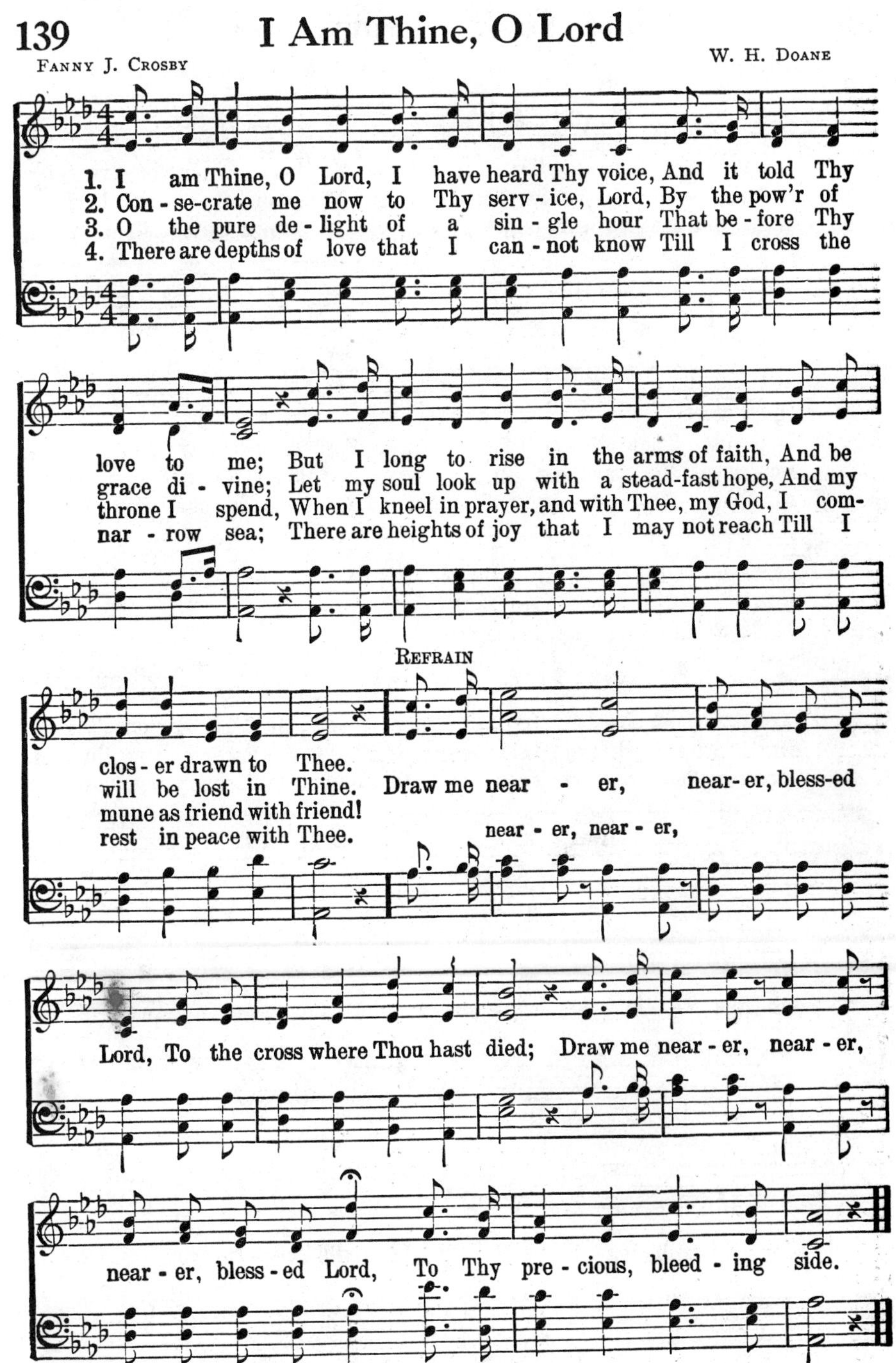

139
I Am Thine, O Lord
Fanny J. Crosby
W. H. Doane
1. I am Thine, O Lord, I have heard Thy voice, And it told Thy
2. Con - se-crate me now to Thy serv - ice, Lord, By the pow'r of
3. O the pure de - light of a sin - gle hour That be - fore Thy
4. There are depths of love that I can - not know Till I cross the
love to me; But I long to rise in the arms of faith, And be
grace di - vine; Let my soul look up with a stead-fast hope, And my
throne I spend, When I kneel in prayer, and with Thee, my God, I com-
nar - row sea; There are heights of joy that I may not reach Till I
Refrain
clos - er drawn to Thee.
will be lost in Thine.
mune as friend with friend!
rest in peace with Thee.
Draw me near - er, near - er, bless-ed
near - er, near - er,
Lord, To the cross where Thou hast died; Draw me near - er, near - er,
near - er, bless - ed Lord, To Thy pre - cious, bleed - ing side.

140
Yield Not To Temptation
H. R. Palmer
H. R. Palmer
1. Yield not to temp-ta-tion, For yield-ing is sin; Each vic-t'ry will
2. Shun e-vil com-pan-ions, Bad lan-guage dis-dain; God's name hold in
3. To him that o'er-com-eth, God giv-eth a crown; Thro' faith we will
help you Some oth-er to win; Fight man-ful-ly on-ward,
rev-'rence, Nor take it in vain; Be thought-ful and ear-nest,
con-quer, Tho' oft-en cast down; He who is our Sav-ior,
Dark pas-sions sub-due; Look ev-er to Je-sus, He'll car-ry you through.
Kind-heart-ed and true; Look ev-er to Je-sus, He'll car-ry you through.
Our strength will re-new; Look ev-er to Je-sus, He'll car-ry you through.
Chorus
Ask the Sav-ior to help you, Com-fort, strength-en, and keep you;
He is will-ing to aid you, He will car-ry you through.

141 The Way Of The Cross Leads Home

Jessie Brown Pounds
Chas. H. Gabriel
1. I must needs go home by the way of the cross, There's no oth - er
2. I must needs go on in the blood-sprinkled way, The path that the
3. Then I bid fare-well to the way of the world, To walk in it
way but this; I shall ne'er get sight of the Gates of Light,
Sav - ior trod, If I ev - er climb to the heights sub-lime,
nev - er - more; For my Lord says "Come," and I seek my home,
Chorus.
If the way of the cross I miss.
Where the soul is at home with God.
Where He waits at the o - pen door.
The way of the cross leads
home, The way of the cross leads home; It is
leads home,
leads home;
sweet to know, as I on-ward go, The way of the cross leads home. A - men.

142 I'll Go Where You Want Me To Go

MARY BROWN — CARRIE E. ROUNSEFELL

1. It may not be on the mountain's height, Or o - ver the storm - y sea;
2. Per-haps to - day there are lov - ing words Which Jesus would have me speak;
3. There's surely somewhere a low - ly place In earth's harvest-fields so wide,
It may not be at the bat - tle's front My Lord will have need of me;
There may be now, in the paths of sin, Some wand'rer whom I should seek.
Where I may la - bor thro' life's short day For Je - sus, the Cru - ci - fied.
But if by a still, small voice He calls To paths I do not know,
O Sav - ior, if Thou wilt be my Guide, Tho' dark and rug-ged the way,
So, trust-ing my all un - to Thy care, I know Thou lov - est me!
I'll answer, dear Lord, with my hand in Thine, I'll go where you want me to go.
My voice shall ech - o the mes-sage sweet, I'll say what you want me to say.
I'll do Thy will with a heart sin-cere, I'll be what you want me to be.
REFRAIN
I'll go where you want me to go, dear Lord, O'er mountain, or plain, or sea;

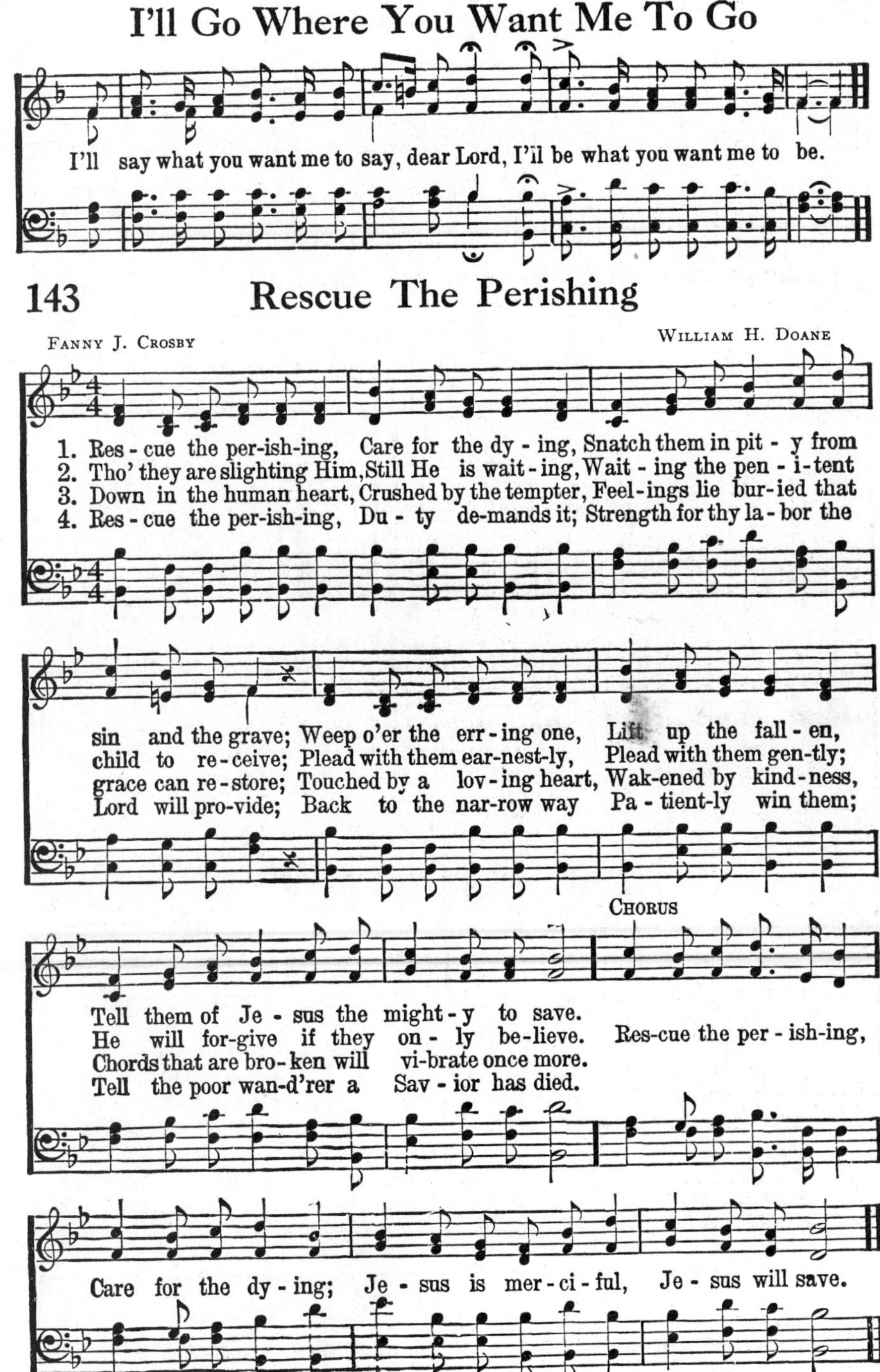
I'll Go Where You Want Me To Go
I'll say what you want me to say, dear Lord, I'll be what you want me to be.
143
Rescue The Perishing
Fanny J. Crosby
William H. Doane
1. Res - cue the per-ish-ing, Care for the dy - ing, Snatch them in pit - y from
2. Tho' they are slighting Him, Still He is wait - ing, Wait - ing the pen - i-tent
3. Down in the human heart, Crushed by the tempter, Feel-ings lie bur-ied that
4. Res - cue the per-ish-ing, Du - ty de-mands it; Strength for thy la - bor the
sin and the grave; Weep o'er the err - ing one, Lift up the fall - en,
child to re-ceive; Plead with them ear-nest-ly, Plead with them gen-tly;
grace can re-store; Touched by a lov - ing heart, Wak-ened by kind-ness,
Lord will pro-vide; Back to the nar-row way Pa - tient-ly win them;
Chorus
Tell them of Je - sus the might - y to save.
He will for-give if they on - ly be-lieve.
Chords that are bro- ken will vi-brate once more.
Tell the poor wan-d'rer a Sav - ior has died.
Res-cue the per - ish-ing,
Care for the dy - ing; Je - sus is mer - ci - ful, Je - sus will save.

144 I Am Coming To The Cross

William McDonald | William G. Fischer

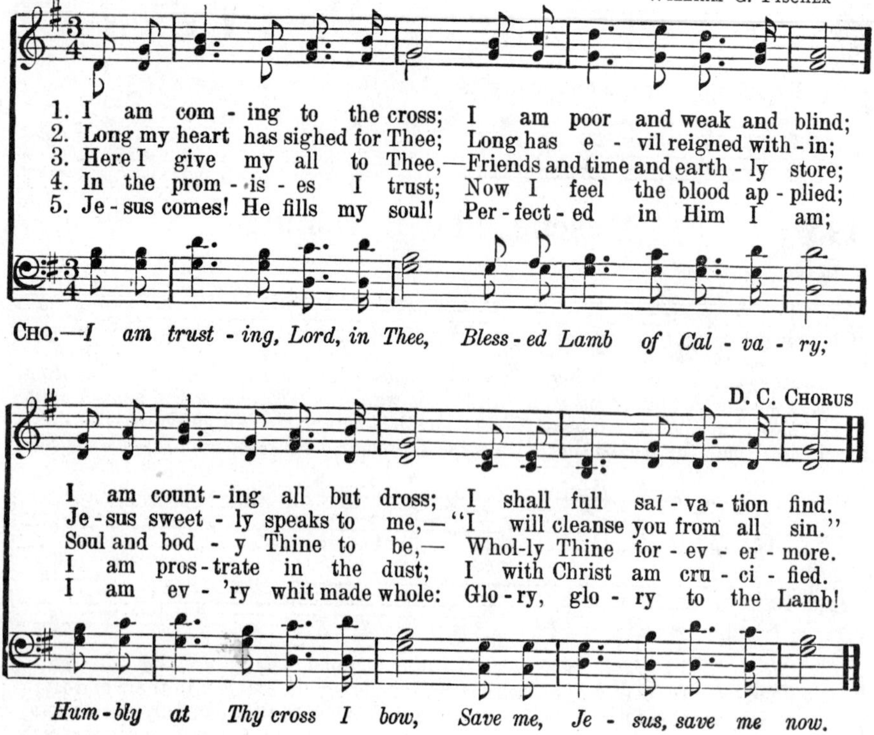

1. I am com - ing to the cross; I am poor and weak and blind;
I am count - ing all but dross; I shall full sal - va - tion find.

2. Long my heart has sighed for Thee; Long has e - vil reigned with - in;
Je - sus sweet - ly speaks to me,— "I will cleanse you from all sin."

3. Here I give my all to Thee,—Friends and time and earth - ly store;
Soul and bod - y Thine to be,— Whol-ly Thine for - ev - er - more.

4. In the prom - is - es I trust; Now I feel the blood ap - plied;
I am pros - trate in the dust; I with Christ am cru - ci - fied.

5. Je - sus comes! He fills my soul! Per - fect - ed in Him I am;
I am ev - 'ry whit made whole: Glo - ry, glo - ry to the Lamb!

Cho.—*I am trust - ing, Lord, in Thee, Bless - ed Lamb of Cal - va - ry;*
Hum - bly at Thy cross I bow, Save me, Je - sus, save me now.

D. C. Chorus

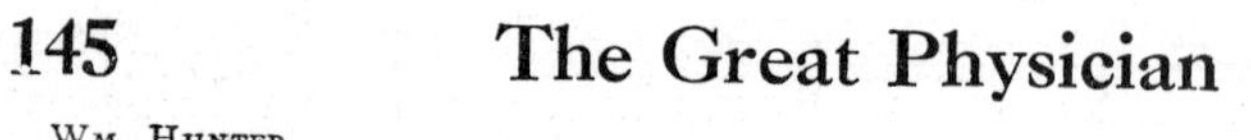

145 The Great Physician

Wm. Hunter | J. H. Stockton

Fine
1. {The great Phy - si - cian now is here, The sym - pa - thiz - ing Je - sus;
He speaks the droop - ing heart to cheer, O hear the voice of Je - sus.}
2. {Your man - y sins are all for - giv'n, O hear the voice of Je - sus;
Go on your way in peace to heav'n, And wear a crown with Je - sus.}
3. {All glo - ry to the dy - ing Lamb! I now be - lieve in Je - sus;
I love the bless - ed Sav - ior's name, I love the name of Je - sus.}
4. {And when to that bright world a - bove, We rise to be with Je - sus,
We'll sing a - round the throne of love, His name, the name of Je - sus.}
D. S.—Sweet - est car - ol ev - er sung, Je - sus, bless - ed Je - sus.

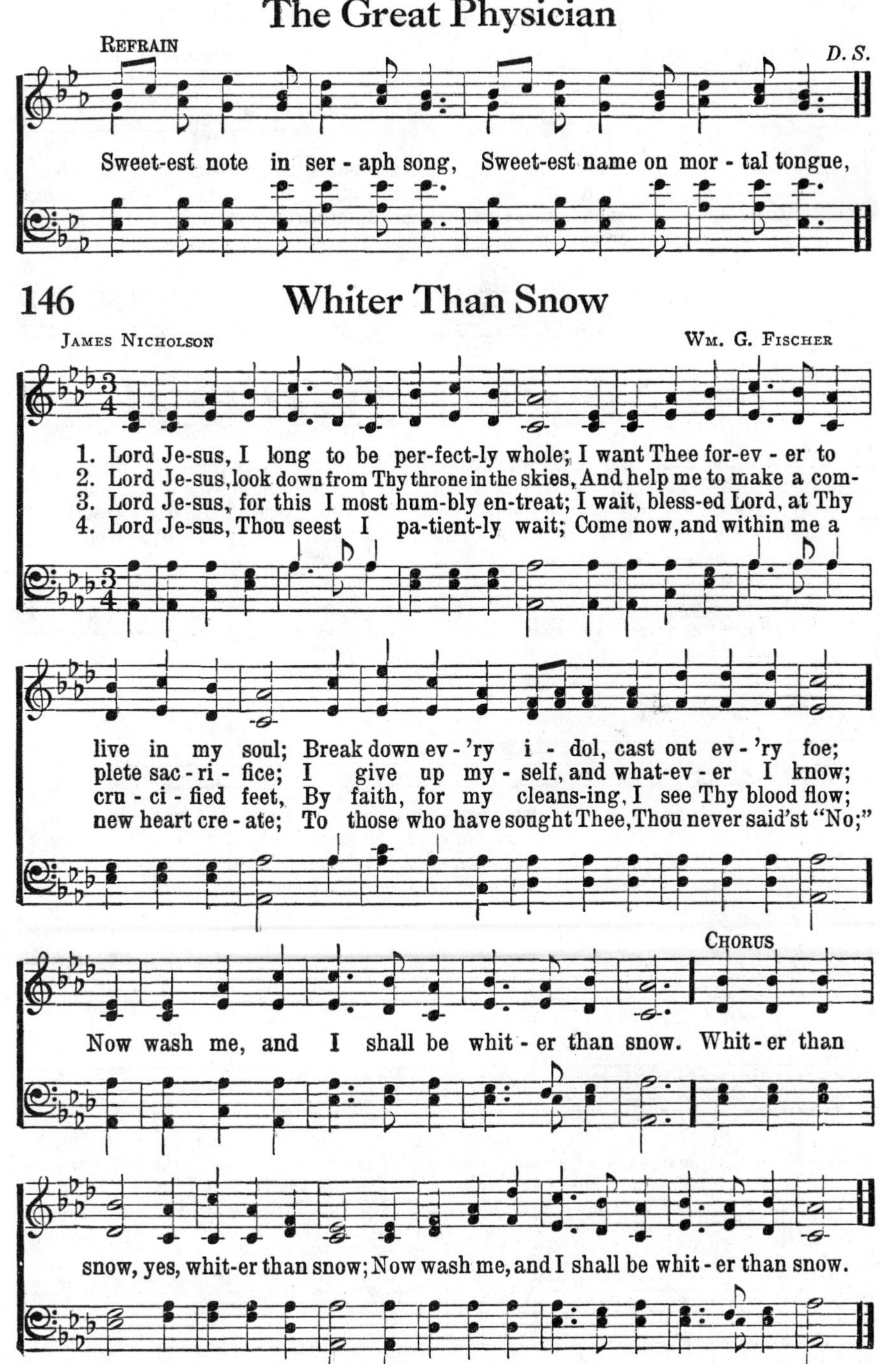
The Great Physician
Refrain
D. S.
Sweet-est note in ser - aph song, Sweet-est name on mor - tal tongue,
146
Whiter Than Snow
James Nicholson
Wm. G. Fischer
1. Lord Je-sus, I long to be per-fect-ly whole; I want Thee for-ev - er to
2. Lord Je-sus, look down from Thy throne in the skies, And help me to make a com-
3. Lord Je-sus, for this I most hum-bly en-treat; I wait, bless-ed Lord, at Thy
4. Lord Je-sus, Thou seest I pa-tient-ly wait; Come now, and within me a
live in my soul; Break down ev - 'ry i - dol, cast out ev - 'ry foe;
plete sac - ri - fice; I give up my - self, and what-ev - er I know;
cru - ci - fied feet, By faith, for my cleans-ing, I see Thy blood flow;
new heart cre - ate; To those who have sought Thee, Thou never said'st "No;"
Chorus
Now wash me, and I shall be whit - er than snow. Whit - er than
snow, yes, whit-er than snow; Now wash me, and I shall be whit - er than snow.

147
Rise Up, O Men Of God
William P. Merrill
William H. Walter
1. Rise up, O men of God! Have done with less - er things; Give
2. Rise up, O men of God! His king-dom tar - ries long: Bring
3. Rise up, O men of God! The Church for you doth wait, Her
4. Lift high the cross of Christ! Tread where His feet have trod: As
heart and soul and mind and strength To serve the King of kings.
in the day of broth - er - hood And end the night of wrong.
strength un - e - qual to her task: Rise up, and make her great!
broth - ers of the Son of Man Rise up, O men of God!
148
I Surrender All
J. W. Van Deventer
W. S. Weeden
1. All to Je - sus I sur-ren-der, All to Him I free - ly give;
2. All to Je - sus I sur-ren-der, Hum-bly at His feet I bow,
3. All to Je - sus I sur-ren-der, Make me, Sav-iour, whol - ly Thine;
4. All to Je - sus I sur-ren-der, Lord, I give my-self to Thee;
5. All to Je - sus I sur-ren-der, Now I feel the sa - cred flame;
I will ev - er love and trust Him, In His pres-ence dai - ly live.
World-ly pleas-ures all for-sak-en, Take me, Je - sus, take me now.
Let me feel the Ho - ly Spir - it,—Tru - ly know that Thou art mine.
Fill me with Thy love and pow-er, Let Thy bless-ing fall on me.
Oh, the joy of full sal - va - tion! Glo - ry, glo - ry to His name!

I Surrender All
Chorus
I sur-ren-der all, I sur-ren-der all,
I sur-ren-der all, I sur-ren-der all,
All to Thee, my bless-ed Sav-iour, I sur-ren-der all.
149
Pass Me Not
Fanny J. Crosby
William H. Doane
1. Pass me not, O gen-tle Sav-iour, Hear my hum-ble cry,
2. Let me at a throne of mer-cy Find a sweet re-lief;
3. Trust-ing on-ly in Thy mer-it, Would I seek Thy face;
4. Thou the Spring of all my com-fort, More than life to me,
While on oth-ers Thou art call-ing, Do not pass me by.
Kneel-ing there in deep con-tri-tion, Help my un-be-lief.
Heal my wounded, bro-ken spir-it, Save me by Thy grace.
Whom have I on earth be-side Thee? Whom in heav'n but Thee?
Refrain
Sav-iour, Sav-iour,
Hear my humble cry; While on others Thou art call-ing, Do not pass me by.

150 O Happy Day

PHILIP DODDRIDGE

E. F. RIMBAULT

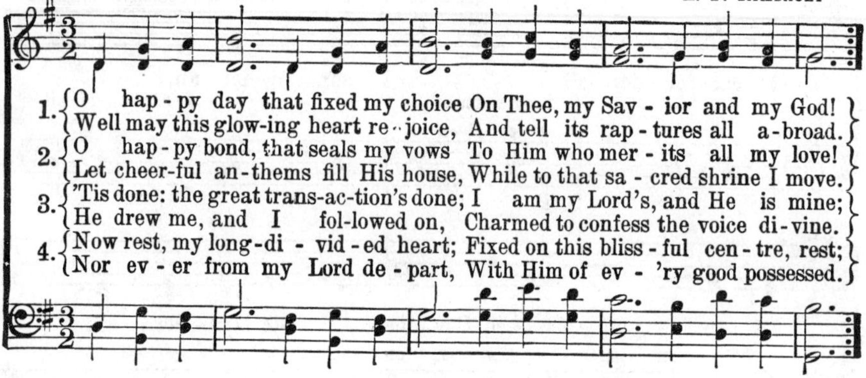

1. O hap - py day that fixed my choice On Thee, my Sav - ior and my God!
Well may this glow-ing heart re - joice, And tell its rap - tures all a-broad.
2. O hap - py bond, that seals my vows To Him who mer - its all my love!
Let cheer-ful an-thems fill His house, While to that sa - cred shrine I move.
3. 'Tis done: the great trans-ac-tion's done; I am my Lord's, and He is mine;
He drew me, and I fol-lowed on, Charmed to confess the voice di-vine.
4. Now rest, my long-di - vid - ed heart; Fixed on this bliss - ful cen - tre, rest;
Nor ev - er from my Lord de - part, With Him of ev - 'ry good possessed.

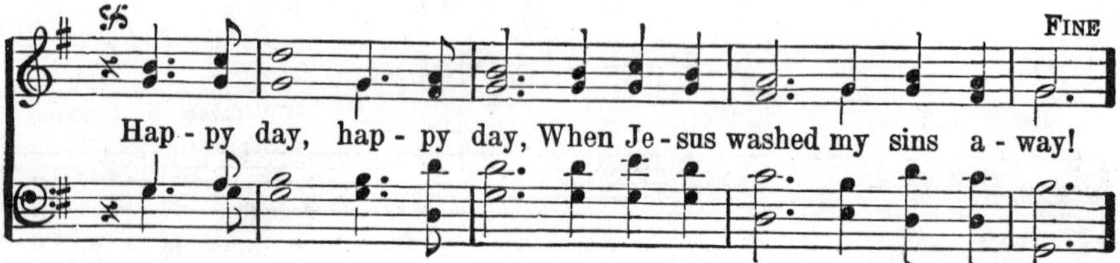

𝄋 Hap - py day, hap - py day, When Je - sus washed my sins a - way! FINE

He taught me how to watch and pray, And live re - joic - ing ev - 'ry day; D. S.

151 Just As I Am

CHARLOTTE ELLIOTT

WILLIAM B. BRADBURY

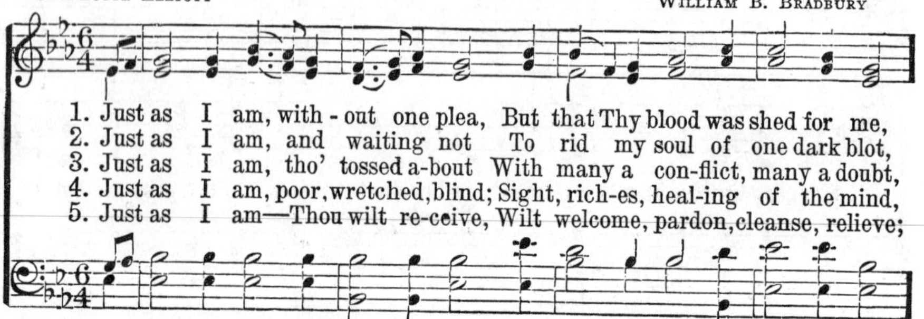
1. Just as I am, with - out one plea, But that Thy blood was shed for me,
2. Just as I am, and waiting not To rid my soul of one dark blot,
3. Just as I am, tho' tossed a-bout With many a con-flict, many a doubt,
4. Just as I am, poor, wretched, blind; Sight, rich-es, heal-ing of the mind,
5. Just as I am—Thou wilt re-ceive, Wilt welcome, pardon, cleanse, relieve;

Just As I Am

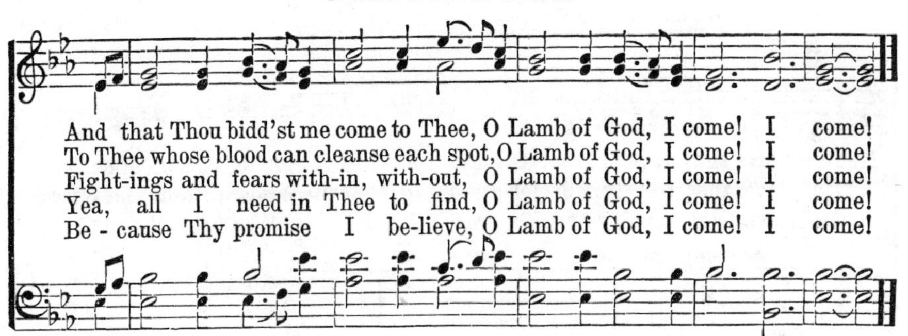
And that Thou bidd'st me come to Thee, O Lamb of God, I come! I come!
To Thee whose blood can cleanse each spot, O Lamb of God, I come! I come!
Fight-ings and fears with-in, with-out, O Lamb of God, I come! I come!
Yea, all I need in Thee to find, O Lamb of God, I come! I come!
Be - cause Thy promise I be-lieve, O Lamb of God, I come! I come!

152 Almost Persuaded

P. P. B. — P. P. Bliss

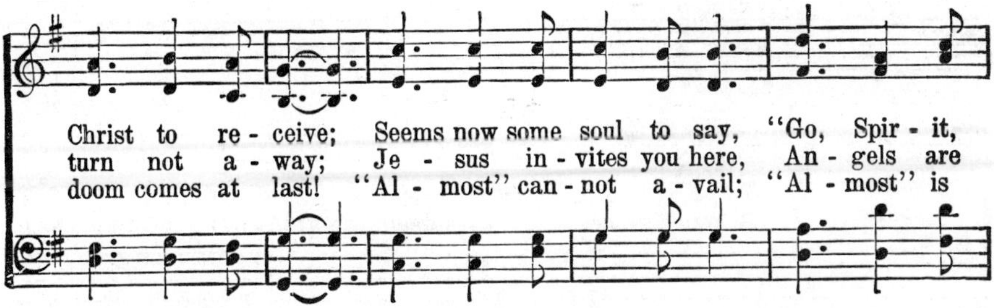

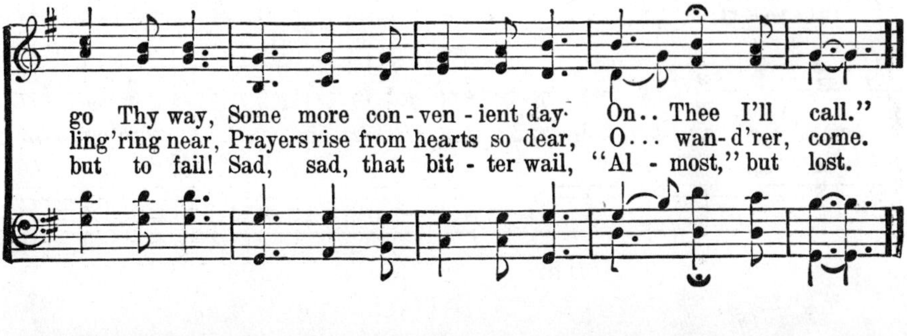

1. "Al - most per-suad - ed," now to be - lieve; "Al - most per-suad - ed," Christ to re - ceive; Seems now some soul to say, "Go, Spir - it, go Thy way, Some more con - ven - ient day On.. Thee I'll call."
2. "Al - most per-suad - ed," come, come to - day; "Al - most per-suad - ed," turn not a - way; Je - sus in - vites you here, An - gels are ling'ring near, Prayers rise from hearts so dear, O... wan-d'rer, come.
3. "Al - most per-suad - ed," har - vest is past! "Al - most per-suad - ed," doom comes at last! "Al - most" can - not a - vail; "Al - most" is but to fail! Sad, sad, that bit - ter wail, "Al - most," but lost.

153 Love, Mercy And Grace

C. A. M. C. AUSTIN MILES

1. 'Twas Love that gave at great-est cost A Life, that mine should not be lost.
2. The love that free-ly all for-gives In full-ness now with-in me lives;
3. God's love, His mer-cy and His grace, Com-bine to raise a fall-en race;
The Love that died in deep de-spair My debt ful-ly sat-is-fied there.
Thro' ev-'ry tri-al this I see; His grace is suf-fi-cient for me.
His hand is read-y, ere we call, Held out with for-give-ness for all.
CHORUS
It was Love . . . that took my place On the cross of Cal-va-
It was Love that took my place
the cross of
ry; It was grace, . . . re-deem-ing grace, That
It was grace, re-deem-ing grace,
Cal-va-ry;
paid my ran-som full and free. O-ver sin, ... with-out, with-
O-ver sin,

Love, Mercy And Grace

154 Rise, Crowned With Light

10. 10. 10. 10.

Alexander Pope, 1688-1744
Stanza 3, line 4, alt.

Russian Hymn
Alexis T. Lwoff

With majesty
in, I have . . . . . the vic - to - ry,
with-out, with-in, I have the vic - to - ry, I have the vic - to - ry,
Thro' grace, mar-vel-ous grace, that lives in me.
Thro' grace, mar-vel - ous grace,
1. Rise, crowned with light, im - pe - rial cit - y, rise! Ex - alt thy tow-'ring head and lift thine eyes! See heav'n its spar-kling por-tals wide dis-play, And break up - on thee in a flood of day!
2. See a long race thy spa-cious courts a-dorn; See fu - ture sons, and daugh-ters yet un - born, In crowd-ing ranks on ev - 'ry side a-rise, De - mand-ing life, im - pa-tient for the skies.
3. The seas shall waste, the skies in smoke de - cay, Rocks fall to dust, and moun-tains melt a - way; But fixed His word, His sav - ing pow'r re-mains; Thy realm shall last, thy own Mes - si - ah reigns! A - MEN.

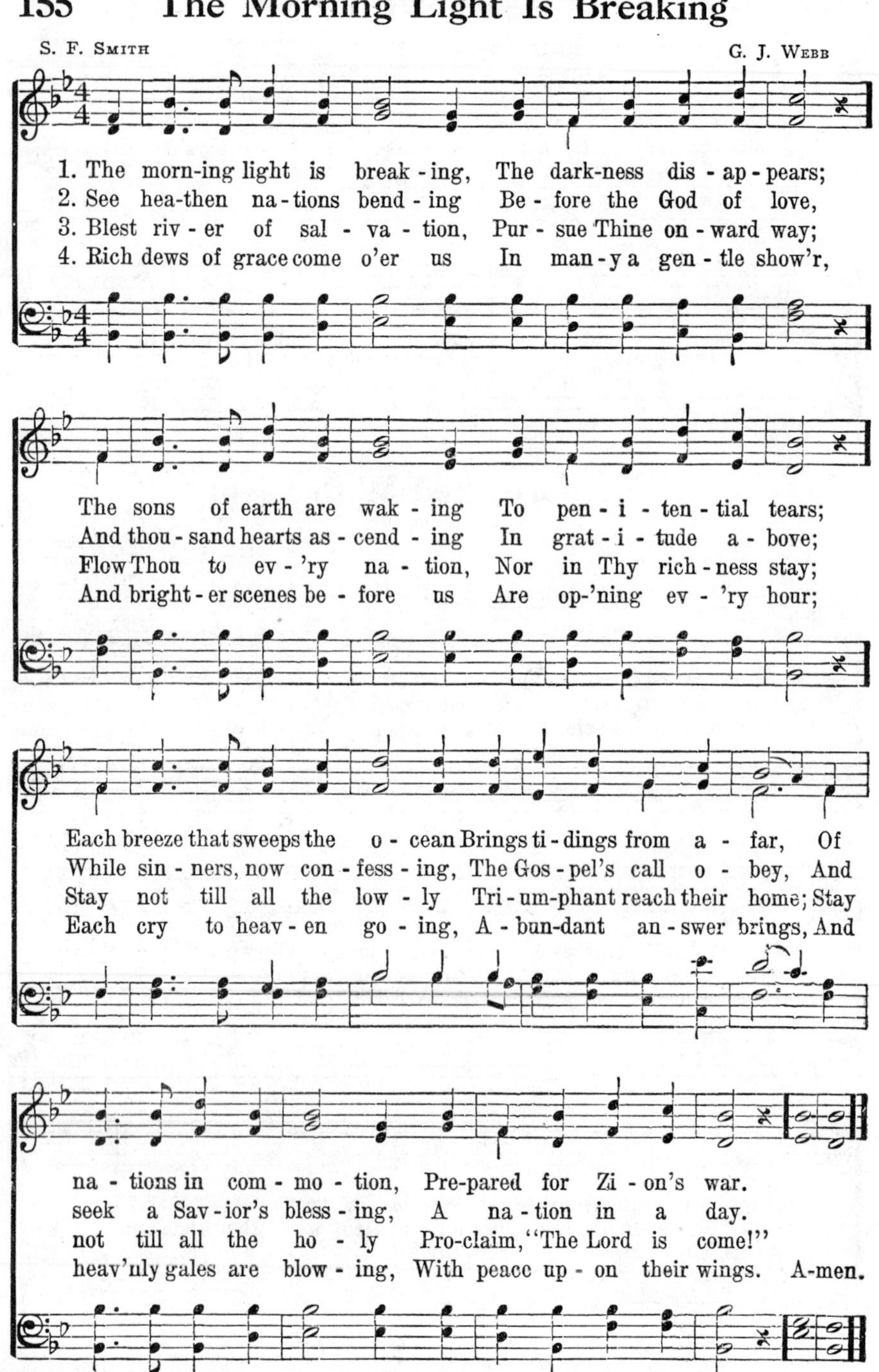
155 The Morning Light Is Breaking
S. F. Smith
G. J. Webb
1. The morn-ing light is break - ing, The dark-ness dis - ap - pears;
2. See hea-then na - tions bend - ing Be - fore the God of love,
3. Blest riv - er of sal - va - tion, Pur - sue Thine on - ward way;
4. Rich dews of grace come o'er us In man - y a gen - tle show'r,
The sons of earth are wak - ing To pen - i - ten - tial tears;
And thou - sand hearts as - cend - ing In grat - i - tude a - bove;
Flow Thou to ev - 'ry na - tion, Nor in Thy rich - ness stay;
And bright - er scenes be - fore us Are op-'ning ev - 'ry hour;
Each breeze that sweeps the o - cean Brings ti - dings from a - far, Of
While sin - ners, now con - fess - ing, The Gos - pel's call o - bey, And
Stay not till all the low - ly Tri - um-phant reach their home; Stay
Each cry to heav - en go - ing, A - bun-dant an - swer brings, And
na - tions in com - mo - tion, Pre-pared for Zi - on's war.
seek a Sav - ior's bless - ing, A na - tion in a day.
not till all the ho - ly Pro-claim, "The Lord is come!"
heav'nly gales are blow - ing, With peace up - on their wings. A-men.

156 At Length There Dawns The Glorious Day

ST. MICHEL'S. C. M. D.
OZORA S. DAVIS, 1866-1931
From W. GAWLER'S HYMNS AND PSALMS, 1789
1. At length there dawns the glo - rious day By proph-ets long fore - told;
2. For what are sun-d'ring strains of blood, Or an-cient caste and creed?
3. One com - mon faith u - nites us all, We seek one com - mon goal,
At length the cho - rus clear - er grows That shep - herds heard of old.
One claim u - nites all men in God To serve each hu - man need.
One ten - der com-fort broods up - on The strug - gling hu - man soul.
The day of dawn-ing Broth - er - hood Breaks on our ea - ger eyes,
Then here to - geth - er, broth - er - men, We pledge the Lord a - new
To this clear call of Broth - er - hood Our hearts re - spon - sive ring;
And hu - man ha - treds flee be - fore The ra - diant east-ern skies.
Our loy - al love, our stal-wart faith, Our serv-ice strong and true.
We join the glo - rious new cru - sade Of our great Lord and King. A-MEN.

157 Forward Through The Ages

ST. GERTRUDE. 6, 5, 6, 5, D. WITH REFRAIN

FREDERICK L. HOSMER — ARTHUR S. SULLIVAN

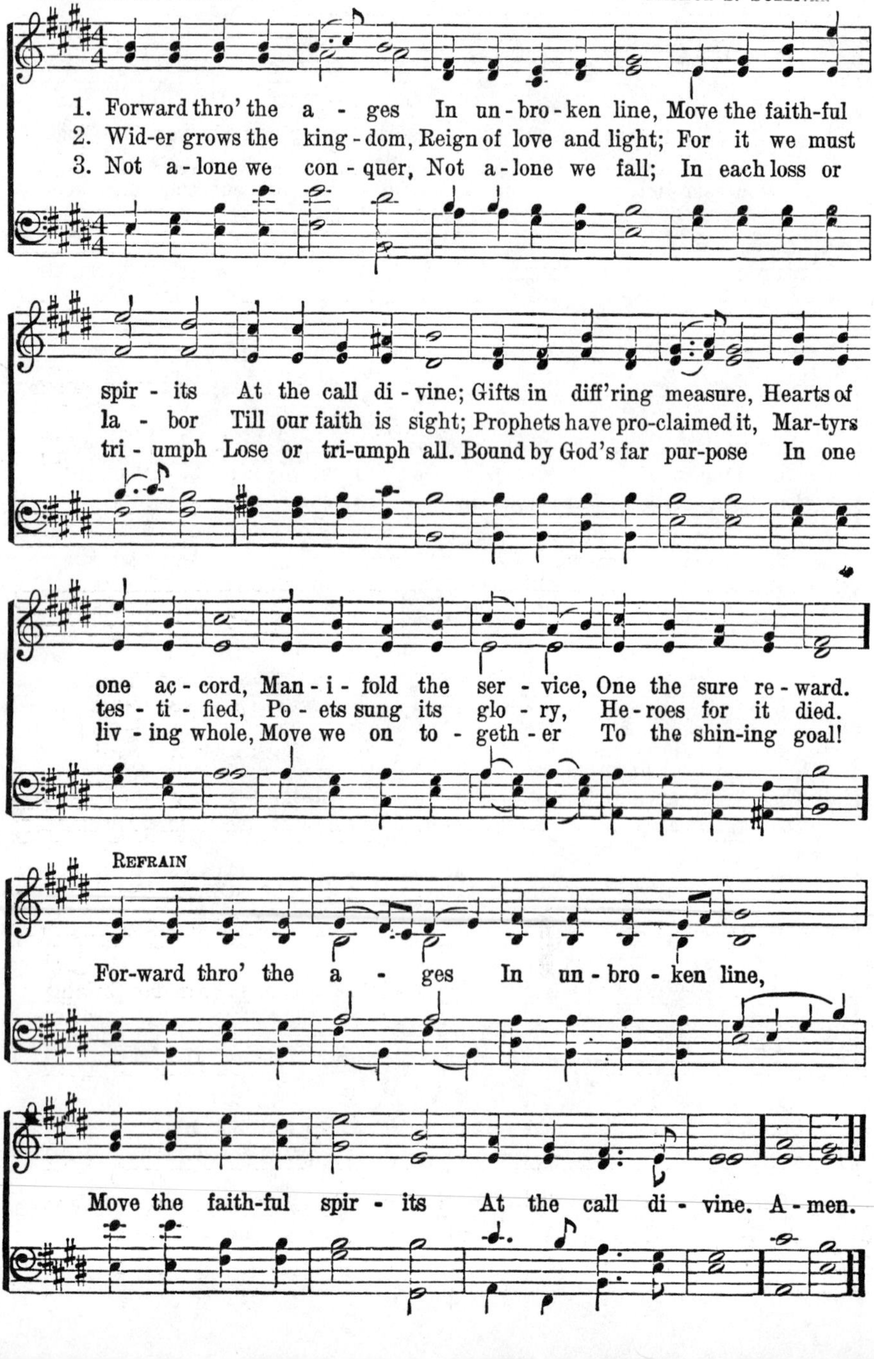

1. Forward thro' the a - ges In un-bro-ken line, Move the faith-ful spir - its At the call di - vine; Gifts in diff'ring measure, Hearts of one ac - cord, Man - i - fold the ser - vice, One the sure re - ward.
2. Wid-er grows the king - dom, Reign of love and light; For it we must la - bor Till our faith is sight; Prophets have pro-claimed it, Mar-tyrs tes - ti - fied, Po - ets sung its glo - ry, He-roes for it died.
3. Not a-lone we con - quer, Not a-lone we fall; In each loss or tri - umph Lose or tri-umph all. Bound by God's far pur-pose In one liv - ing whole, Move we on to - geth - er To the shin-ing goal!

REFRAIN

For-ward thro' the a - ges In un-bro-ken line, Move the faith-ful spir - its At the call di - vine. A - men.

158 We've A Story To Tell

Colin Sterne
H. E. Nichol
Voices in Unison
1. We've a sto - ry to tell to the na - tions, That shall turn their hearts to the right; A sto - ry of truth and sweet - ness, A sto - ry of peace and light,.. A sto - ry of peace and light.
2. We've a song to be sung to the na - tions, That shall lift their hearts to the Lord; A song that shall con - quer e - vil And shat-ter the spear and sword,. And shat - ter the spear and sword.
3. We've a mes - sage to give to the na - tions, That the Lord who reign- eth a - bove, Hath sent us His Son to save us, And show us that God is love,.. And show us that God is love.
4. We've a Sav - ior to show to the na - tions, Who the path of sor - row has trod, That all of the world's great peo - ple Might come to the truth of God,.. Might come to the truth of God!
Refrain
For the darkness shall turn to dawn - ing, And the dawning to noon-day bright,
And Christ's great kingdom shall come on earth, The kingdom of love and light.

159 Heralds Of Christ

NATIONAL HYMN. 10. 10. 10. 10.

Laura Scherer Copenhaver, 1868-
George W. Warren, 1828-1902
Trumpets, before each stanza
1. Her - alds of Christ, who bear the King's com-mands,
2. Thro' des-ert ways, dark fen, and deep mo - rass,
3. Lord, give us faith and strength the road to build,
Im - mor - tal ti-dings in your mor-tal hands,
Thro' jungles, sluggish seas, and mountain pass,
To see the prom-ise of the day ful - filled,
Pass on and car - ry swift the news ye bring:
Build ye the road, and fal - ter not, nor stay;
When war shall be no more and strife shall cease
Make straight, make straight the highway of the King.
Pre - pare a - cross the earth the King's highway.
Up - on the high-way of the Prince of Peace. A - MEN.
160 One Sweetly Solemn Thought
DULCE DOMUM. Irregular
Phoebe Cary, 1824-1871
R. S. Ambrose?
1. One sweet - ly sol - emn thought Comes to me o'er and o'er;
2. Near - er my Fa - ther's house, Where man - y man - sions be;
3. Near - er the bound of life, Where bur - dens are laid down;
4. Fa - ther, per - fect my trust! Strength-en my pow'r of faith!

One Sweetly Solemn Thought

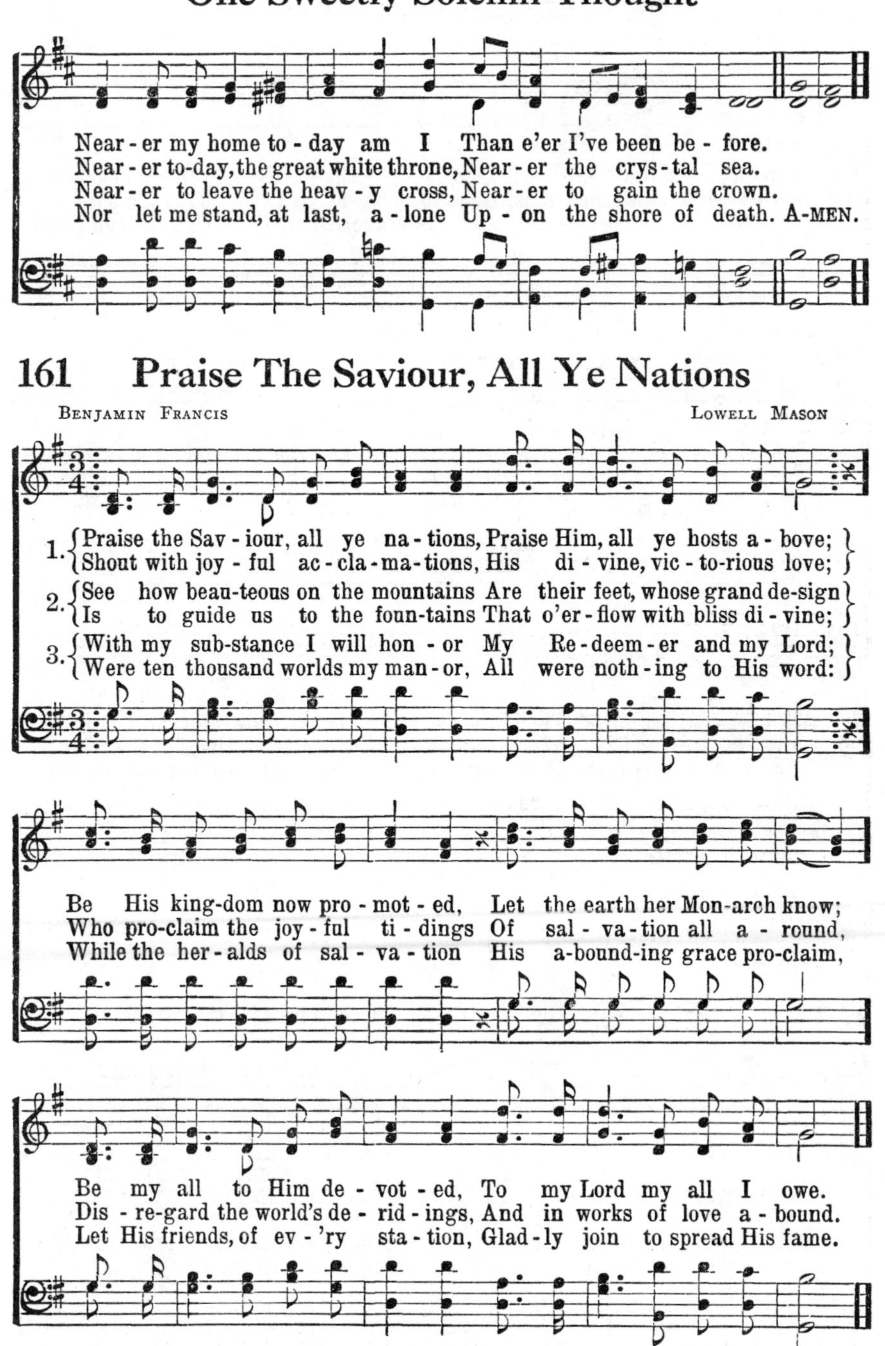
Near - er my home to - day am I Than e'er I've been be - fore.
Near - er to-day, the great white throne, Near - er the crys - tal sea.
Near - er to leave the heav - y cross, Near - er to gain the crown.
Nor let me stand, at last, a - lone Up - on the shore of death. A-MEN.
161 Praise The Saviour, All Ye Nations
BENJAMIN FRANCIS
LOWELL MASON
1. Praise the Sav - iour, all ye na - tions, Praise Him, all ye hosts a - bove;
Shout with joy - ful ac - cla - ma - tions, His di - vine, vic - to-rious love;
2. See how beau-teous on the mountains Are their feet, whose grand de-sign
Is to guide us to the foun-tains That o'er - flow with bliss di - vine;
3. With my sub-stance I will hon - or My Re - deem - er and my Lord;
Were ten thousand worlds my man - or, All were noth - ing to His word:
Be His king-dom now pro - mot - ed, Let the earth her Mon-arch know;
Who pro-claim the joy - ful ti - dings Of sal - va - tion all a - round,
While the her - alds of sal - va - tion His a-bound-ing grace pro-claim,
Be my all to Him de - vot - ed, To my Lord my all I owe.
Dis - re-gard the world's de - rid - ings, And in works of love a - bound.
Let His friends, of ev - 'ry sta - tion, Glad - ly join to spread His fame.

162 Marching With The Heroes

William George Tarrant — Adam Geibel

Unison
1. Marching with the he - roes, Com-rades of the strong, Lift we hearts and voic - es As we march a - long; O the joy - ful mu - sic All in cho - rus raise! Theirs the song of tri-umph, Ours the song of praise.
2. Glo - ry to the he - roes, Who in days of old Trod the path of du - ty, Faith-ful, wise, and bold; For the right un - flinch - ing, Strong the weak to save, War - riors all and free-men, Fighting for the slave.
3. So we sing the sto - ry Of the brave and true, Till a - mong the he - roes We are he - roes, too; Loy - al to our Cap - tain Like the men of yore, March-ing with the he - roes, On-ward ev - er - more.
Refrain. Harmony
March - ing with the he - roes, Com - rades of the strong,
March-ing, march-ing
Lift we hearts and voic - es As we march a - long.

163 My Savior's Love

C. H. G.
Chas. H. Gabriel
1. I stand a-mazed in the pres-ence Of Je - sus the Naz - a - rene,
2. For me it was in the gar - den He prayed: "Not My will, but Thine;"
3. In pit - y an - gels be - held Him, And came from the world of light
4. He took my sins and my sor - rows, He made them His ver - y own;
5. When with the ransomed in glo - ry His face I at last shall see,
And won - der how He could love me, A sin-ner, condemned, un-clean.
He had no tears for His own griefs, But sweat-drops of blood for mine.
To com - fort Him in the sor - rows He bore for my soul that night.
He bore the bur - den to Cal - v'ry, And suf-fered, and died a - lone.
'Twill be my joy thro' the a - ges To sing of His love for me.
Chorus.
How mar-vel-ous! how won-der-ful! And my song shall ev - er be:
Oh, how mar-vel-ous! oh, how won-der-ful!
How mar-vel-ous! how won-der-ful Is my Sav-ior's love for me! A-men.
Oh, how mar-vel-ous! oh, how won-der - ful

164 The Kingdom Coming

Mrs. M. B. C. Slade R. M. McIntosh

1. From all the dark pla - ces Of earth's hea-then ra - ces, O see how the
2. The sun-light is glanc-ing O'er ar - mies ad-vanc - ing, To con - quer the
3. With shout-ing and sing-ing, And ju - bi - lant ring-ing, Their arms of re-
thick shad-ows fly! The voice of sal - va - tion A-wakes ev - 'ry na - tion,
king-doms of sin; Our Lord shall pos-sess them, His presence shall bless them,
bel - lion cast down, At last ev - 'ry na - tion The Lord of sal - va - tion,
Chorus
Come o - ver and help us, they cry.
His beau - ty shall en - ter them in.
Their King and Re-deem - er shall crown!
The king - dom is com - ing, O
tell ye the sto - ry, God's ban-ner ex - alt - ed shall be! The earth shall be
full of His knowledge and glo-ry, As wa-ters that cov-er the sea. A-men.

165 Bringing In The Sheaves

Knowles Shaw — George A. Minor

1. Sow-ing in the morn-ing, sow-ing seeds of kind-ness, Sow-ing in the noon-tide and the dew-y eve; Wait-ing for the har-vest, and the time of reap-ing, We shall come re-joic-ing, bring-ing in the sheaves.
2. Sow-ing in the sun-shine, sow-ing in the shad-ows, Fear-ing nei-ther clouds nor win-ter's chill-ing breeze; By and by the har-vest, and the la-bor end-ed, We shall come re-joic-ing, bring-ing in the sheaves.
3. Go-ing forth with weep-ing, sow-ing for the Mas-ter, Tho' the loss sus-tained our spir-it oft-en grieves; When our weep-ing's o-ver, He will bid us wel-come, We shall come re-joic-ing, bring-ing in the sheaves.
Chorus
Bring-ing in the sheaves, bring-ing in the sheaves, We shall come re-joic-ing, bring-ing in the sheaves;
Bring-ing in the sheaves, bring-ing in the sheaves, We shall come re-joic-ing, bring-ing in the sheaves.

166 In Christ There Is No East Or West
John Oxenham
Alexander R. Reinagle
1. In Christ there is no East or West, In Him no South or North;
2. In Him shall true hearts ev-'ry-where Their high com-mun-ion find;
3. Join hands then, broth-ers of the faith, What-e'er your race may be:
4. In Christ now meet both East and West, In Him meet South and North:
But one great fel-low-ship of love Through-out the whole wide earth.
His serv-ice is the gold-en cord Close-bind-ing all man-kind.
Who serves my Fa-ther as a son is sure-ly kin to Me.
All Christ-ly souls are one in Him Through-out the whole wide earth.
167 Lord, Speak To Me, That I May Speak
CANONBURY. L. M.
Frances R. Havergal
Robert A. Schumann
1. Lord, speak to me, that I may speak In liv-ing ech-oes of Thy tone;
2. Oh! teach me, Lord, that I may teach The pre-cious things Thou dost im-part;
3. Oh! give Thine own sweet rest to me, That I may speak with sooth-ing pow'r
4. Oh! fill me with Thy full-ness, Lord, Un-til my ver-y heart o'er-flow
5. Oh! use me, Lord, use e-ven me, Just as Thou wilt, and when, and where;
As Thou hast sought, so let me seek, The err-ing chil-dren lost and lone.
And wing my words, that they may reach The hid-den depths of man-y a heart.
A word in sea-son, as from Thee, To wea-ry ones in need-ful hour.
In kindling tho't and glow-ing word, Thy love to tell, Thy praise to show.
Un-til Thy bless-ed face I see, Thy rest, Thy joy, Thy glo-ry share. A-MEN.

168 The Voice Of God Is Calling

WORDS USED BY PERMISSION OF JOHN HAYNES HOLMES

JOHN HAYNES HOLMES, 1913 SAMUEL S. WESLEY, 1864

1. The voice of God is call - ing Its sum - mons un - to men;
2. I hear My peo - ple cry - ing In cot and mine and slum;
3. We heed, O Lord, Thy sum - mons, And an - swer, "Here are we!
4. From ease and pleas-ure save us, From pride of place ab - solve;
As once He spoke in Zi - on, So now He speaks a - gain.
No field or mart is si - lent, No cit - y street is dumb.
Send us up - on Thine er - rand, Let us Thy serv - ants be.
Purge us of low de - si - re, Lift us to high re - solve.
Whom shall I send to suc - cor My peo - ple in their need?
I see My peo - ple fall - ing In dark - ness and de - spair,
Our strength is dust and ash - es, Our years a pass - ing hour—
Take us, and make us ho - ly, Teach us Thy will and way,
Whom shall I send to loos - en The bonds of lust and greed?
Whom shall I send to shat - ter The fet - ters which they bear?
But Thou canst use our weak - ness, To mag - ni - fy Thy pow'r."
Speak, and be - hold! we an - swer, Com - mand and we o - bey! A - MEN.

169 That Cause Can Neither Be Lost Nor Stayed

CHRISTIAN OSTERGAARD
Translated by J. A. AABERG
Danish Folk Tune
1. That cause can nei - ther be lost nor stayed Which takes the course of what God has made; And is not trust - ing in walls and tow - ers, But slow - ly grow - ing from seeds to flow - ers.
2. Each no - ble serv - ice that men have wrought Was first con- ceived as a fruit - ful thought; Each wor - thy cause with a fu - ture glo - rious By quiet - ly grow - ing be - comes vic - to - rious.
3. There - by it - self like a tree it shows: That high it reach - es, as deep it grows; And when the storms are its branch - es shak - ing, It deep - er root in the soil is tak - ing.
4. Be then no more by a storm dis - mayed, For by it the full-grown seeds are laid; And though the tree by its might it shat - ters, What then, if thou - sands of seeds it scat - ters!
170 Fairest Lord Jesus
CRUSADER'S HYMN. 5. 6. 8. 5. 5. 8.
From SCHLEISCHEN VOLKSLIEDER, 1842
From the German, 17th Century
Arr. by RICHARD S. WILLIS, 1819-1900
1. Fair-est Lord Je - sus, Rul-er of all na - ture, O Thou of God and man the Son,
2. Fair are the meadows, Fairer still the woodlands, Robed in the blooming garb of spring;
3. Fair is the sunshine, Fairer still the moonlight, And all the twinkling star-ry host:

Fairest Lord Jesus

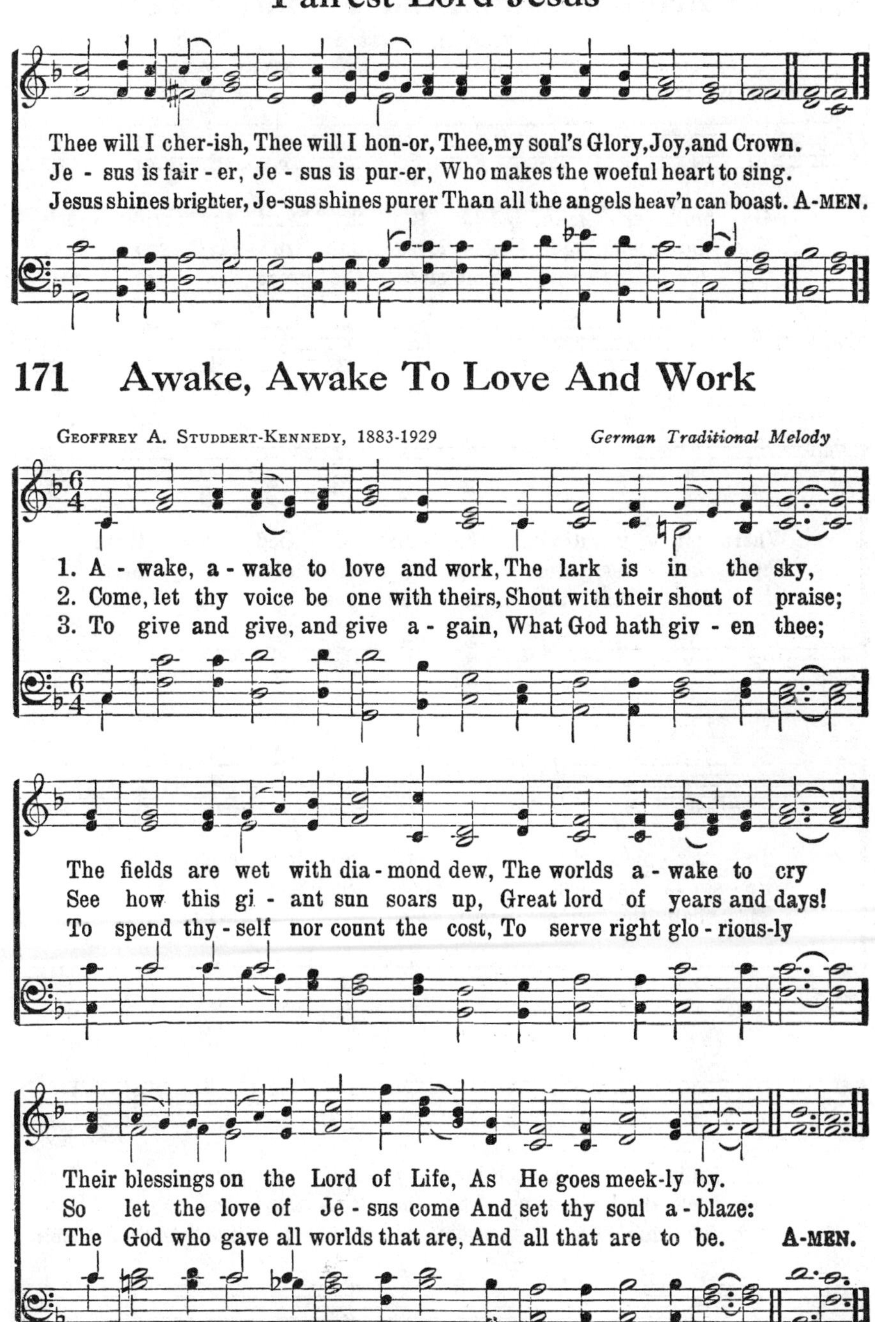
Thee will I cher-ish, Thee will I hon-or, Thee, my soul's Glory, Joy, and Crown.
Je - sus is fair - er, Je - sus is pur-er, Who makes the woeful heart to sing.
Jesus shines brighter, Je-sus shines purer Than all the angels heav'n can boast. A-MEN.
171 Awake, Awake To Love And Work
GEOFFREY A. STUDDERT-KENNEDY, 1883-1929
German Traditional Melody
1. A - wake, a - wake to love and work, The lark is in the sky,
2. Come, let thy voice be one with theirs, Shout with their shout of praise;
3. To give and give, and give a - gain, What God hath giv - en thee;
The fields are wet with dia - mond dew, The worlds a - wake to cry
See how this gi - ant sun soars up, Great lord of years and days!
To spend thy - self nor count the cost, To serve right glo - rious-ly
Their blessings on the Lord of Life, As He goes meek-ly by.
So let the love of Je - sus come And set thy soul a - blaze:
The God who gave all worlds that are, And all that are to be. A-MEN.

172 O Brother Man, Fold To Thy Heart

ILONA. 11. 10. 11. 10.

MUSIC USED BY PERMISSION OF D. APPLETON-CENTURY COMPANY

John G. Whittier, 1807-1892 J. W. Lerman, 1864-

1. O broth - er man, fold to thy heart thy broth - er!
2. For he whom Je - sus loved hath tru - ly spo - ken:
3. Fol - low with rev - 'rent steps the great ex - am - ple
Where pit - y dwells, the peace of God is there;
The ho - lier wor - ship which He deigns to bless
Of Him whose ho - ly work was do - ing good;
To wor - ship right - ly is to love each oth - er,
Re - stores the lost, and binds the spir - it bro - ken,
So shall the wide earth seem our Fa - ther's tem - ple,
Each smile a hymn, each kind - ly deed a prayer.
And feeds the wid - ow and the fa - ther - less.
Each lov - ing life a psalm of grat - i - tude.
A - men.

173 Living For Jesus

T. O. CHISHOLM
C. HAROLD LOWDEN

Not fast

1. Liv-ing for Je-sus a life that is true, Striving to please Him in all that I do,
Yielding allegiance, glad-hearted and free, This is the pathway of blessing for me.

2. Liv-ing for Je-sus who died in my place, Bearing on Calv'ry my sin and disgrace,
Such love constrains me to answer His call, Follow His leading and give Him my all.

3. Liv-ing for Je-sus wher-ev-er I am, Do-ing each du-ty in His Ho-ly Name,
Will-ing to suf-fer af-flic-tion or loss, Deeming each trial a part of my cross.

4. Living for Jesus thro' earth's little while, My dearest treasure, the light of His smile,
Seek-ing the lost ones He died to redeem, Bringing the weary to find rest in Him.

* CHORUS. UNISON. *A little slower.*

O Je-sus, Lord and Savior, I give my-self to Thee; For Thou, in Thy a-tonement, Didst give Thyself for me; I own no oth-er Mas-ter, My heart shall be Thy throne, My life I give, henceforth to live, O Christ, for Thee alone.

rit.

*Melody in lower notes. A two-part effect may be had by having the men sing the melody, the women taking the middle notes.

174 The Call Of The Christ

W. C. Poole
H. A. Henry
1. The call of the Christ rings out to-day, Who will make re-ply? For la-bor, or serv-ice, or bat-tle fray, Or seek-ing the lost who have gone a-stray, O Mas-ter, I'm read-y to go or stay—Here am I!
2. The call of the Christ rings sweet and clear, Who will make re-ply? Thy call-ing, O Mas-ter, to-day I hear, And glad-ly will fol-low Thee, far or near; With Thee as my Lead-er, no harm I fear, Here am I!
3. The call of the Christ is now for you, Will you make re-ply? I'm wait-ing, O Mas-ter, Thy will to do; Count me on the side of the brave and true, I'll fol-low Thee all of the bat-tle thro', Here am I!
Chorus
Here am I for serv-ice, what-so-e'er it be; I am wait-ing or-ders, Mas-ter, now from Thee;
I have heard Thy summons from dark Cal-va-ry, (Omit . . . .) And I glad-ly an-swer, "Mas-ter, here am I!"
1
2

175 Just When I Need Him Most

Rev. Wm. Poole
Chas. H. Gabriel
1. Just when I need Him, Je - sus is near, Just when I fal - ter,
2. Just when I need Him, Je - sus is true, Nev - er for - sak - ing
3. Just when I need Him, Je - sus is strong, Bear - ing my bur - dens
4. Just when I need Him, He is my all, An - swer-ing when up-
just when I fear; Read - y to help me, read - y to cheer,
all the way thro'; Giv - ing for bur - dens pleas - ures a - new,
all the day long; For all my sor - row giv - ing a song,
on Him I call; Ten - der - ly watch - ing lest I should fall,
Just when I need Him most.
Chorus.
Just when I need Him most,
Just when I need Him most; Je - sus is near to
com - fort and cheer, Just when I need Him most. A - men.

176 I Heard The Voice Of Jesus Say

Horatius Bonar
Old English Air
Slowly
1. I heard the voice of Je - sus say, "Come un - to Me and rest;
2. I heard the voice of Je - sus say, "Be - hold, I free - ly give
3. I heard the voice of Je - sus say, "I am this dark world's Light;
Lay down, thou wea - ry one, lay down thy head up - on My breast."
The liv - ing wa - ter; thirst - y one, Stoop down, and drink, and live!"
Look un - to Me, thy morn shall rise, And all thy days be bright."
I came to Je - sus as I was, Wea-ry and worn and sad;
I came to Je - sus, and I drank Of that life - giv - ing stream;
I looked to Je - sus, and I found In Him my Star, my Sun,
I found in Him a rest - ing place, And He has made me glad.
My thirst was quenched, my soul re - vived, And now I live in Him.
And in that light of life I'll walk, Till trav-'ling days are done.

177 Others

C. D. Meigs
Elizabeth McE. Shields
1. Lord, help me live from day to day In such a self-for-get-ful way
2. Help me in all the work I do To ev-er be sin-cere and true
3. Let "Self" be cru-ci-fied and slain And bur-ied deep: and all in vain
4. And when my work on earth is done, And my new work in heav'n's begun,
That e-ven when I kneel to pray My prayer shall be for—Oth-ers.
And know that all I'd do for You Must needs be done for—Oth-ers.
May ef-forts be to rise a-gain, Un-less to live for—Oth-ers.
May I for-get the crown I've won, While think-ing still of—Oth-ers.
Chorus
Oth-ers, Lord, yes, oth-ers, Let this my mot-to
be, Help me to live for oth-ers, That I may live like Thee.
rit.

178 Now, On Land And Sea Descending

VESPER HYMN (Bortniansky). 8. 7. 8. 7. 8. 6. 8. 7.

SAMUEL LONGFELLOW, 1819-1892, alt. DIMITRI S. BORTNIANSKY, 1752-1825

1. Now, on land and sea de-scend-ing, Brings the night its peace pro-found;
2. Soon as dies the sun - set glo - ry, Stars of heav'n shine out a - bove,
3. Now, our wants and bur-dens leav - ing To His care who cares for all,
4. As the dark-ness deep-ens o'er us, Lo! e - ter - nal stars a - rise;

Let our ves - per hymn be blend-ing With the ho - ly calm a - round.
Tell-ing still the an - cient sto - ry—Their Cre - a - tor's changeless love.
Cease we fear - ing, cease we griev-ing: At His touch our bur - dens fall.
Hope and faith and love rise glo - rious, Shin-ing in the spir - it's skies.

Ju - bi - la - te! Ju - bi - la - te! Ju - bi - la - te! A - men!

Let our ves - per hymn be blending With the ho - ly calm a - round.
Tell-ing still the an - cient sto-ry—Their Cre - a-tor's changeless love.
Cease we fear-ing, cease we grieving: At His touch our bur-dens fall.
Hope and faith and love rise glorious, Shin -ing in the spir - it's skies. A-MEN.

179 O Young And Fearless Prophet

BLAIRGOWRIE (Dykes). 13. 13. 13. 13.

WORDS USED BY PERMISSION OF S. RALPH HARLOW

S. RALPH HARLOW, 1885- JOHN B. DYKES, 1823-1876

1. O young and fear - less Proph - et of an - cient Gal - i - lee:
2. We mar - vel at the pur - pose that held Thee to Thy course
3. O help us stand un - swerv - ing a - gainst war's blood-y way,
4. Cre - ate in us the splen - dor that dawns when hearts are kind,
5. O young and fear - less Proph - et, we need Thy pres - ence here,
Thy life is still a sum - mons to serve hu - man - i - ty,
While ev - er on the hill - top be - fore Thee loomed the cross;
Where hate and lust and false - hood hold back Christ's ho - ly sway;
That knows not race nor sta - tion as boun-daries of the mind;
A - mid our pride and glo - ry to see Thy face ap - pear;
To make our thoughts and ac - tions less prone to please the crowd,
Thy stead-fast face set for - ward where love and du - ty shone,
For - bid false love of coun - try, that blinds us to His call
That learns to val - ue beau - ty, in heart, or brain, or soul,
Once more to hear Thy chal - lenge a - bove our noi - sy day,
To stand with hum - ble cour - age for Truth with hearts un-cowed.
While we be - tray so quick - ly and leave Thee there a - lone.
Who lifts a - bove the na - tion the broth - er - hood of all.
And longs to bind God's chil - dren in - to one per-fect whole.
A - gain to lead us for - ward a - long God's ho - ly way. A - MEN.

180 Does Jesus Care

Frank E. Graeff
J. Lincoln Hall
1. Does Je-sus care when my heart is pained Too deep-ly for mirth or song,
2. Does Je-sus care when my way is dark With a nameless dread and fear?
3. Does Jesus care when I've tried and failed To resist some temptation strong;
4. Does Jesus care when I've said "goodbye" To the dearest on earth to me,
As the burdens press, And the cares distress, And the way grows weary and long?
As the daylight fades Into deep night shades, Does He care enough to be near?
When for my deep grief There is no relief, Tho' my tears flow all the night long?
And my sad heart aches Till it nearly breaks, Is it aught to Him? does He see?
Refrain
O yes, He cares, I know He cares, His heart is touched with my grief;...
When the days are weary, The long night dreary, I know my Saviour cares....
He cares.

181 The Cross Is Not Greater

B. B. BALLINGTON BOOTH

1. The cross that He gave may be heav-y, But it ne'er outweighs His grace;
2. The thorns in my path are not sharper Than composed His crown for me;
3. The light of His love shin-eth brighter, As it falls on paths of woe;
4. His will I have joy in ful-fill-ing, As I'm walk-ing in His sight;
The storm that I feared may surround me, But it ne'er ex-cludes His face.
The cup that I drink not more bit-ter Than He drank in Geth-sem-a-ne.
The toil of my work grow-eth light-er, As I stoop to raise the low.
My all to the blood I am bring-ing, It a-lone can keep me right.
CHORUS
The cross is not great-er than His grace, The storm can-not
hide His bless-ed face; I am sat-is-fied to know That with
Je-sus here be-low, I can con-quer ev-'ry foe.

182 Follow The Gleam

Silver Bay Prize Song, BRYN MAWR COLLEGE
SALLIE HUME DOUGLAS
1. To the Knights in the days of old, Keep-ing watch on the mountain height,
2. And we who would serve the King And loy-al-ly Him o-bey,
Came a vi-sion of Ho-ly Grail And a voice thro' the wait-ing night.
In the con-se-crate si-lence know That the challenge still holds to-day.
REFRAIN
Fol-low, fol-low, fol-low the gleam, Ban-ners un-furled o'er all the world,
Fol-low, fol-low, fol-low the gleam, Stand-ards of worth o'er all the earth,
Fol-low, fol-low, fol-low the gleam Of the Chal-ice that is the Grail.
Fol-low, fol-low, fol-low the gleam Of the light that shall bring the dawn.
183 Just As I Am, Thine Own To Be
MARIANNE HEARN
JOSEPH BARNBY
1. Just as I am, Thine own to be, Friend of the young, who lov-est me.
2. In the glad morn-ing of my day, My life to give, my vows to pay,
3. I would live ev-er in the light, I would work ev-er for the right,
4. Just as I am, young, strong, and free, To be the best that I can be,

Just As I Am, Thine Own To Be
Unison
To con-se-crate my-self to Thee, O Je-sus Christ, I come.
With no re-serve and no de-lay, With all my heart I come.
I would serve Thee with all my might; Therefore, to Thee I come.
For truth, and righteousness, and Thee, Lord of my life, I come. A-men.
184
I Would Be True
Howard Arnold Walter
Joseph Yates Peek
1. I would be true, for there are those who trust me; I would be pure, for there are those who care; I would be strong, for there is much to suf-fer; I would be brave, for there is much to dare, I would be brave, for there is much to dare.
2. I would be friend of all— the foe, the friend-less; I would be giv-ing, and for-get the gift; I would be hum-ble, for I know my weak-ness; I would look up, and laugh, and love, and lift, I would look up, and laugh, and love, and lift.

185 In Thee Do I Live

C. A. M. C. AUSTIN MILES

1. All that I am or hope to be, O son of God, I owe to Thee,
2. Thy blessed cross has sealed my peace, Thy sorrows make my own to cease;
3. Thy cruel wounds my own have healed; Thy broken heart my par-don sealed;
For Thou has bought me; I am Thine, And by Thy mer-cy Thou art mine.
Thy pow'r has cleansed me from all sin, Thy presence keeps my conscience clean.
Thy death, O Christ, means life for me, A life for all e-ter-ni-ty.
CHORUS
Thy mer-cy sought me, Thy love has bought me, Thy grace has
taught me to be-lieve. Then, in be-liev-ing, Thy peace re-
ceiv-ing, Now in Thee on-ly, do I live....

186 Are Ye Able, Said The Master

Earl Marlatt — Harry S. Mason

1. "Are ye a - ble," said the Mas - ter, "To be cru - ci - fied with me?"
2. "Are ye a - ble," to re- mem - ber, When a thief lifts up his eyes,
3. "Are ye a - ble," when the shad - ows Close a - round you with the sod,
4. "Are ye a - ble," still the Mas - ter Whis-pers down e - ter - ni - ty,
"Yea," the stur - dy dream-ers an-swered, "To the death we fol - low Thee."
That His par-doned soul is wor - thy Of a place in Par - a - dise?
To be- lieve that spir - it tri- umphs, To commend your soul to God?
And he - ro - ic spir - its an - swer, Now, as then in Gal - i - lee.
Refrain
"Lord, we are a - ble," Our spir - its are Thine, Re - mold them,
make us like Thee, di - vine. Thy guid - ing ra - diance a - bove
us shall be A bea - con to God, To love and loy - al - ty.

187 Give Of Your Best To The Master

H. B. G. — Mrs. Charles Barnard

1. Give of your best to the Mas - ter; Give of the strength of your youth;
2. Give of your best to the Mas - ter; Give Him first place in your heart;
3. Give of your best to the Mas - ter; Naught else is wor- thy His love;
Ref.—Give of your best to the Mas - ter; Give of the strength of your youth;
Fine
Throw your soul's fresh, glowing ar - dor In - to the bat - tle for truth.
Give Him first place in your serv - ice, Con - se - crate ev - 'ry part.
He gave Him - self for your ran - som, Gave up His glo - ry a - bove:
Clad in sal - va-tion's full ar - mor, Join in the bat - tle for truth.
Je - sus has set the ex - am - ple; Dauntless was He, young and brave;..
Give, and to you shall be giv - en; God His be - lov - ed Son gave;..
Laid down His life with-out mur - mur, You from sin's ru - in to save;...
rall.
D. C.
Give Him your loy- al de - vo - tion, Give Him the best that you have.....
Grate-ful - ly seek-ing to serve Him, Give Him the best that you have.....
Give Him your heart's ad-o - ra - tion, Give Him the best that you have.....

188 Jesus Is Always There

B. M. L. BERTHA MAE LILLENAS

1. Some-times our skies are cloud-y and drear-y, Some-times our hearts are bur-dened with care; But we may know, what-e'er may be-fall us,
2. When in the midst of life with its prob-lems, Bent with our toil and bur-dens we bear; Won-der-ful thought and deep con-so-la-tion:
3. When we are walk-ing thru the green pastures, Or o-ver moun-tains rug-ged and bare; Pre-cious the thought and sweet the as-sur-ance,
4. "Lo, I am with you al-way," is writ-ten, God will not fail to an-swer our prayer; Trust-ing His word we rest in His prom-ise,—
Je-sus is al-ways there.
CHORUS
Nev-er a bur-den that He doth not car-ry, Nev-er a sor-row that He doth not share; Wheth-er the days may be sun-ny or drear-y, Je-sus is al-ways there.

189 Close To Thee

Fanny J. Crosby — Silas J. Vail

1. Thou, my ev - er - last - ing por - tion, More than friend or life to me;
2. Not for ease or world - ly pleas-ure, Nor for fame my prayer shall be;
3. Lead me thro' the vale of shad-ows, Bear me o'er life's fit - ful sea;

D.S.—All a - long my pil - grim jour - ney, Sav - ior, let me walk with Thee.
D.S.—Glad-ly will I toil and suf - fer, On - ly let me walk with Thee.
D.S.—Then the gate of life e - ter - nal May I en - ter, Lord, with Thee.

Fine

Refrain

Close to Thee, close to Thee, Close to Thee, close to Thee;

D. S.

190 Into My Heart

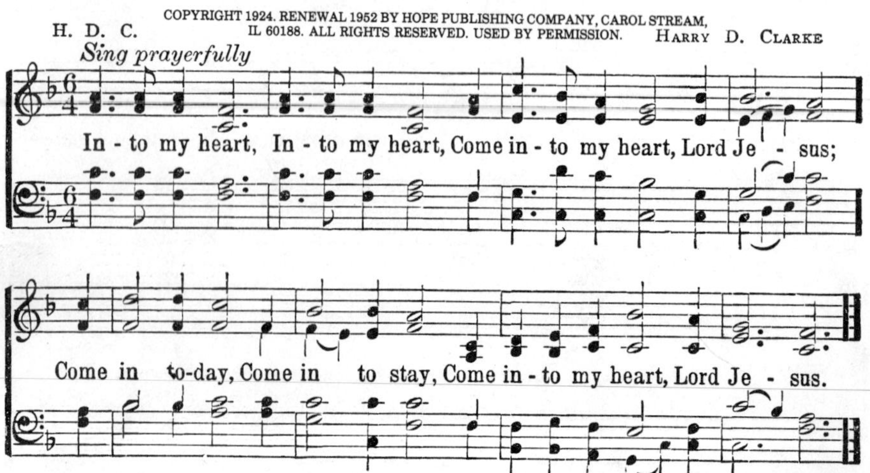

COPYRIGHT 1924. RENEWAL 1952 BY HOPE PUBLISHING COMPANY, CAROL STREAM, IL 60188. ALL RIGHTS RESERVED. USED BY PERMISSION.
H. D. C.
Harry D. Clarke
Sing prayerfully
In - to my heart, In - to my heart, Come in - to my heart, Lord Je - sus;
Come in to-day, Come in to stay, Come in - to my heart, Lord Je - sus.

191 Ivory Palaces

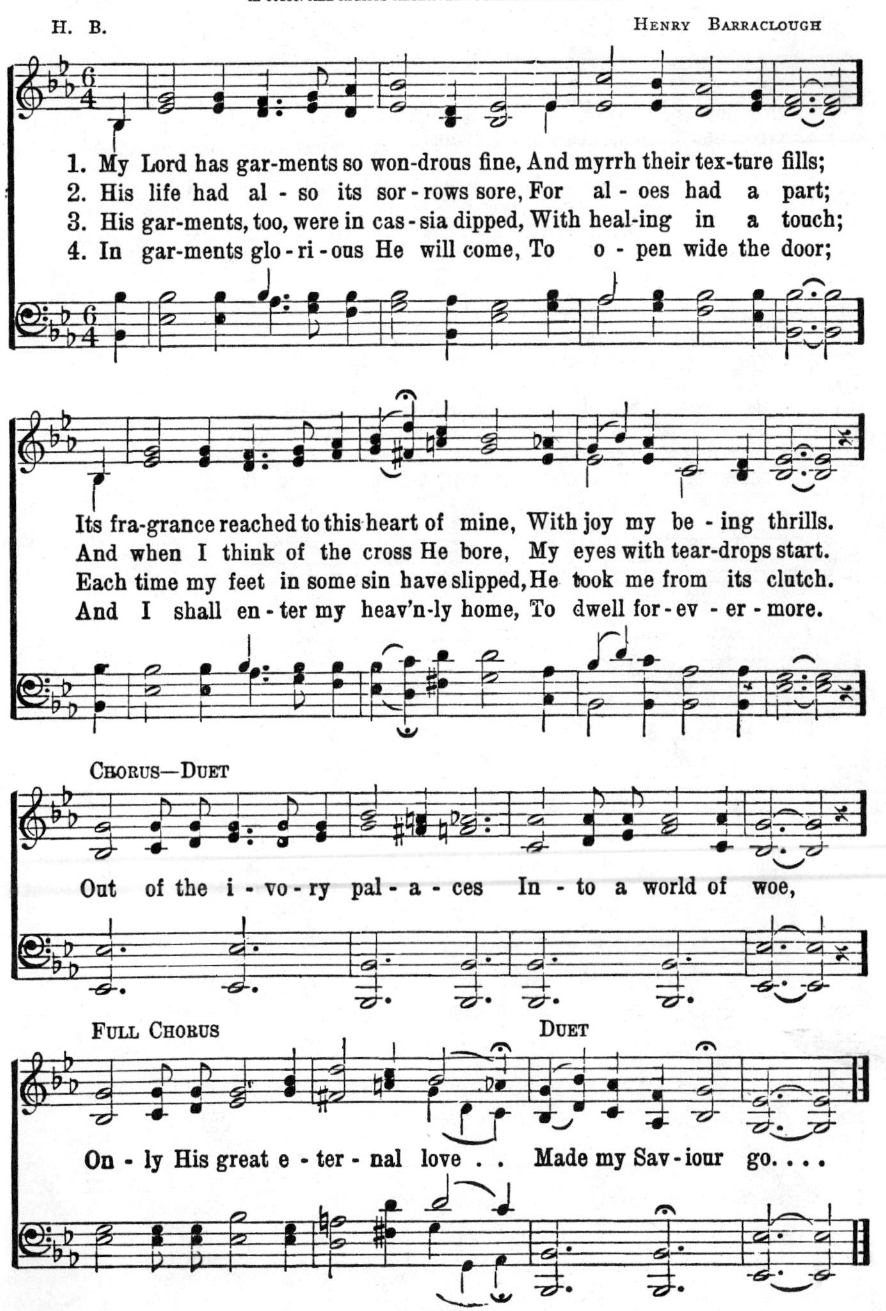
H. B.
HENRY BARRACLOUGH
1. My Lord has gar-ments so won-drous fine, And myrrh their tex-ture fills;
2. His life had al - so its sor - rows sore, For al - oes had a part;
3. His gar-ments, too, were in cas - sia dipped, With heal-ing in a touch;
4. In gar-ments glo - ri - ous He will come, To o - pen wide the door;
Its fra-grance reached to this heart of mine, With joy my be - ing thrills.
And when I think of the cross He bore, My eyes with tear-drops start.
Each time my feet in some sin have slipped, He took me from its clutch.
And I shall en - ter my heav'n-ly home, To dwell for - ev - er - more.
CHORUS—DUET
Out of the i - vo - ry pal - a - ces In - to a world of woe,
FULL CHORUS
DUET
On - ly His great e - ter - nal love . . Made my Sav - iour go. . . .

192 He Lifted Me

Charlotte G. Homer
Chas. H. Gabriel
1. In lov-ing kind-ness Je-sus came, My soul in mer-cy to re-claim,
2. He called me long be-fore I heard, Be-fore my sin-ful heart was stirred,
3. His brow was pierced with man-y a thorn, His hands by cru-el nails were torn,
4. Now on a high-er plane I dwell, And with my soul I know 'tis well;
And from the depths of sin and shame Thro' grace He lift-ed me. . . . . . .
But when I took Him at His word, For-giv'n He lift-ed me. . . . . . .
When from my guilt and grief, for-lorn, In love He lift-ed me. . . . . . .
Yet how or why, I can-not tell, He should have lift-ed me. . . . . . .
He lift-ed me.
Chorus
From sink-ing sand He lift-ed me, With ten-der hand He lift-ed me,
From shades of night to planes of light, O praise His name, He lift-ed me!
193 Everybody Ought To Love Jesus
Copyright, 1917, by H. D. Loes. W. Elmer Bailey, owner
Harry Dixon Loes
Ev-'ry-bod-y ought to love Je-sus, Je-sus, Je-sus; He
Je-sus Christ, the won-der-ful Sav-iour;

Everybody Ought To Love Jesus

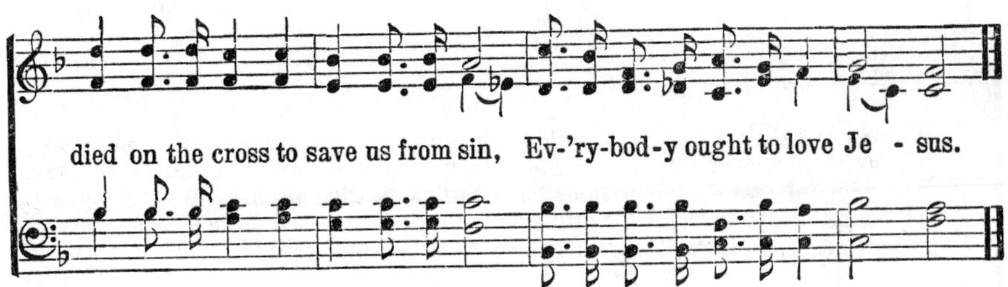
died on the cross to save us from sin, Ev-'ry-bod-y ought to love Je - sus.

194 Near To The Heart Of God

C. B. McAfee

1. There is a place of qui - et rest, Near to the heart of God,
A place where sin can - not mo - lest, Near to the heart of God.

2. There is a place of com - fort sweet, Near to the heart of God,
A place where we our Sav - ior meet, Near to the heart of God.

3. There is a place of full re - lease, Near to the heart of God,
A place where all is joy and peace, Near to the heart of God.

Refrain

O Je - sus, blest Re - deem - er, Sent from the heart of God,
Hold us, who wait be - fore Thee, Near to the heart of God.

195 Where Cross The Crowded Ways Of Life
F. Mason North
Beethoven
1. Where cross the crowded ways of life, Where sounds the cries of race and clan,
2. In haunts of wretch-ed - ness and need, On shadowed thresholds dark with fears,
3. The cup of wa - ter giv'n for Thee Still holds the freshness of Thy grace;
4. O Mas-ter, from the mountain side, Make haste to heal these hearts of pain,
5. Till sons of men shall learn Thy love And fol-low where Thy feet have trod:
A - bove the noise of self-ish strife, We hear Thy voice, O Son of man!
From paths where hide the lures of greed, We catch the vi - sion of Thy tears.
Yet long these mul - ti - tudes to see The sweet com-pas-sion of Thy face.
A - mong these restless throngs a-bide, O tread the cit - y's streets a - gain.
Till glo - rious from Thy heav'n above Shall come the cit - y of our God.
196 O God, Our Help
Isaac Watts
ST. ANNE C. M.
William Croft
1. O God, our help in a - ges past, Our hope for years to come,
2. Un - der the shad - ow of Thy throne Still may we dwell se - cure;
3. Be - fore the hills in or - der stood, Or earth re - ceived her frame;
4. Time, like an ev - er - roll - ing stream, Bears all its sons a - way;
5. O God, our help in a - ges past, Our hope for years to come;
Our shel - ter from the storm - y blast, And our e - ter - nal home!
Suf - fi - cient is Thine arm a - lone, And our de - fense is sure.
From ev - er - last - ing Thou art God, To end - less years the same.
They fly, for - got - ten, as a dream Dies at the opening day.
Be Thou our guide while life shall last, And our e - ter - nal home.

197 Somebody Knows

ALFRED H. ACKLEY
B. D. ACKLEY
Legato
1. Fail-ing in strength when opprest by my foes, Somebody knows, Somebody knows;
2. Why should I fear when the care-bil-lows roll? Somebody knows, Somebody knows;
3. Wounded and helpless and sick with distress, Somebody knows, Somebody knows;
Wait-ing for some-one to ban-ish my woes, Some-bod-y knows,–'tis Je - sus.
When the deep shadows sweep o-ver my soul, Some-bod-y knows,–'tis Je - sus.
Long-ing for home and a mother's ca-ress, Some-bod-y knows,–'tis Je - sus.
CHORUS OR QUARTET
Some-bod-y knows, Some-bod-y knows When I am tempted and tried by my foes;
He is the One who will keep me— Some-bod-y knows—'tis Je - sus.

198 Look For The Beautiful

COPYRIGHT 1911. RENEWAL 1938 BY HOPE PUBLISHING COMPANY, CAROL STREAM, IL 60188. ALL RIGHTS RESERVED. USED BY PERMISSION.
T. H.
THORO HARRIS
1. Look for the beau-ti - ful, look for the true, Look for the beau - ti - ful life's jour-ney thro'. Seek-ing true love-li-ness, joy you will know, As to the home a-bove on-ward you go.
2. Think of the beau-ti - ful, think of the pure; On - ly the beau - ti - ful long can en-dure. God to His low - ly ones "giveth more grace"; None but the pure in heart look on His face.
3. Speak of the beau-ti - ful, speak of the pure; These to e - ter - ni-ty, fade-less en-dure. Er - ror shall van-ish soon, e - vil de - cay; God and the beau-ti - ful pass not a - way.
4. Look to the stars of light (not down to earth); All that is beau - ti - ful there had its birth. Up-ward and forward go, look-ing a - bove; There is the dwelling-place of per-fect love.
CHORUS
Look for the beau-ti - ful, seek to find the true, God and the beau-ti - ful will dwell with you; Look for the beau - ti - ful, seek to find the true, You shall be beau - ti - ful, beau - ti - ful with - in.
Harmony

199 Sweet By And By

S. F. Bennett — J. P. Webster

1. There's a land that is fair - er than day, And by faith we can
2. We shall sing on that beau - ti - ful shore The mel - o - di - ous
3. To our boun - ti - ful Fa - ther a - bove, We will of - fer our
see it a - far; For the Fa - ther waits o - ver the way, To pre-
songs of the blest, And our spir - its shall sor - row no more, Not a
trib - ute of praise, For the glo - ri - ous gift of His love, And the
Chorus
pare us a dwell - ing-place there. In the sweet by and
sigh for the bless - ing of rest.
bless-ings that hal - low our days.
In the sweet
by, We shall meet on that beau - ti - ful shore; In the
by and by, by and by,
sweet by and by, We shall meet on that beau - ti - ful shore.
In the sweet by and by,

200 The Home Over There

D. W. C. Huntington — Tullius C. O'Kane

D. W. C. Huntington
Tullius C. O'Kane
1. O think of the home o - ver there, By the side of the riv - er of
2. O think of the friends o - ver there, Who be - fore us the jour-ney have
3. My Sav - ior is now o - ver there, There my kin-dred and friends are at
4. I'll soon be at home o - ver there, For the end of my jour - ney I
light, Where the saints, all im - mor - tal and fair, Are
trod, Of the songs that they breathe on the air, In their
rest; Then a - way from my sor - row and care, Let me
see; Man - y dear to my heart, o - ver there, Are
o - ver there,
robed in their garments of white,
home in the pal - ace of God.
fly to the land of the blest.
watch-ing and wait-ing for me.
Refrain.
O - ver there, o - ver
O - ver there, o - ver
O - ver there, o - ver
O - ver there, o - ver
o - ver there.
O - ver there,
there, O think of the home o - ver there,
there, O think of the friends o - ver there,
there, My Sav - ior is now o - ver there,
there, I'll soon be at home o - ver there,
O - ver
O - ver
O - ver
O - ver
o - ver there,
o - ver there,

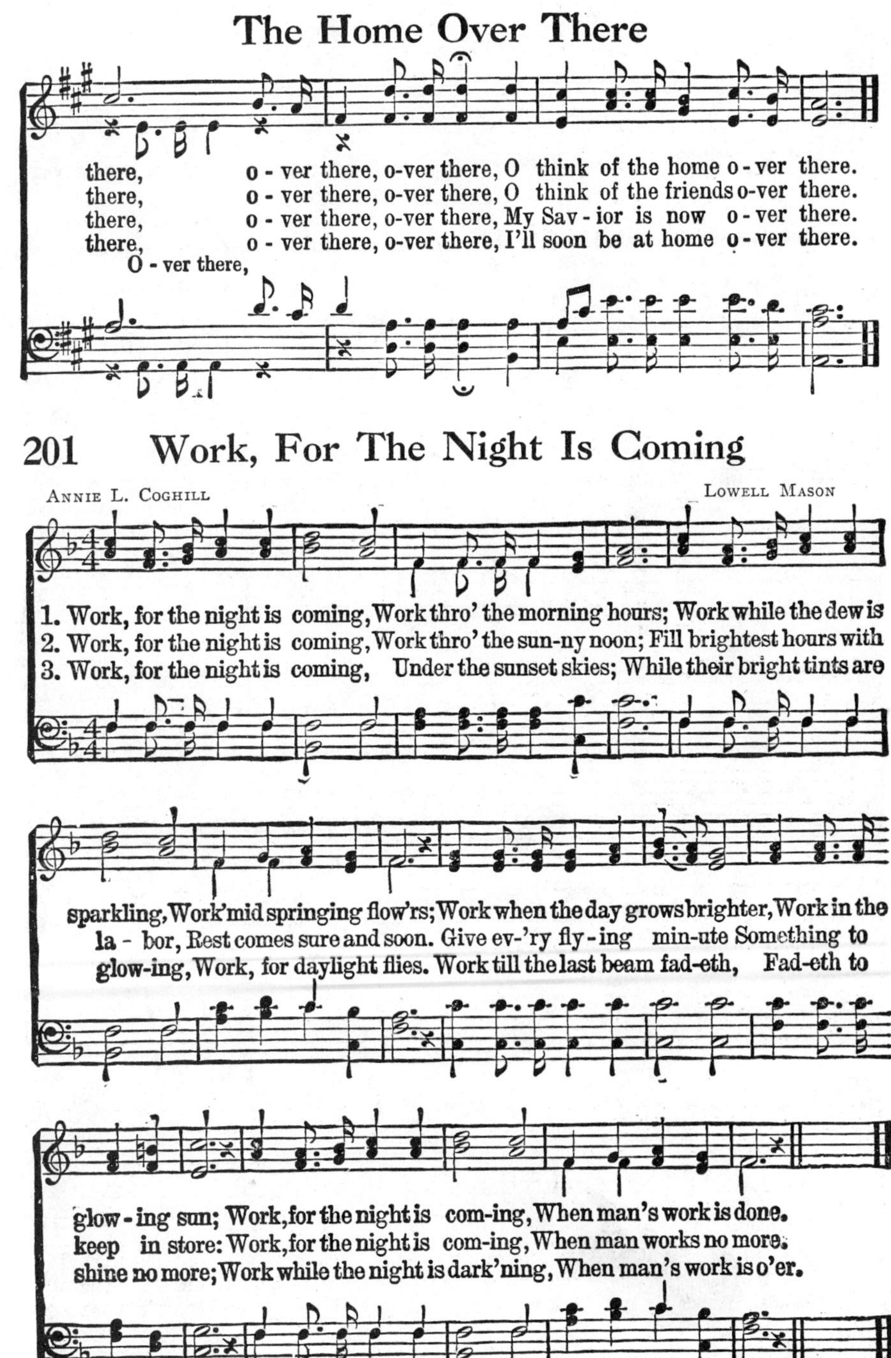
The Home Over There
there, o - ver there, o-ver there, O think of the home o - ver there.
there, o - ver there, o-ver there, O think of the friends o-ver there.
there, o - ver there, o-ver there, My Sav - ior is now o - ver there.
there, o - ver there, o-ver there, I'll soon be at home o - ver there.
O - ver there,
201 Work, For The Night Is Coming
Annie L. Coghill
Lowell Mason
1. Work, for the night is coming, Work thro' the morning hours; Work while the dew is
2. Work, for the night is coming, Work thro' the sun-ny noon; Fill brightest hours with
3. Work, for the night is coming, Under the sunset skies; While their bright tints are
sparkling, Work 'mid springing flow'rs; Work when the day grows brighter, Work in the
la - bor, Rest comes sure and soon. Give ev-'ry fly - ing min-ute Something to
glow-ing, Work, for daylight flies. Work till the last beam fad-eth, Fad-eth to
glow - ing sun; Work, for the night is com-ing, When man's work is done.
keep in store: Work, for the night is com-ing, When man works no more.
shine no more; Work while the night is dark'ning, When man's work is o'er.

202 Beautiful River

R. L. — Robert Lowry

1. Shall we gath-er at the riv-er, Where bright an-gel feet have trod;
With its crys-tal tide for-ev-er Flow-ing by the throne of God?
2. On the bos-om of the riv-er, Where the Sav-ior-King we own,
We shall meet, and sor-row nev-er, 'Neath the glo-ry of the throne.
3. Ere we reach the shin-ing riv-er, Lay we ev-'ry bur-den down;
Grace our spir-its will de-liv-er, And pro-vide a robe and crown.
4. Soon we'll reach the shining riv-er, Soon our pil-grim-age will cease;
Soon our hap-py hearts will qui-ver With the mel-o-dy of peace.
Chorus
p
Yes, we'll gather at the riv-er, The beau-ti-ful, the beau-ti-ful riv-er,
Gath-er with the saints at the riv-er That flows by the throne of God.

203 Lead, Kindly Light

John H. Newman — John B. Dykes

1. Lead, kindly Light, amid th'encircling gloom, Lead Thou me on! The night is
2. I was not ev-er thus, nor prayed that Thou Shouldst lead me on; I loved to
3. So long Thy pow'r hath blest me, sure it still Will lead me on O'er moor and

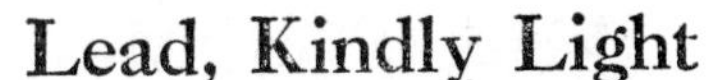

Lead, Kindly Light

dark, and I am far from home; Lead Thou me on! Keep Thou my feet; I
choose and see my path; but now Lead Thou me on! I loved the gar - ish
fen, o'er crag and torrent, till The night is gone, And with the morn those

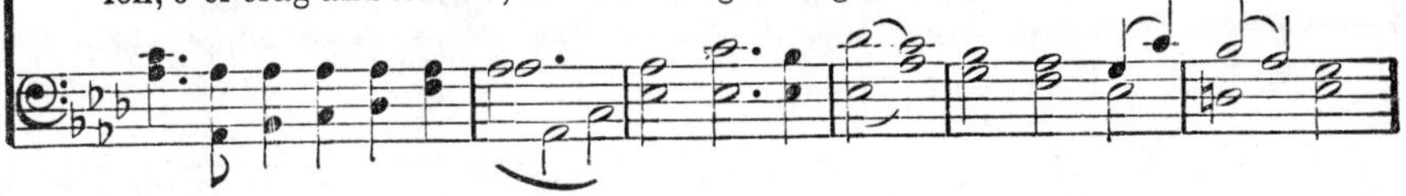

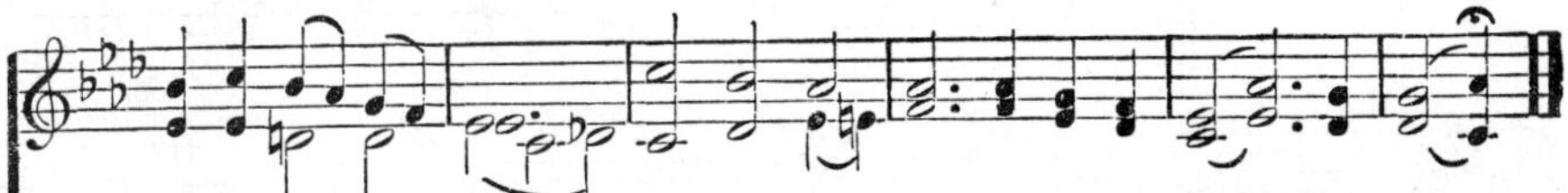

do not ask to see . . . The dis-tant scene; one step e - nough for me.
day, and, spite of fears, . . Pride ruled my will. Remember not past years!
an-gel fa - ces smile, . Which I have loved long since, and lost a - while!

204 Sun Of My Soul

John Keble — Peter Ritter

1. Sun of my soul! Thou Sav-ior dear, It is not night if Thou be near;
2. When the soft dews of kind-ly sleep My wear - y eye - lids gen-tly steep,
3. A - bide with me from morn till eve, For with-out Thee I can-not live;
4. Be near to bless me when I wake, Ere thro' the world my way I take;

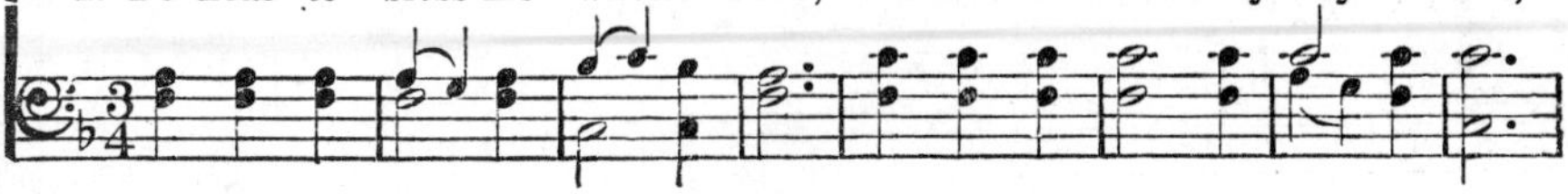

Oh, may no earth-born cloud a - rise To hide Thee from Thy servant's eyes!
Be my last tho't–how sweet to rest For-ev - er on my Sav-ior's breast!
A-bide with me when night is nigh, For with-out Thee I dare not die.
A-bide with me till in Thy love I lose my-self in Heav'n a-bove.

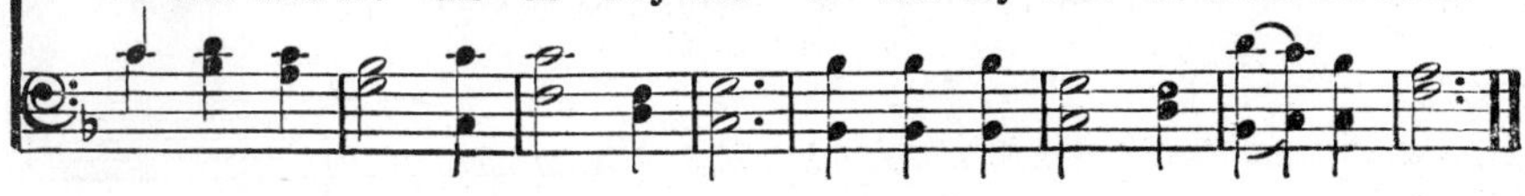

205 Abide With Me

H. F. Lyte | W. H. Monk

1. A - bide with me: fast falls the e - ven - tide;
2. Swift to its close ebbs out life's lit - tle day;
3. I need Thy pres - ence ev - 'ry pass - ing hour:
4. Hold Thou Thy cross be - fore my clos - ing eyes,
The dark - ness deep - ens; Lord, with me a - bide:
Earth's joys grow dim, its glo - ries pass a - way;
What but Thy grace can foil the temp - ter's pow'r?
Shine through the gloom, and point me to the skies:
When oth - er help - ers fail, and com - forts flee,
Change and de - cay in all a - round I see:
Who like Thy - self my guide and stay can be?
Heav'n's morn - ing breaks, and earth's vain shad - ows flee—
Help of the help - less, O a - bide with me!
O Thou who chang - est not, a - bide with me!
Through cloud and sun - shine, O a - bide with me!
In life, in death, O Lord, a - bide with me!

206

I Will Sing You A Song

Ellen H. Gates

Philip Phillips

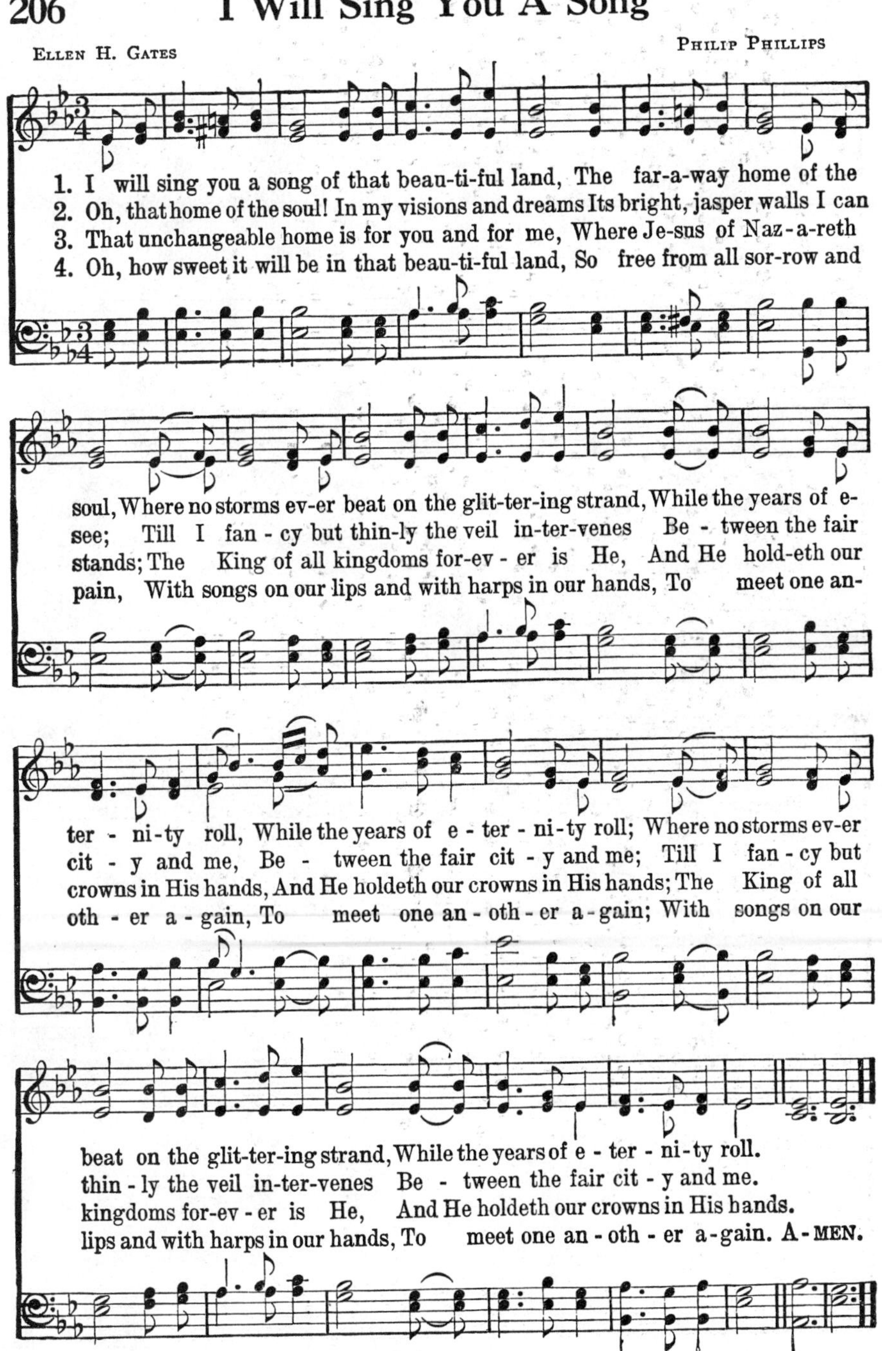
1. I will sing you a song of that beau-ti-ful land, The far-a-way home of the
2. Oh, that home of the soul! In my visions and dreams Its bright, jasper walls I can
3. That unchangeable home is for you and for me, Where Je-sus of Naz-a-reth
4. Oh, how sweet it will be in that beau-ti-ful land, So free from all sor-row and
soul, Where no storms ev-er beat on the glit-ter-ing strand, While the years of e-
see; Till I fan - cy but thin-ly the veil in-ter-venes Be - tween the fair
stands; The King of all kingdoms for-ev - er is He, And He hold-eth our
pain, With songs on our lips and with harps in our hands, To meet one an-
ter - ni-ty roll, While the years of e - ter - ni-ty roll; Where no storms ev-er
cit - y and me, Be - tween the fair cit - y and me; Till I fan - cy but
crowns in His hands, And He holdeth our crowns in His hands; The King of all
oth - er a - gain, To meet one an - oth - er a - gain; With songs on our
beat on the glit-ter-ing strand, While the years of e - ter - ni-ty roll.
thin - ly the veil in-ter-venes Be - tween the fair cit - y and me.
kingdoms for-ev - er is He, And He holdeth our crowns in His hands.
lips and with harps in our hands, To meet one an - oth - er a-gain. A-MEN.

207 The Unclouded Day

J. K. A.
Rev. J. K. Alwood
1. O they tell me of a home far be - yond the skies, O they
2. O they tell me of a home where my friends have gone, O they
3. O they tell me of a King in His beau - ty there, And they
4. O they tell me that He smiles on His chil - dren there, And His
tell me of a home far a - way; O they tell me of a home
tell me of that land far a - way, Where the tree of life
tell me that mine eyes shall be - hold Where He sits on the throne
smile drives their sor-rows all a - way; And they tell me that no tears
D. S.—O they tell me of a home
Fine.
where no storm-clouds rise, O they tell me of an un - cloud-ed day.
in e - ter - nal bloom Sheds its fragrance thro' the un - cloud-ed day.
that is whit-er than snow, In the cit - y that is made of gold.
ev - er come a - gain, In that love - ly land of un - cloud-ed day.
where no storm-clouds rise, O they tell me of an un - cloud-ed day.
Chorus
D. S.
O the land of cloud-less day, O the land of an un-cloud - ed day;

208 Gathering Home

Miss Mariana B. Slade
R. M. M'Intosh
1. Up to the boun-ti-ful Giv-er of life, Gath-er-ing home! gath-er-ing home!
2. Up to the cit - y where falleth no night, Gath-er-ing home! gath-er-ing home!
3. Up to the beau-ti-ful mansions a-bove, Gath-er-ing home! gath-er-ing home!
Up to the dwelling, where cometh no strife, The dear ones are gathering home.
Up where the Sav-ior's own face is the light, The dear ones are gathering home.
Safe in the arms of His in - fi-nite love, The dear ones are gathering home.
Chorus.
Gath-er-ing home,............ Gath-er-ing home,............
Gath - er - ing home, Gath - er - ing home,
Nev-er to sor-row more, nev-er to roam; Gath-er-ing home,...........
Gath-er-ing home,
Gath-er-ing home,......... God's children are gath-er-ing home. A - men.
Gath-er-ing home,

The Christian's "Good-Night"

Sarah Doudney — Ira D. Sankey

1. Sleep on, be - lov - ed, sleep, and take thy rest; Lay down thy head up - on thy Sav-iour's breast; We love thee well, but Je - sus loves thee best— Good-night! Good-night! Good-night!
2. Calm is thy slum - ber as an in - fant's sleep; But thou shalt wake no more to toil and weep: Thine is a per - fect rest, se - cure and deep— Good-night! Good-night! Good-night!
3. Un - til the shad - ows from this earth are cast, Un- til He gath - ers in His sheaves at last; Un - til the twi - light gloom be o - ver - past— Good-night! Good-night! Good-night!
4. Un - til the Eas - ter glo - ry lights the skies, Un- til the dead in Je - sus shall a - rise, And He shall come, but not in low - ly guise— Good-night! Good-night! Good-night!
rit.

5 Until, made beautiful by Love Divine,
Thou, in the likeness of thy Lord shalt shine,
And He shall bring that golden crown of thine—
Good-night!

6 Only "Good-night," beloved—not "farewell!"
A little while, and all His saints shall dwell
In hallowed unison indivisible—
Good-night!

7 Until we meet again before His throne,
Clothed in the spotless robe He gives His own,
Until we know even as we are known—
Good-night!

210 Into The Woods

Sidney Lanier, 1842-1881

Peter C. Lutkin, 1858-1931

mp
1. In - to the woods my Mas - ter went,.. Clean for-spent, for - spent;
2. Out of the woods my Mas - ter went, And He was well con - tent;
In - to the woods my Mas - ter came, For-spent with love and shame.
Out of the woods my Mas - ter came, Con-tent with death and shame.
But the ol - ives they were not blind to Him, The lit - tle grey leaves were
When death and shame would woo Him last, From un-der the trees they
cres.
rit.
kind to Him, The thorn-tree had a mind to Him, When in-to the woods He came.
drew Him last,'Twas on a tree they slew Him—last When out of the woods He came.

211 O Love That Wilt Not Let Me Go

George Matheson
A. L. Peace
1. O Love that wilt not let me go, I rest my wea - ry soul in Thee; I give Thee back the life I owe, That in Thine o - cean depths its flow May rich - er, full - er be.
2. O Light that fol - low'st all my way, I yield my flick-'ring torch to Thee; My heart re - stores its bor - rowed ray, That in Thy sun-shine's glow its day May bright-er, fair - er be.
3. O Joy that seek - est me thro' pain, I can - not close my heart to Thee; I trace the rain - bow thro' the rain, And feel the prom - ise is not vain That morn shall tear - less be.
4. O Cross that lift - est up my head, I dare not ask to hide from Thee; I lay in dust life's glo - ry dead, And from the ground there blossoms red Life that shall end - less be.
212
Silent Night! Holy Night!
Joseph Mohr
P. M.
Franz Gruber
1. Si - lent night! ho - ly night! All is calm, all is bright 'Round yon
2. Si - lent night! ho - ly night! Shep - herds quake at the sight! Glo - ries
3. Si - lent night! ho - ly night! Son of God, love's pure light Ra - diant

Silent Night

vir - gin moth - er and Child! Ho - ly In - fant, so ten - der and mild,
stream from heav-en a - far, Heav'n-ly hosts sing Al - le - lu - ia;
beams from Thy ho - ly face, With the dawn of re - deem - ing grace,
Sleep in heav - en - ly peace, Sleep in heav - en - ly peace.
Christ, the Sav - iour is born, Christ the Sav-iour is born.
Je - sus, Lord, at Thy birth, Je - sus, Lord, at Thy birth. A - MEN.

213 While Shepherds Watched Their Flocks

CHRISTMAS, C. M.

NAHUM TATE — GEORGE F. HANDEL

1. While shepherds watched their flocks by night, All seat-ed on the ground, The an - gel
2. "Fear not," said he; for might-y dread Had seized their troubled mind, "Glad tidings
3. "To you, in Da-vid's town, this day Is born, of Da - vid's line, The Sav-iour,
4. "The heav'n-ly Babe you there shall find To hu-man view dis - played, All mean-ly
5. "All glo - ry be to God on high, And to the earth be peace; Good-will hence-

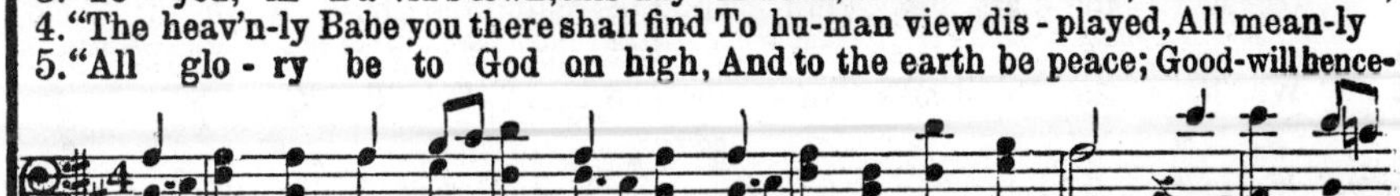

of the Lord came down, And glory shone a-round, And glo-ry shone a - round.
of great joy I bring, To you and all man-kind, To you and all man-kind.
who is Christ the Lord; And this shall be the sign, And this shall be the sign:
wrapped in swathing bands, And in a man-ger laid, And in a man-ger laid."
forth from heav'n to men Be-gin, and nev-er cease, Be-gin, and nev-er cease!" AMEN.

214 O Little Town Of Bethlehem

Phillips Brooks — Lewis H. Redner

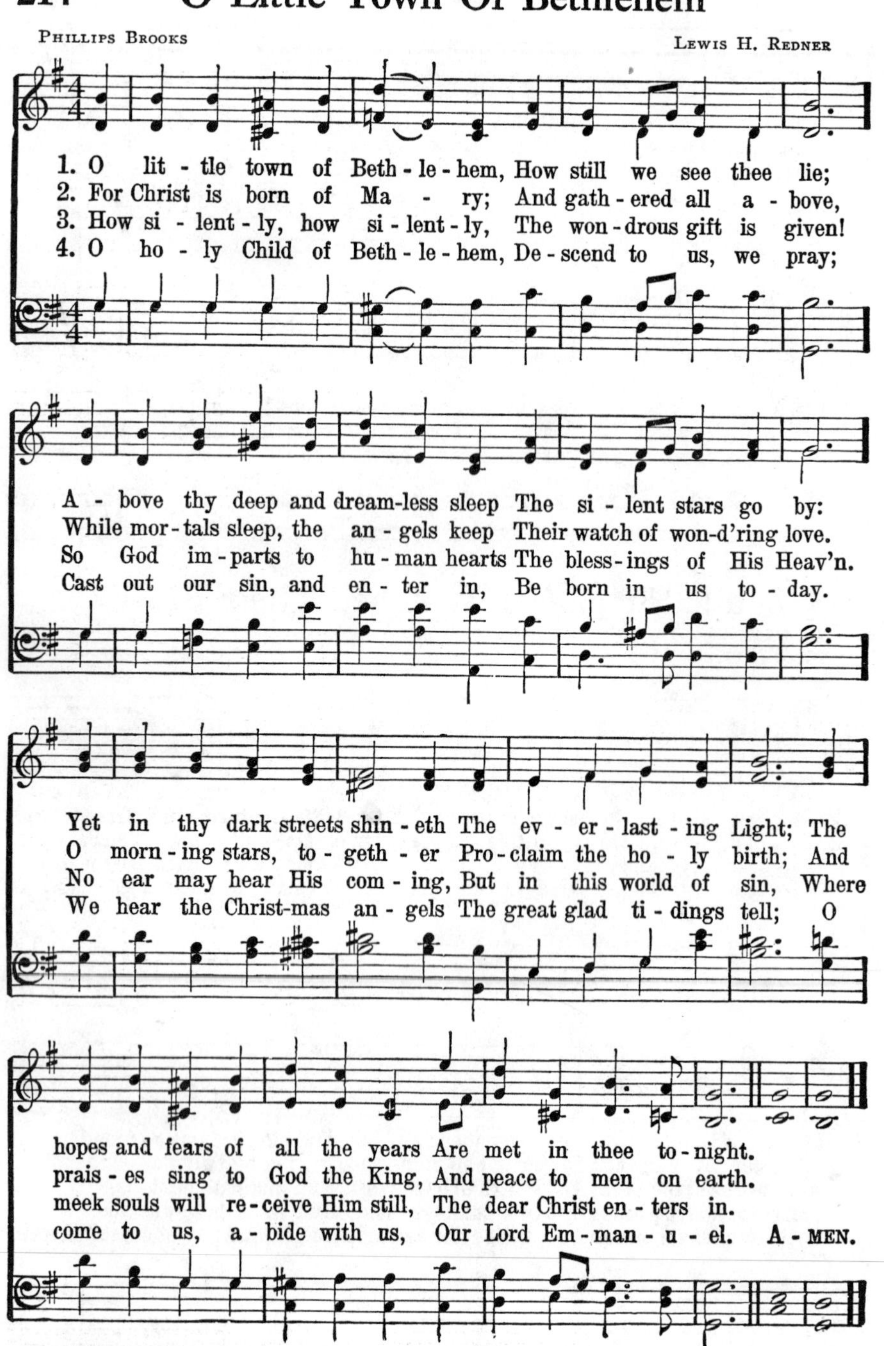
1. O lit - tle town of Beth - le - hem, How still we see thee lie;
2. For Christ is born of Ma - ry; And gath - ered all a - bove,
3. How si - lent - ly, how si - lent - ly, The won - drous gift is given!
4. O ho - ly Child of Beth - le - hem, De - scend to us, we pray;
A - bove thy deep and dream-less sleep The si - lent stars go by:
While mor - tals sleep, the an - gels keep Their watch of won-d'ring love.
So God im - parts to hu - man hearts The bless - ings of His Heav'n.
Cast out our sin, and en - ter in, Be born in us to - day.
Yet in thy dark streets shin - eth The ev - er - last - ing Light; The
O morn - ing stars, to - geth - er Pro - claim the ho - ly birth; And
No ear may hear His com - ing, But in this world of sin, Where
We hear the Christ-mas an - gels The great glad ti - dings tell; O
hopes and fears of all the years Are met in thee to - night.
prais - es sing to God the King, And peace to men on earth.
meek souls will re - ceive Him still, The dear Christ en - ters in.
come to us, a - bide with us, Our Lord Em - man - u - el. A - MEN.

215 It Came Upon The Midnight Clear

Edmund H. Sears — Richard S. Willis

1. It came up - on the mid-night clear, That glo-rious song of old,
2. Still thro' the clo-ven skies they come, With peaceful wings un - furled,
3. And ye, be - neath life's crushing load, Whose forms are bending low,
4. For lo, the days are has - t'ning on, By prophet bards fore-told,
From an - gels bending near the earth To touch their harps of gold:
And still their heav'nly mu - sic floats O'er all the wea - ry world:
Who toil a - long the climb - ing way With pain - ful steps and slow,
When with the ev - er - cir - cling years Comes 'round the age of gold:
"Peace on the earth, good-will to men, From heav'ns all-gracious King:" The
A - bove its sad and low - ly plains They bend on hov'ring wing: And
Look now! for glad and gold - en hours Come swift-ly on the wing; O
When peace shall o - ver all the earth Its an - cient splendors fling, And
world in sol - emn still-ness lay To hear the an - gels sing.
ev - er o'er its Ba - bel sounds The bless-ed an - gels sing.
rest be - side the wea - ry road, And hear the an - gels sing.
the whole world give back the song Which now the an - gels sing. A - men.

216 There's A Song In The Air

Josiah G. Holland
Karl P. Harrington
Andante con moto
1. There's a song in the air! There's a star in the sky!
2. There's a tu - mult of joy O'er the won - der - ful birth,
3. In the light of that star Lie the a - ges im - pearled;
4. We re - joice in the light, And we ech - o the song
ritard.
There's a moth - er's deep prayer, And a ba - by's low cry!
For the Vir - gin's sweet boy Is the Lord of the earth.
And that song from a - far Has swept o - ver the world.
That comes down through the night From the heav - en - ly throng.
piu mosso
And the star rains its fire while the beau - ti - ful sing,
Ay! the star rains its fire while the beau - ti - ful sing,
Ev - 'ry hearth is a - flame, and the beau - ti - ful sing,
Ay! we shout to the love - ly e - van - gel they bring,
ritard.
For the man - ger of Beth - le - hem cra - dles a King!
For the man - ger of Beth - le - hem cra - dles a King!
In the homes of the na - tions that Je - sus is King!
And we greet in His cra - dle our Sav - ior and King!

217 Joy To The World!

ISAAC WATTS
GEORGE F. HANDEL
1. Joy to the world! the Lord is come; Let earth re-
2. Joy to the earth! the Savior reigns; Let men their
3. No more let sins and sor - rows grow, Nor thorns in-
4. He rules the world with truth and grace, And makes the
ceive her King; Let ev - 'ry heart pre - pare Him room,
songs em - ploy; While fields and floods, rocks, hills and plains
fest the ground; He comes to make His bless - ings flow
na - tions prove The glo - ries of His right - eous - ness,
And Heav'n and na - ture sing, And Heav'n and na - ture
Re - peat the sound - ing joy, Re - peat the sound - ing
Far as the curse is found, Far as the curse is
And won - ders of His love, And won - ders of His
1. And Heav'n and na - ture sing,......... And
sing, And Heav'n, and Heav'n and na - ture sing.
joy, Re - peat, re - peat the sound - ing joy.
found, Far as, far as the curse is found.
love, And won - ders, and won - ders of His love.
Heav'n and na - ture sing,

218 Hark! The Herald Angels Sing

Charles Wesley — Mendelssohn

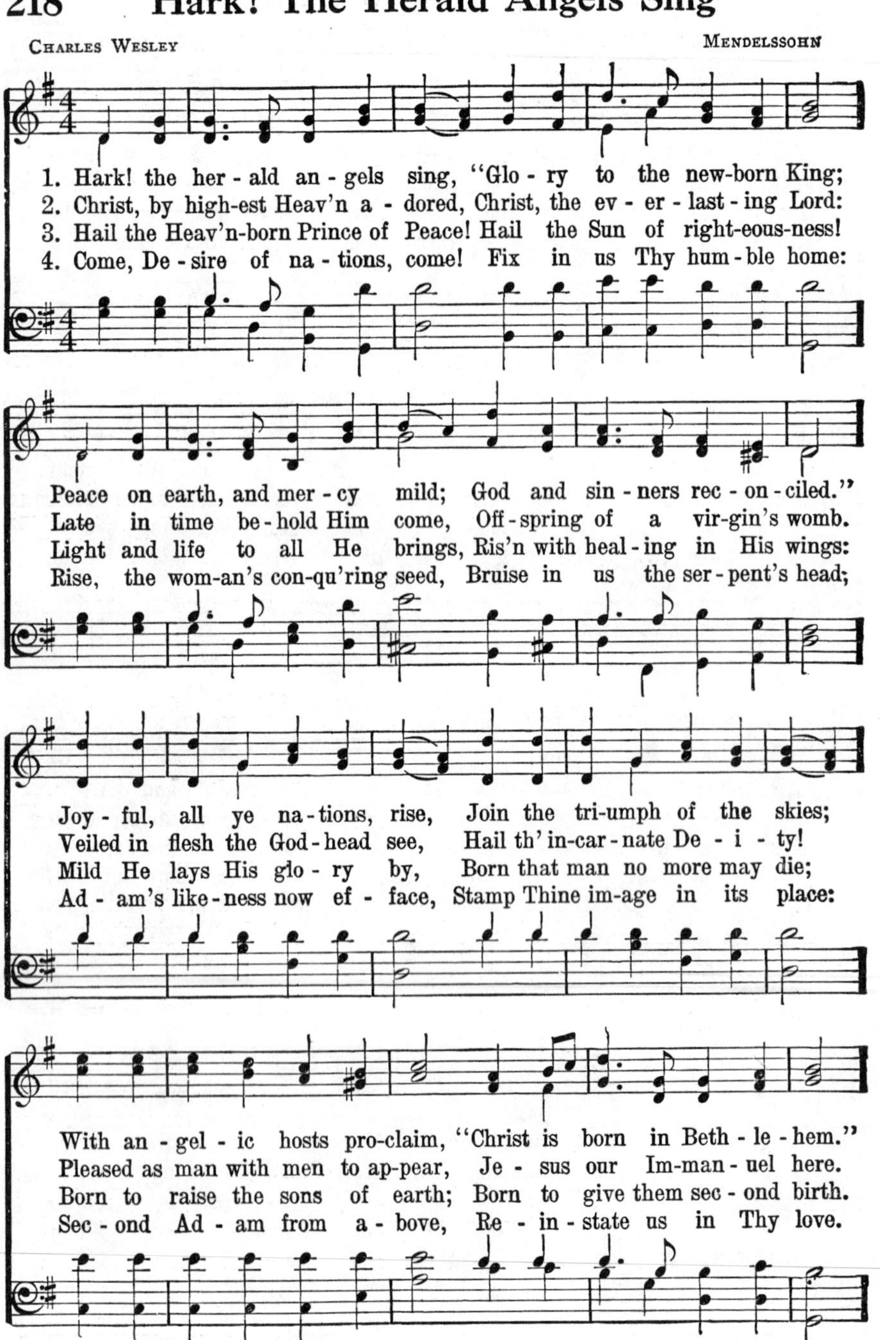
1. Hark! the her - ald an - gels sing, "Glo - ry to the new-born King;
2. Christ, by high-est Heav'n a - dored, Christ, the ev - er - last - ing Lord:
3. Hail the Heav'n-born Prince of Peace! Hail the Sun of right-eous-ness!
4. Come, De - sire of na - tions, come! Fix in us Thy hum - ble home:
Peace on earth, and mer - cy mild; God and sin - ners rec - on - ciled."
Late in time be - hold Him come, Off - spring of a vir-gin's womb.
Light and life to all He brings, Ris'n with heal - ing in His wings:
Rise, the wom-an's con-qu'ring seed, Bruise in us the ser - pent's head;
Joy - ful, all ye na - tions, rise, Join the tri-umph of the skies;
Veiled in flesh the God - head see, Hail th' in-car - nate De - i - ty!
Mild He lays His glo - ry by, Born that man no more may die;
Ad - am's like - ness now ef - face, Stamp Thine im-age in its place:
With an - gel - ic hosts pro-claim, "Christ is born in Beth - le - hem."
Pleased as man with men to ap-pear, Je - sus our Im-man - uel here.
Born to raise the sons of earth; Born to give them sec - ond birth.
Sec - ond Ad - am from a - bove, Re - in - state us in Thy love.

Hark! The Herald Angels Sing
Hark! the her - ald an-gels sing, "Glo - ry to the new-born King." Amen.
219
O Come, All Ye Faithful
Tr. by Frederick Oakeley
Wade's Cantus Diversi
1. O come, all ye faith - ful, joy - ful and tri - um-phant, O
2. Sing, choirs of an - gels, sing in ex - ul - ta - tion, O
3. Yea, Lord, we greet Thee, born this hap - py morn-ing,
come ye, O come ye to Beth - le - hem; Come and be - hold Him;
sing, all ye bright hosts of heav'n a - bove; Glo - ry to God, all
Je - sus, to Thee be all glo - ry giv'n; Word of the Fa - ther,
Refrain
born the King of an - gels.
glo - ry in the high-est. O come, let us a-dore Him, O come, let us a -
now in flesh ap - pear-ing.
dore Him, O come, let us a - dore Him, Christ, the Lord. A - men.

220 Christ Arose

Robert Lowry — Robert Lowry

1. Low in the grave He lay— Je - sus my Sav - ior! Wait-ing the com-ing day—
2. Vain-ly they watch His bed—Je - sus my Sav - ior! Vain-ly they seal the dead—
3. Death cannot keep his prey— Je - sus my Sav - ior! He tore the bars a - way—
Refrain Faster
Je - sus my Lord! Up from the grave He a - rose, (He a-rose,) With a
might-y tri-umph o'er His foes; (He a-rose!) He a - rose a Vic - tor from the
dark do - main, And He lives for - ev - er with His saints to reign. He a-
rose! He a - rose! He a - rose! Hal - le - lu - jah! Christ a - rose!
He a - rose!
rit.

221 Christ The Lord Is Risen Today

7. 7. 7. 7. WITH ALLELUIAS
Charles Wesley
Worgan
From Lyra Davidica
1. Christ the Lord is ris'n to - day, Al - le - lu - ia!
2. Lives a - gain our glo - rious King: Al - le - lu - ia!
3. Love's re - deem - ing work is done, Al - le - lu - ia!
4. Soar we now, where Christ has led, Al - le - lu - ia!
Sons of men and an - gels say: Al - le - lu - ia!
Where, O death, is now thy sting? Al - le - lu - ia!
Fought the fight, the bat - tle won; Al - le - lu - ia!
Fol - l'wing our ex - alt - ed Head; Al - le - lu - ia!
Raise your joys and tri - umphs high, Al - le - lu - ia!
Once He died our souls to save: Al - le - lu - ia!
Death in vain for - bids Him rise; Al - le - lu - ia!
Made like Him, like Him we rise; Al - le - lu - ia!
Sing, ye heav'ns, and earth re - ply, Al - le - lu - ia!
Where thy vic - to - ry, O grave? Al - le - lu - ia!
Christ has o - pened Par - a - dise. Al - le - lu - ia!
Ours the cross, the grave, the skies. Al - le - lu - ia!

222 Come, Ye Thankful People

HENRY ALFORD GEORGE J. ELVEY

1. Come, ye thank - ful peo - ple, come, Raise the song of har - vest - home:
2. All the world is God's own field, Fruit un - to His praise to yield;
3. For the Lord our God shall come, And shall take His har - vest home;
4. E - ven so, Lord, quick - ly come To Thy fi - nal har - vest - home;
All is safe - ly gath - ered in, Ere the win - ter storms be - gin;
Wheat and tares to - geth - er sown, Un - to joy or sor - row grown;
From His field shall in that day All of - fens - es purge a - way;
Gath - er Thou Thy peo - ple in, Free from sor - row, free from sin;
God, our Ma - ker, doth pro - vide For our wants to be sup - plied:
First the blade, and then the ear, Then the full corn shall ap - pear:
Give His an - gels charge at last In the fire the tares to cast;
There, for - ev - er pu - ri - fied, In Thy pres-ence to a - bide:
Come to God's own tem - ple, come, Raise the song of har - vest-home.
Lord of har - vest, grant that we Wholesome grain and pure may be.
But the fruit - ful ears to store In His gar - ner ev - er - more.
Come, with all Thine an - gels, come, Raise the glo-rious har - vest-home.

223 We Plough The Fields, And Scatter

MATTHIAS CLAUDIUS, DRESDEN. 7, 6, 7, 6. WITH REFRAIN

Tr. Jane M. Campbell — Johann A. P. Schulz

1. We plough the fields, and scat-ter The good seed on the land, But it is fed and wa-tered By God's al-might-y hand; He sends the snow in win-ter, The warmth to swell the grain, The breez-es and the sun-shine: And soft refreshing rain.
2. He on-ly is the Mak-er Of all things near and far; He paints the way-side flow-er, He lights the ev-'ning star; The winds and waves o-bey Him, By Him the birds are fed; Much more to us, His chil-dren, He gives our dai-ly bread.
3. We thank Thee, then, O Fa-ther, For all things bright and good; The seed-time and the har-vest, Our life, our health, our food; No gifts have we to of-fer For all Thy love im-parts, But that which Thou de-sir-est, Our hum-ble, thankful hearts.
Refrain
All good gifts around us Are sent from heav'n a-bove; Then thank the Lord, O thank the Lord for all His love. A-men.

224 Stand Up, Stand Up For Jesus

George Duffield
Adam Geibel
Solo or Unison
1. Stand up, stand up for Je - sus, Ye sol-diers of the cross; Lift high His roy-al
2. Stand up, stand up for Je - sus, The trump-et call o - bey, Forth to the mighty
3. Stand up, stand up for Je - sus, Stand in His strength alone; The arm of flesh will
4. Stand up, stand up for Je - sus, The strife will not be long; This day the noise of
ban - ner, It must not suf - fer loss; From vic - t'ry un - to vic - t'ry His
con - flict, In this His glo-rious day; "Ye that are men now serve Him" A-
fail you, Ye dare not trust your own; Put on the gos - pel ar - mor, Each
bat - tle, The next, the vic-tor's song: To him that o - ver-com - eth, A
rit.
ar - my shall He lead, Till ev - 'ry foe is vanquished And Christ is Lord in - deed.
gainst unnumbered foes; Let courage rise with dan-ger, And strength to strength oppose.
piece put on with prayer; Where du-ty calls or dan - ger, Be nev - er want-ing there.
crown of life shall be; He with the King of glo - ry Shall reign e - ter - nal-ly.
Chorus Harmony
Stand up for Je - sus, Ye sol - diers of the cross; . . Lift
stand up

Stand Up, Stand Up For Jesus

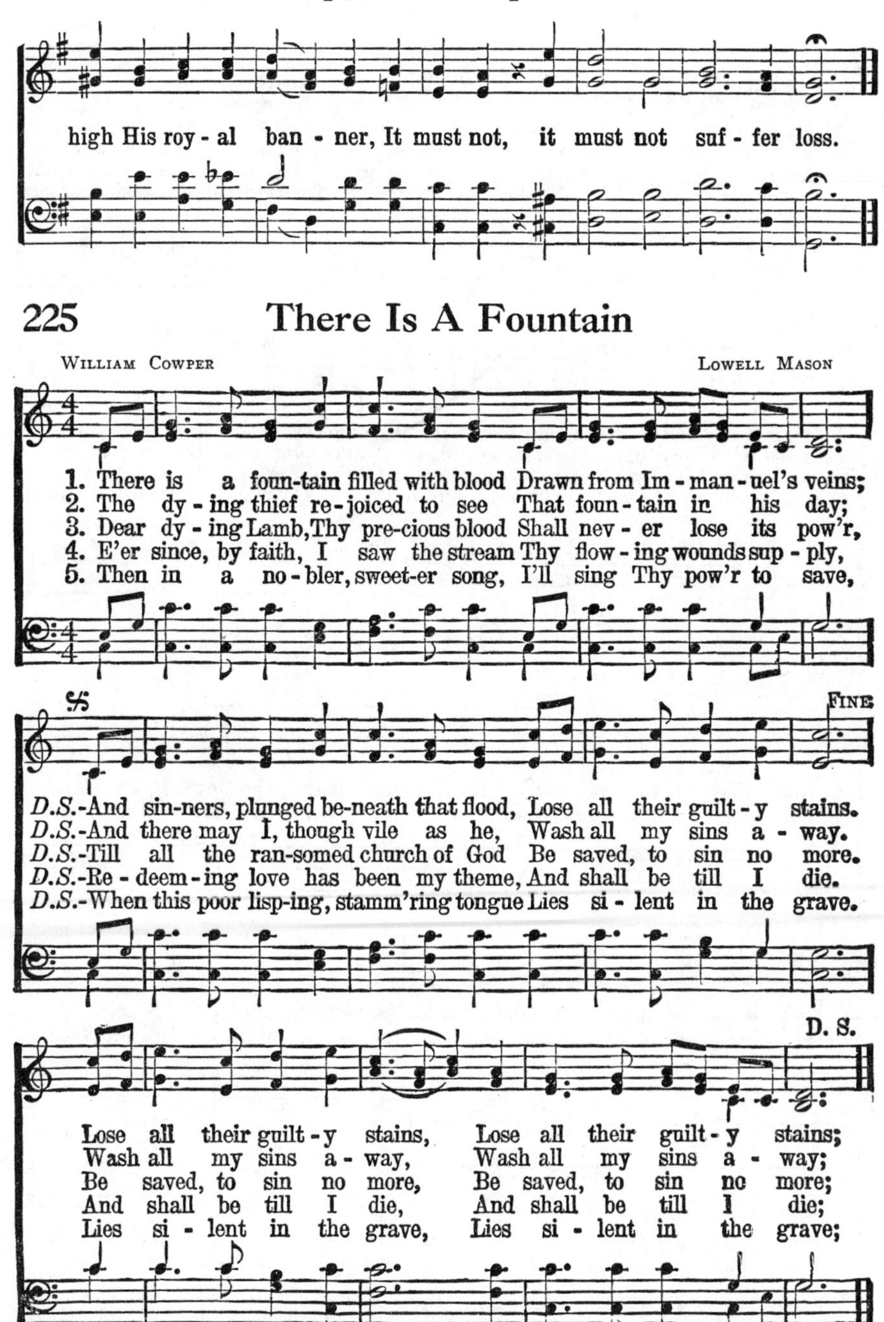

high His roy - al ban - ner, It must not, it must not suf - fer loss.
225 There Is A Fountain
William Cowper
Lowell Mason
1. There is a foun-tain filled with blood Drawn from Im - man - uel's veins;
2. The dy - ing thief re - joiced to see That foun - tain in his day;
3. Dear dy - ing Lamb, Thy pre-cious blood Shall nev - er lose its pow'r,
4. E'er since, by faith, I saw the stream Thy flow - ing wounds sup - ply,
5. Then in a no - bler, sweet-er song, I'll sing Thy pow'r to save,
Fine
D.S.-And sin-ners, plunged be-neath that flood, Lose all their guilt - y stains.
D.S.-And there may I, though vile as he, Wash all my sins a - way.
D.S.-Till all the ran-somed church of God Be saved, to sin no more.
D.S.-Re - deem - ing love has been my theme, And shall be till I die.
D.S.-When this poor lisp-ing, stamm'ring tongue Lies si - lent in the grave.
D. S.
Lose all their guilt - y stains, Lose all their guilt - y stains;
Wash all my sins a - way, Wash all my sins a - way;
Be saved, to sin no more, Be saved, to sin no more;
And shall be till I die, And shall be till I die;
Lies si - lent in the grave, Lies si - lent in the grave;

226 My Country, 'Tis Of Thee

S. F. Smith
Henry Carey
1. My coun-try, 'tis of thee, Sweet land of lib - er - ty, Of thee I sing: Land where my fa - thers died, Land of the pilgrims' pride, From ev - 'ry mountain side Let free-dom ring!
2. My na-tive coun-try thee, Land of the no - ble, free, Thy name I love: I love thy rocks and rills, Thy woods and templed hills; My heart with rapture thrills Like that a - bove.
3. Let mu-sic swell the breeze, And ring from all the trees Sweet freedom's song: Let mor-tal tongues awake; Let all that breathe partake; Let rocks their silence break, The sound pro-long.
4. Our fa-thers' God! to Thee, Au - thor of lib - er - ty, To Thee we sing: Long may our land be bright With freedom's ho-ly light; Pro-tect us by Thy might, Great God, our King!
227 God Bless Our Native Land
C. T. Brooks
Lowell Mason
1. God bless our na - tive land; Firm may she ev - er stand Thro' storm and night; When the wild tem - pests rave, Rul - er of wind and wave, Do Thou our coun - try save By Thy great might.
2. For her our prayers shall rise To God a - bove the skies; On Him we wait; Thou who art ev - er nigh, Guard-ing with watch - ful eye, To Thee a - loud we cry, God save the State.

228 America The Beautiful

KATHERINE LEE BATES
SAMUEL A. WARD
1. O beau - ti - ful for spa-cious skies, For am - ber waves of grain; . . .
2. O beau - ti - ful for pil - grim feet, Whose stern, im-pas-sioned stress . . .
3. O beau - ti - ful for he - roes proved In lib - er - at - ing strife, . . .
4. O beau - ti - ful for pa - triot dream That sees be - yond the years . . . .
For pur - ple moun-tain maj - es - ties A - bove the fruit - ed plain!
A thor-ough-fare for free - dom beat A - cross the wil - der - ness!
Who more than self their coun-try loved, And mer - cy more than life!
Thine al - a - bas - ter cit - ies gleam Un-dimmed by hu - man tears!
A - mer - i - ca! A - mer - i - ca! God shed His grace on thee,
A - mer - i - ca! A - mer - i - ca! God mend thine ev - 'ry flaw,
A - mer - i - ca! A - mer - i - ca! May God thy gold re - fine
A - mer - i - ca! A - mer - i - ca! God shed His grace on thee,
And crown thy good with broth - er - hood From sea to shin - ing sea!
Con - firm thy soul in self - con - trol, Thy lib - er - ty in law!
Till all suc-cess be no - ble - ness, And ev - 'ry gain di - vine!
And crown thy good with broth - er - hood From sea to shin - ing sea!

229 The Star-Spangled Banner
Francis Scott Key
1. Oh, say, can you see, by the dawn's ear-ly light, What so proud-ly we
2. On the shore, dim-ly seen thro' the mists of the deep, Where the foe's haughty
3. And where is that band, who so vaunt-ing-ly swore That the hav-oc of
4. Oh, thus be it ev - er when free-men shall stand Be - tween their loved
hailed at the twilight's last gleaming? Whose broad stripes and bright stars, thro' the
host in dread si-lence re - pos - es, What is that which the breeze, o'er the
war and the bat-tle's con-fu - sion, A home and a coun - try should
homes and the war's des - o - la - tion; Blest with vic - t'ry and peace, may the
per - il - ous fight, O'er the ramparts we watched, were so gal-lant-ly stream-ing?
tow - er - ing steep, As it fit - ful - ly blows, half conceals, half dis-clos - es?
leave us no more? Their blood has washed out their foul footsteps' pol - lu - tion;
Heav'n-rescued land Praise the Pow'r that hath made and preserved us a na - tion!
And the rock-ets' red glare, the bombs bursting in air, Gave proof thro' the
Now it catch-es the gleam of the morning's first beam, In full glo - ry re-
No ref-uge could save the hire-ling and slave From the ter - ror of
Then con-quer we must, when our cause it is just; And this be our

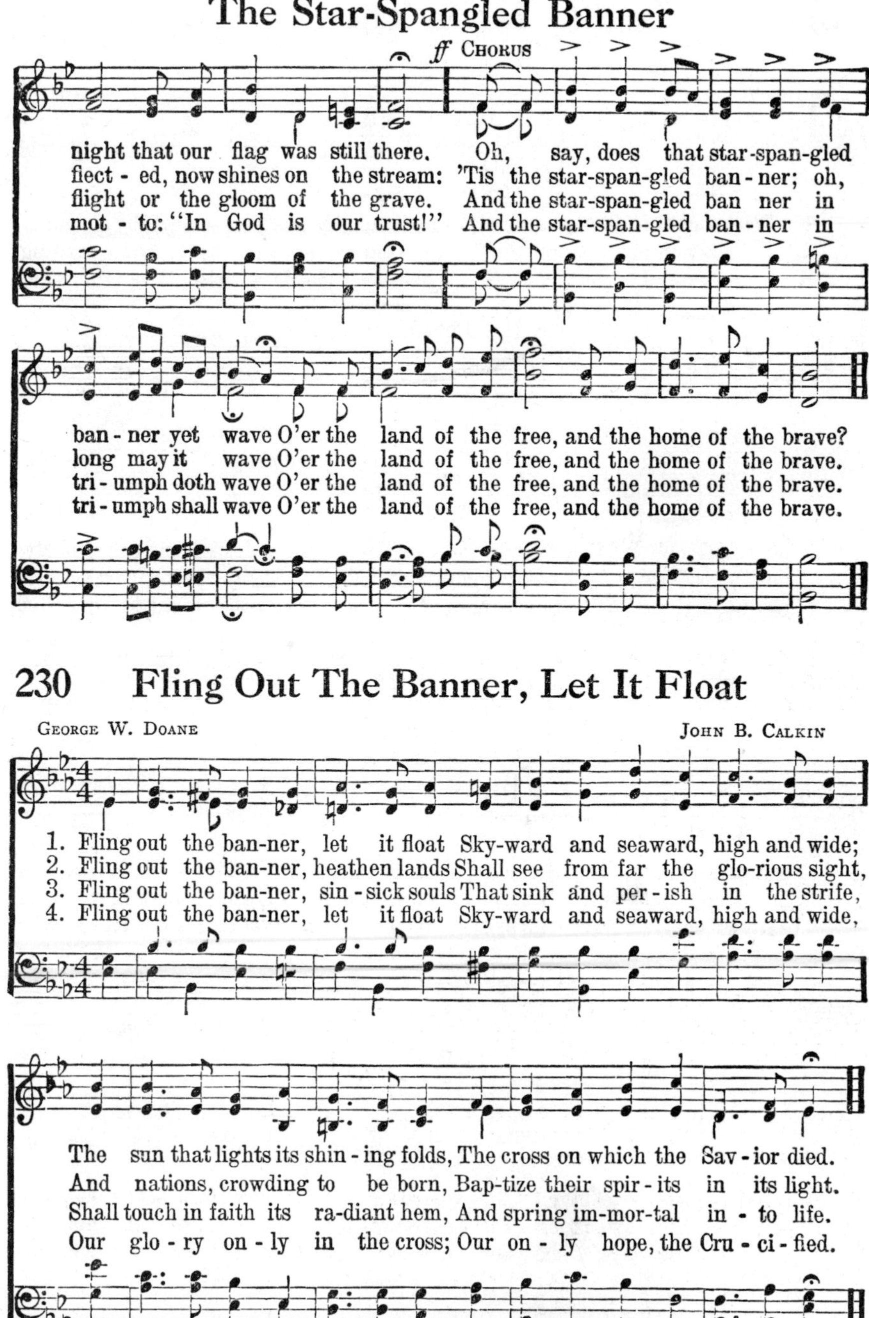
The Star-Spangled Banner
ff Chorus
night that our flag was still there. Oh, say, does that star-span-gled
fiect - ed, now shines on the stream: 'Tis the star-span-gled ban - ner; oh,
flight or the gloom of the grave. And the star-span-gled ban ner in
mot - to: "In God is our trust!" And the star-span-gled ban - ner in
ban - ner yet wave O'er the land of the free, and the home of the brave?
long may it wave O'er the land of the free, and the home of the brave.
tri - umph doth wave O'er the land of the free, and the home of the brave.
tri - umph shall wave O'er the land of the free, and the home of the brave.
230 Fling Out The Banner, Let It Float
George W. Doane
John B. Calkin
1. Fling out the ban-ner, let it float Sky-ward and seaward, high and wide;
2. Fling out the ban-ner, heathen lands Shall see from far the glo-rious sight,
3. Fling out the ban-ner, sin - sick souls That sink and per - ish in the strife,
4. Fling out the ban-ner, let it float Sky-ward and seaward, high and wide,
The sun that lights its shin - ing folds, The cross on which the Sav - ior died.
And nations, crowding to be born, Bap-tize their spir - its in its light.
Shall touch in faith its ra-diant hem, And spring im-mor-tal in - to life.
Our glo - ry on - ly in the cross; Our on - ly hope, the Cru - ci - fied.

231 His Eye Is On The Sparrow

Mrs. C. D. Martin
Chas. H. Gabriel
1. Why should I feel discouraged, Why should the shadows come, Why should my heart be lonely And long for Heav'n and home, When Jesus is my portion? My constant Friend is He: His eye is on the spar-row, And I know He watches me; His eye is on the sparrow, And I know He watches me.
2. "Let not your heart be troubled," His ten-der word I hear, And rest-ing on His goodness, I lose my doubts and fears; Tho' by the path He leadeth But one step I may see: His eye is on the spar-row, And I know He watches me; His eye is on the sparrow, And I know He watches me.
3. When-ev-er I am temp-ted, When-ev-er clouds a - rise, When songs give place to sighing, When hope within me dies, I draw the clo-ser to Him, From care He sets me free; His eye is on the spar-row, And I know He cares for me; His eye is on the sparrow, And I know He cares for me.

His Eye Is On The Sparrow
CHORUS
I sing be-cause I'm hap-py, (I'm hap-py,) I sing because I'm free, (I'm free,)
rall.
For His eye is on the spar-row, And I know He watches me. A-MEN.
232 Come, Ye Sinners, Poor And Needy
GREENVILLE. 8. 7. 8. 7. 8. 7.
JOSEPH HART, 1712-1768
JEAN J. ROUSSEAU, 1712-1778
1. Come, ye sin-ners, poor and need-y, Weak and wound-ed, sick and sore;
2. Now, ye need-y, come and wel-come; God's free boun-ty glo-ri-fy;
3. Let not con-science make you lin-ger, Nor of fit-ness fond-ly dream;
4. Come, ye wea-ry, heav-y-la-den, Bruised and mangled by the fall;
Je-sus read-y stands to save you, Full of pit-y, love and pow'r:
True be-lief and true re-pent-ance, Ev-'ry grace that brings you nigh,
All the fit-ness He re-quir-eth Is to feel your need of Him:
If you tar-ry till you're bet-ter, You will nev-er come at all;
He is a-ble, He is a-ble, He is will-ing: doubt no more.
With-out mon-ey, With-out mon-ey, Come to Je-sus Christ and buy.
This He gives you, This He gives you; 'Tis the Spir-it's glimm'ring beam.
Not the righteous, Not the righteous—Sin-ners Je-sus came to call. A-MEN.

233 Love Lifted Me

© COPYRIGHT 1911. RENEWAL 1939 BY JOHN T. BENSON, JR. ASSIGNED TO SINGSPIRATION (ASCAP), DIVISION OF THE ZONDERVAN CORP. ALL RIGHTS RESERVED. USED BY PERMISSION.
JAMES ROWE
HOWARD E. SMITH
1. I was sink-ing deep in sin, Far from the peaceful shore, Ver - y deep-ly
2. All my heart to Him I give, Ev - er to Him I'll cling, In His bless-ed
3. Souls in dan-ger, look a-bove, Je - sus com-plete-ly saves; He will lift you
stained with-in, Sink-ing to rise no more; But the Mas - ter of the sea
pres - ence live, Ev - er His prais - es sing. Love so might-y and so true
by His love Out of the an - gry waves. He's the Mas - ter of the sea,
Heard my despairing cry, From the wa - ters lift - ed me, Now safe am I.
Mer-its my soul's best songs; Faith-ful, lov-ing serv-ice, too, To Him be - longs.
Bil-lows His will o - bey; He your Sav-ior wants to be—Be saved to - day.
CHORUS
Love lift-ed me! . . . . Love lift - ed me! . . . . When noth-ing
e - ven me! e - ven me!
else could help, Love lift - ed me. Love lift - ed me.
1
2

234 All Hail The Power Of Jesus' Name

DIADEM. C. M.

E. PERRONET | JAMES ELLOR

1. All hail the pow'r of Je - sus' name! Let an-gels pros-trate fall,
2. Ye cho - en seed of Is - rael's race, Ye ransomed from the fall,
3. Let ev - 'ry kin dred, ev - 'ry tribe, On this ter - res - trial ball,
4. O that with yon - der sa - cred throng We at His feet may fall,
Let an - gels pros-trate fall; Bring forth the roy - al di - a - dem,
Ye ran-somed from the fall, Hail Him who saves you by His grace,
On this ter - res - trial ball, To Him all maj - es - ty as - cribe,
We at His feet may fall! We'll join the ev - er - last - ing song,
And crown . . . . Him, Crown Him,
And crown Him, crown Him, crown Him, crown Him, And crown Him Lord of
And crown . . . . Him, Crown Him,
And crown Him, crown Him crown Him, Crown . . . .
crown Him, crown Him;
all, crown Him; And crown Him Lord of all! A - MEN.
crown . . . . Him;
. . . . Him; And crown Him Lord of all!

235 God Of Grace And God Of Glory

CWM RHONDDA. 8. 7. 8. 7. 8. 7.

WORDS USED BY PERMISSION OF HARRY EMERSON FOSDICK

Welsh Hymn Melody

HARRY EMERSON FOSDICK, 1878– JOHN HUGHES, 1873–1932

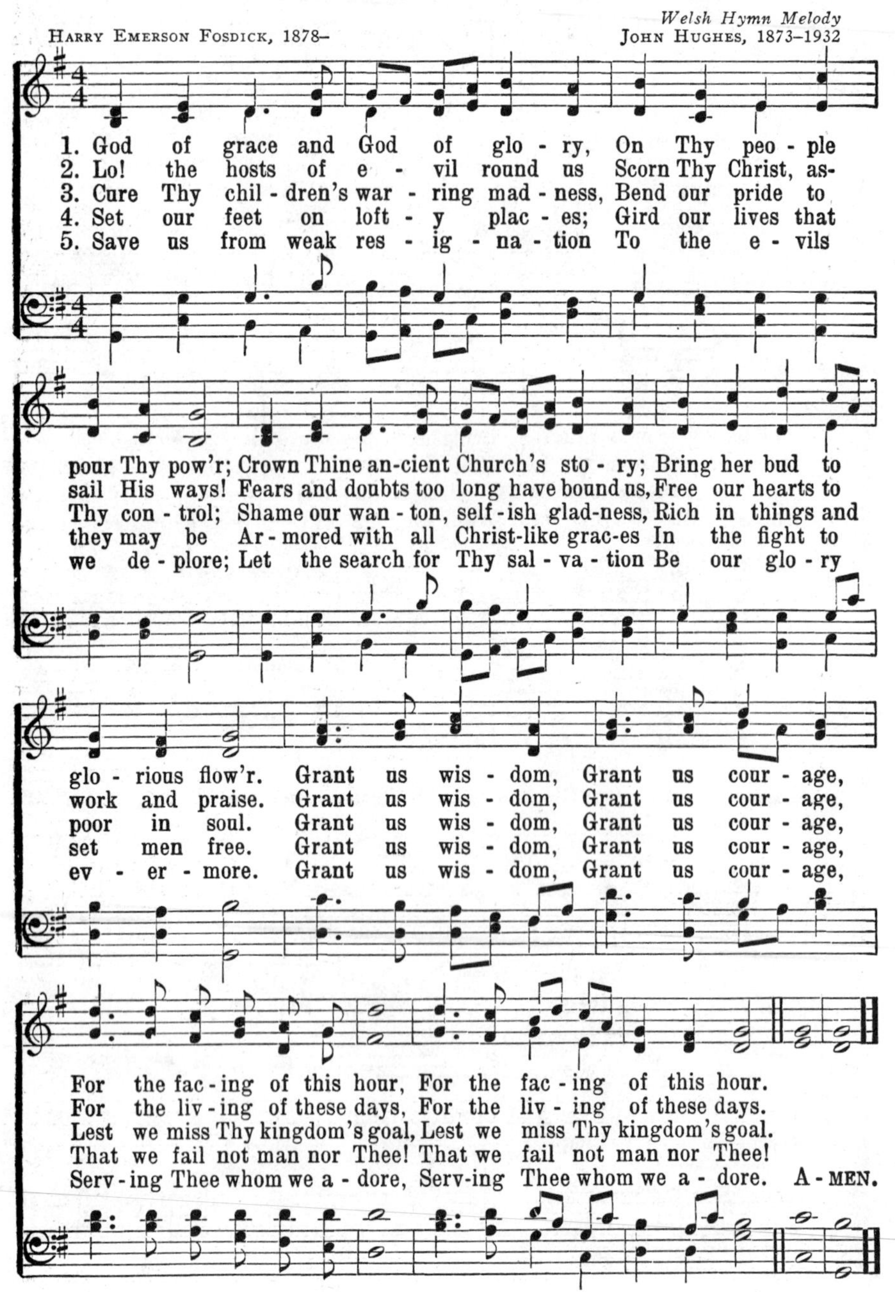

1. God of grace and God of glo - ry, On Thy peo - ple
2. Lo! the hosts of e - vil round us Scorn Thy Christ, as-
3. Cure Thy chil - dren's war - ring mad - ness, Bend our pride to
4. Set our feet on loft - y plac - es; Gird our lives that
5. Save us from weak res - ig - na - tion To the e - vils
pour Thy pow'r; Crown Thine an-cient Church's sto - ry; Bring her bud to
sail His ways! Fears and doubts too long have bound us, Free our hearts to
Thy con - trol; Shame our wan - ton, self - ish glad-ness, Rich in things and
they may be Ar - mored with all Christ-like grac-es In the fight to
we de - plore; Let the search for Thy sal - va - tion Be our glo - ry
glo - rious flow'r. Grant us wis - dom, Grant us cour - age,
work and praise. Grant us wis - dom, Grant us cour - age,
poor in soul. Grant us wis - dom, Grant us cour - age,
set men free. Grant us wis - dom, Grant us cour - age,
ev - er - more. Grant us wis - dom, Grant us cour - age,
For the fac - ing of this hour, For the fac - ing of this hour.
For the liv - ing of these days, For the liv - ing of these days.
Lest we miss Thy kingdom's goal, Lest we miss Thy kingdom's goal.
That we fail not man nor Thee! That we fail not man nor Thee!
Serv - ing Thee whom we a - dore, Serv-ing Thee whom we a - dore. A - MEN.

236 All Creatures Of Our God And King

LASST UNS ERFREUEN. 8. 8. 4. 4. 8. 8. with Alleluias.

St. Francis of Assisi, 1182-1226
Tr. by William H. Draper, 1855-

Melody from Geistliche Kirchengesäng, 1623

In unison
1. All crea-tures of our God and King, Lift up your voice and with us
2. Thou rush-ing wind that art so strong, Ye clouds that sail in heav'n a-
3. Thou flow - ing wa - ter, pure and clear, Make mu - sic for thy Lord to
4. Dear moth-er earth, who day by day Un - fold-est bless-ings on our
5. And all ye men of ten-der heart, For - giv-ing oth - ers, take your
6. Let all things their Cre - a - tor bless, And wor-ship Him in hum-ble-
sing Al-le-lu - ia! Al-le-lu - ia! Thou burn-ing sun with gold-en
long, O praise Him! Al-le-lu - ia! Thou ris - ing morn, in praise re-
hear, Al-le-lu - ia! Al-le-lu - ia! Thou fire so mas-ter-ful and
way, O praise Him! Al-le-lu - ia! The flow'rs and fruits that in thee
part, O sing ye! Al-le-lu - ia! Ye who long pain and sor-row
ness, O praise Him! Al-le-lu - ia! Praise, praise the Father, praise the
beam, Thou sil-ver moon with soft-er gleam! O praise Him! O
joice, Ye lights of eve-ning find a voice! O praise Him! O
bright, Thou giv-est man both warmth and light! O praise Him! O
grow, Let them His glo - ry al - so show! O praise Him! O
bear, Praise God and on Him cast your care! O praise Him! O
Son, And praise the Spir - it, Three in One! O praise Him! O
praise Him! Al-le-lu - ia! Al-le-lu - ia! Al-le-lu - - ia! A-MEN.

237 Though Your Sins Be As Scarlet

FANNY J. CROSBY — W. H. DOANE

DUET Gently
1 2
1. "Tho' your sins be as scar-let, They shall be as white as snow; as snow;
2. Hear the voice that entreats you, O re-turn ye un-to God! to God!
3. He'll for-give your transgressions, And re-mem-ber them no more; no more;
QUARTET
Tho' they be red . . . . . . like crim-son, They shall be as wool;"
He is of great . . . . . . com-pas-sion, And of won-drous love;
"Look un-to Me, ... ye peo-ple," Saith the Lord your God;
1. Tho' they be red
DUET p
QUARTET f
"Tho' your sins be as scar-let, Tho' your sins be as scar-let,
Hear the voice that en-treats you, Hear the voice that en-treats you,
He'll for-give your transgressions, He'll for-give your trans-gres-sions,
p rit.
They shall be as white as snow, They shall be as white as snow."
O re-turn ye un-to God! O re-turn ye un-to God!
And re-mem-ber them no more, And re-mem-ber them no more.

238 Praise Him! Praise Him!

Fanny J. Crosby
Chester G. Allen
1. Praise Him! praise Him! Je-sus, our bless-ed Re-deem-er! Sing, O Earth, His
2. Praise Him! praise Him! Je-sus, our bless-ed Re-deem-er! For our sins He
3. Praise Him! praise Him! Je-sus, our bless-ed Re-deem-er! Heav'nly por - tals
won-der-ful love pro-claim! Hail Him! hail Him! highest archangels in glo-ry;
suffered, and bled, and died; He our Rock, our hope of e - ter-nal sal-va-tion,
loud with ho-san-nas ring! Je - sus, Sav - ior, reigneth for-ev - er and ev - er;
Strength and hon - or give to His ho - ly name! Like a shep-herd, Je-sus will
Hail Him! hail Him! Je-sus the Cru - ci - fied. Sound His praises! Je-sus who
Crown Him! crown Him! Prophet, and Priest, and King! Christ is com-ing! o-ver the
guard His children, In His arms He carries them all day long:
bore our sorrows, Love unbounded, wonderful, deep and strong:
world vic-to-rious, Pow'r and glo-ry un - to the Lord be-long:
Refrain
Praise Him! praise Him!
tell of His ex-cel-lent greatness; Praise Him! praise Him! ev-er in joy-ful song!

239 There Is Glory In My Soul

Grace Weiser Davis

Chas. H. Gabriel

1. Since I lost my sins and I found my Sav-ior, There is glo-ry in my soul!
2. Since He cleansed my heart, gave me sight for blindness, There is glo-ry in my soul!
3. Since with God I've walked, having sweet communion, There is glo-ry in my soul!
4. Since I entered Canaan on my way to heav-en, There is glo-ry in my soul!
Since by faith I sought and obtained God's fa-vor, There is glo-ry in my soul!
Since He touched and healed me in loving kindness, There is glo-ry in my soul!
Brighter grows each day in this heav'nly un - ion, There is glo-ry in my soul!
Since the day my life to the Lord was giv - en, There is glo-ry in my soul!
Chorus
There is glo - ry, glo - ry, there is glo - ry in my soul! Ev - 'ry
day brighter grows, And I con-quer all my foes; There is glo - ry, glo - ry,
there is glo - ry in my soul! There is glo - ry in my soul!
glo - ry in my soul!

Let All The World

GEORGE HERBERT, 1593-1632 JOHN PORTER, 1877.

1. Let all the world in ev - 'ry cor - ner sing: My God and King! The heav'ns are not too high, His praise may thith-er fly; The earth is not too low, His prais-es there may grow. Let all the world in ev - 'ry cor - ner sing: My God and King! 2. Let
all the world in ev - 'ry cor - ner sing: My God and King! The Church with psalms must shout, No door can keep them out: But, more than all, the heart Must bear the long-est part. Let all the world in
1
2
God and King!

241

He Lives

A. H. A. — Rev. A. H. Ackley

1. I serve a ris-en Sav-ior, He's in the world to-day; I know that He is
2. In all the world a-round me I see His lov-ing care, And tho' my heart grows
3. Re-joice, re-joice, O Christian, lift up your voice and sing E-ter-nal hal-le-

liv-ing, what-ev-er men may say; I see His hand of mer-cy, I
wea-ry I nev-er will de-spair; I know that He is lead-ing, thro'
lu-jahs to Je-sus Christ the King! The Hope of all who seek Him, the

hear His voice of cheer, And just the time I need Him He's al-ways near.
all the storm-y blast, The day of His ap-pear-ing will come at last.
Help of all who find, None oth-er is so lov-ing, so good and kind.

Refrain *Spirited*

He lives, He lives, Christ Je-sus lives to-day! He walks with me and
He lives, He lives,

talks with me a-long life's nar-row way. He lives, He lives, sal-
He lives, He lives,

He Lives

rit. ff
va-tion to im - part! You ask me how I know He lives? He lives within my heart.
242
Lead Me To Calvary
COPYRIGHT 1921. RENEWAL 1949 BY HOPE PUBLISHING COMPANY, CAROL STREAM, IL 60188. ALL RIGHTS RESERVED. USED BY PERMISSION.
JENNIE EVELYN HUSSEY
WM. J. KIRKPATRICK
1. King of my life, I crown Thee now, Thine shall the glo - ry be;
2. Show me the tomb where Thou wast laid, Ten - der-ly mourned and wept;
3. Let me like Ma - ry, thru the gloom, Come with a gift to Thee;
4. May I be will - ing, Lord, to bear Dai - ly my cross for Thee;
Lest I for-get Thy thorn-crowned brow, Lead me to Cal - va - ry.
An - gels in robes of light ar - rayed Guard-ed Thee whilst Thou slept.
Show to me now the emp - ty tomb, Lead me to Cal - va - ry.
E - ven Thy cup of grief to share, Thou hast borne all for me.
CHORUS
Lest I for-get Geth-sem - a - ne; Lest I for-get Thine ag - o - ny;
Lest I for-get Thy love for me, Lead me to Cal - va - ry.

243 Pentecostal Power

CHARLOTTE G. HOMER — CHAS. H. GABRIEL

1. Lord, as of old at Pen - te - cost Thou didst Thy pow'r dis - play,
2. For might - y works for Thee pre - pare, And strengthen ev - 'ry heart;
3. All self con-sume, all sin de - stroy! With ear - nest zeal en - due
4. Speak, Lord! be - fore Thy throne we wait, Thy prom-ise we be - lieve,
With cleansing, pur - i - fy - ing flame De-scend on us to - day.
Come, take pos - ses - sion of Thine own, And nev - er - more de - part.
Each wait - ing heart to wait for Thee; O Lord, our faith re - new!
And will not let Thee go un - til The bless - ing we re - ceive.
CHORUS
Lord, send the old-time pow'r, The Pen-te-cost - al pow'r! Thy floodgates of
bless-ing on us throw o - pen wide! Lord, send the old - time pow'r, the
Pen-te-cost - al pow'r, That sinners be converted and Thy name glo-ri-fied!

244

The Lily Of The Valley

English Melody
1. I have found a friend in Je - sus, He's ev - 'ry - thing to me, He's the
2. He all my grief has tak - en, and all my sor-rows borne; In temp-
3. He will nev - er, nev - er leave me, nor yet for - sake me here, While I
fair - est of ten thou-sand to my soul; The Lil - y of the Val - ley, in
ta - tion He's my strong and mighty tow'r; I have all for Him for - sak - en, and
live by faith and do His bless-ed will; A wall of fire a - bout me, I've
D. S.—Lil - y of the Val - ley, the
FINE
Him a - lone I see All I need to cleanse and make me ful - ly whole.
all my i - dols torn From my heart, and now He keeps me by His pow'r.
noth-ing now to fear, With His man - na He my hun - gry soul shall fill.
bright and Morn-ing Star, He's the fair - est of ten thou-sand to my soul.
In sor - row He's my com - fort, in troub - le He's my stay,
Though all the world for - sake me, and Sa - tan tempts me sore,
Then sweep - ing up to glo - ry, to see His bless - ed face,
D. S.
He tells me ev - 'ry care on Him to roll. He's the
Through Je - sus I shall safe - ly reach the goal; He's the
Where riv - ers of de - light shall ev - er roll! He's the
Hal - le - lu - jah!

245 Whispering Hope

Mrs. J. I. McClelland

Arr. by Clyde Willard
From "WHISPERING HOPE"

Duet
1. Like the faint dawn of the morn-ing, Like the sweet freshness of dew,
2. Sing-ing the song of for-give-ness, Soft-ly I hear in my soul,
3. Hope is an an-chor to keep us, Holding both steadfast and sure;
Comes the dear whis-per of Je-sus, Com-fort-ing, ten-der and true.
Je-sus has conquered for-ev-er Sin with its fear-ful con-trol.
Hope brings a won-der-ful cleans-ing, Thru His blood, making us pure.
Dark-ness gives way to the sun-light, While His voice falls on my ear;
Whis-per-ing cour-age for war-fare, Bend-ing Thine ear when I pray;
Whis-per-ing hope of His com-ing, How my heart thrills at His Word!
Sea-sons of heav-en's re-fresh-ing, Call to new glad-ness and cheer.
Glo-ri-ous, ris-en Re-deem-er, O how I praise Thee to-day!
O to be watch-ing and wait-ing, Read-y to wel-come the Lord!
Chorus
Whis-per-ing hope, . . . like the song . . . . of the an-gels,
Whis-per-ing hope, whis-per-ing hope, Angel's sweet song, angel's sweet song,

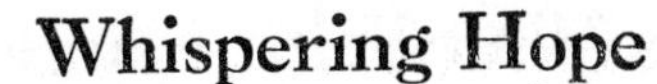
Whispering Hope

rit.
Je - - sus, Thy love, . . . is sweet mu - - - sic to me. . .
Je-sus, Thy love, Je-sus, Thy love is sweet mu-sic, sweet music to me. . .

246 Seal Us, O Holy Spirit

(Inscribed to my friend, Rev. J. F. Carson, D. D.)

I. H. M. — I. H. Meredith

Prayerfully

1. Seal us, O Ho - ly Spir - it, Grant us Thine im - press, we pray;
We would be more like the Sav - ior, Stamped with His im - age to - day.

2. Seal us, O Ho - ly Spir - it, Help us Thy like-ness to show;
Then from our lives un - to oth - ers Streams of rich bless-ings shall flow.

3. Seal us, O Ho - ly Spir - it, Make us Thine own from this hour;
May we be use - ful, dear Mas - ter, Seal us with wit - ness - ing pow'r.

Chorus

Seal us, seal us, Seal us just now, we pray; Seal us, O Ho - ly Spir - it, *rit.* Seal us for serv - ice to - day.

247 It Is Well With My Soul

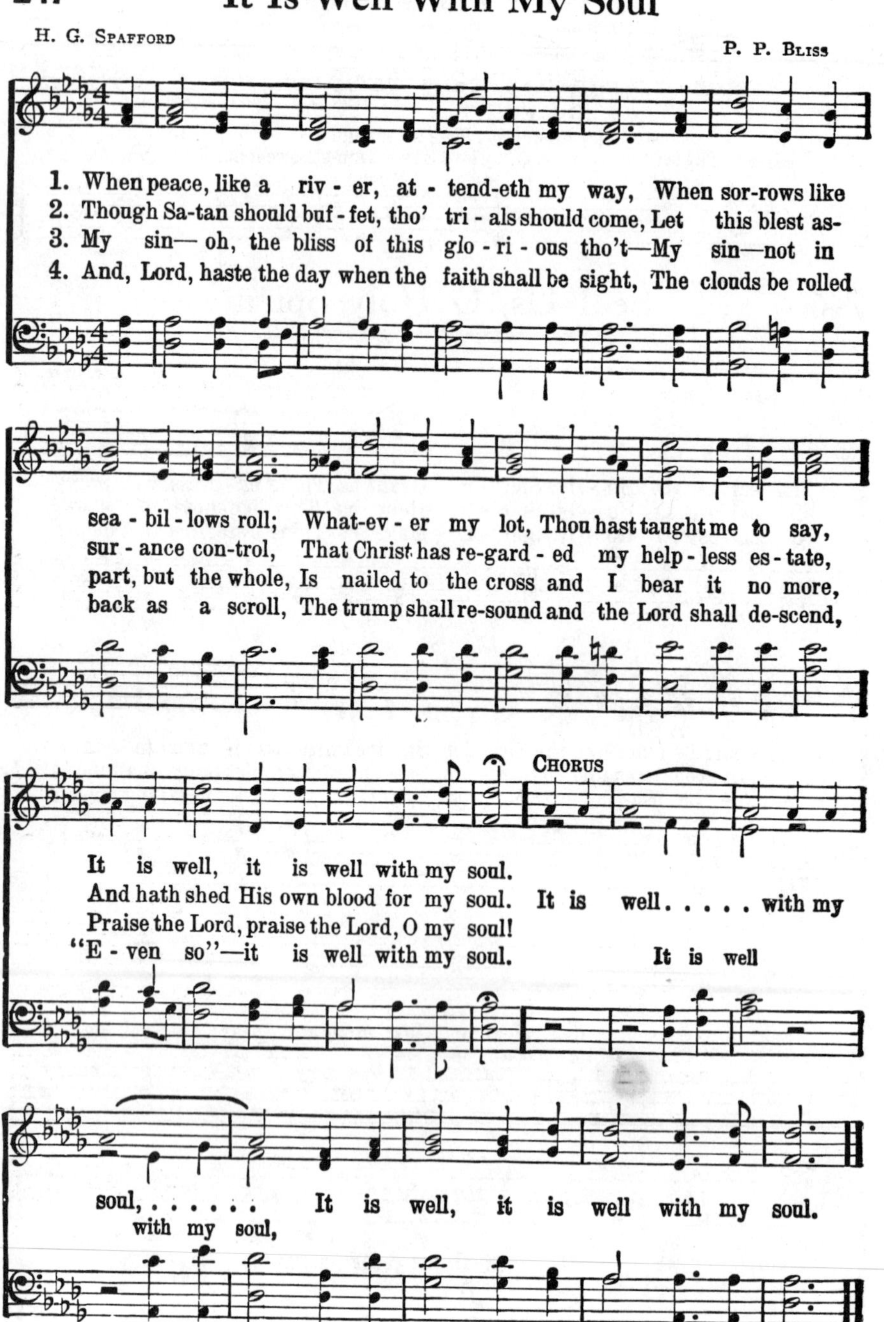
H. G. Spafford
P. P. Bliss
1. When peace, like a riv - er, at - tend-eth my way, When sor-rows like
2. Though Sa-tan should buf - fet, tho' tri - als should come, Let this blest as-
3. My sin— oh, the bliss of this glo - ri - ous tho't—My sin—not in
4. And, Lord, haste the day when the faith shall be sight, The clouds be rolled
sea - bil - lows roll; What-ev - er my lot, Thou hast taught me to say,
sur - ance con-trol, That Christ has re-gard - ed my help - less es - tate,
part, but the whole, Is nailed to the cross and I bear it no more,
back as a scroll, The trump shall re-sound and the Lord shall de-scend,
Chorus
It is well, it is well with my soul.
And hath shed His own blood for my soul.
Praise the Lord, praise the Lord, O my soul!
"E - ven so"—it is well with my soul.
It is well . . . . . with my
It is well
soul, ... It is well, it is well with my soul.
with my soul,

248 The Beautiful Land

F. A. F. White, Arr. — Arr. from Mark M. Jones

1. I have heard of a land On a far - a-way strand—In the Bi - ble the sto - ry is told—Where no sor-row shall come, Nei-ther darkness nor gloom, And noth-ing there ev-er grows old.
2. There are ev-er-green trees That bend low in the breeze, And their fruitage is brighter than gold; There are harps for our hands In the fair - est of lands,
3. There's a home in that land, At the Fa-ther's right hand; There are mansions whose joys are un - told, And per - en - ni - al spring Where the birds ev-er sing,
Chorus
In that beau - ti - ful land, On a far a-way strand, No storms with their blasts ev-er frown; The streets, I am told, Are paved with pure gold, And the sun shall nev - er go down.

249 The Wayside Cross

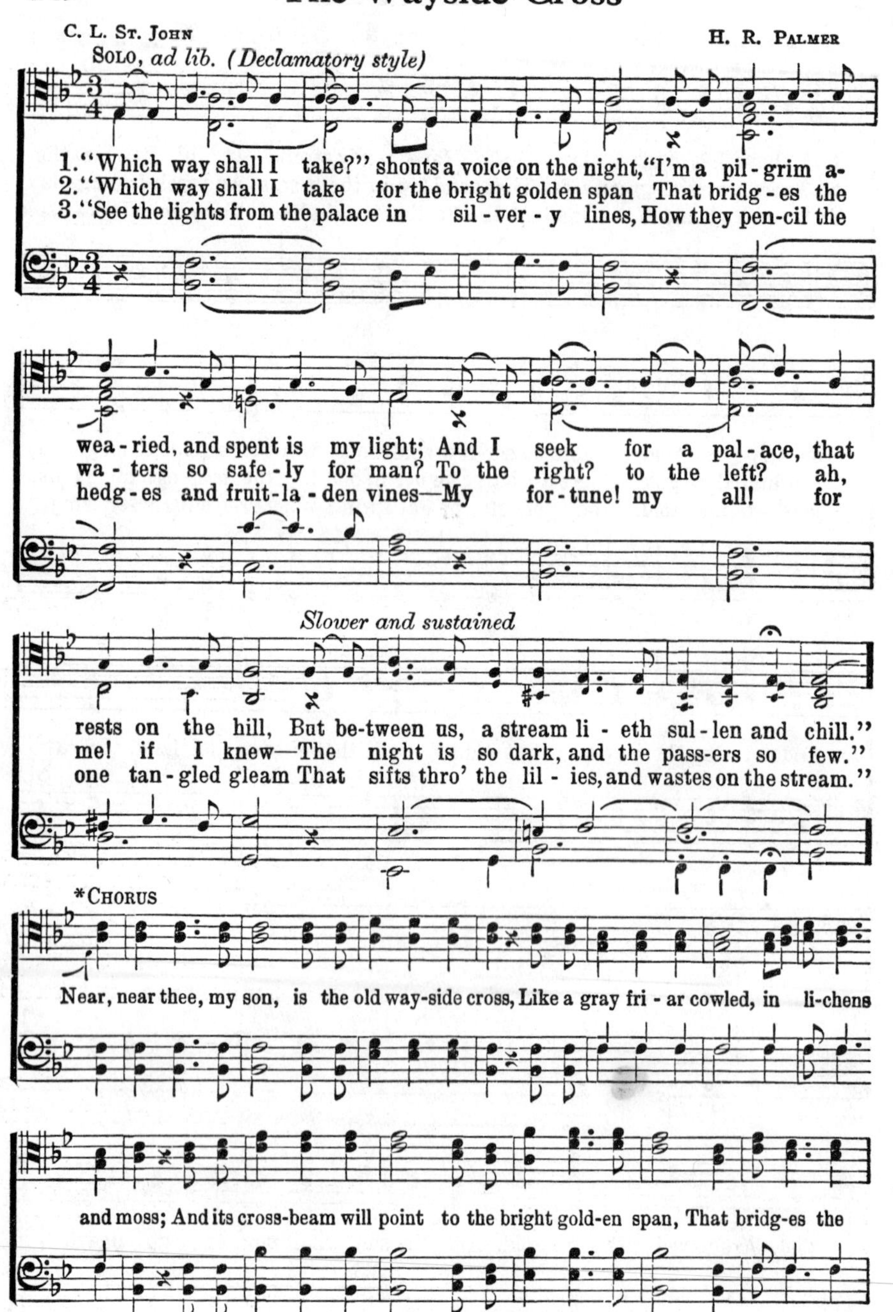
C. L. St. John
H. R. Palmer
Solo, ad lib. (Declamatory style)
1. "Which way shall I take?" shouts a voice on the night, "I'm a pil-grim a-
2. "Which way shall I take for the bright golden span That bridg-es the
3. "See the lights from the palace in sil-ver-y lines, How they pen-cil the
wea-ried, and spent is my light; And I seek for a pal-ace, that
wa-ters so safe-ly for man? To the right? to the left? ah,
hedg-es and fruit-la-den vines—My for-tune! my all! for
Slower and sustained
rests on the hill, But be-tween us, a stream li-eth sul-len and chill."
me! if I knew—The night is so dark, and the pass-ers so few."
one tan-gled gleam That sifts thro' the lil-ies, and wastes on the stream."
*Chorus
Near, near thee, my son, is the old way-side cross, Like a gray fri-ar cowled, in li-chens
and moss; And its cross-beam will point to the bright gold-en span, That bridg-es the

*The chorus should begin while the solo voice is still holding the last note.

The Wayside Cross

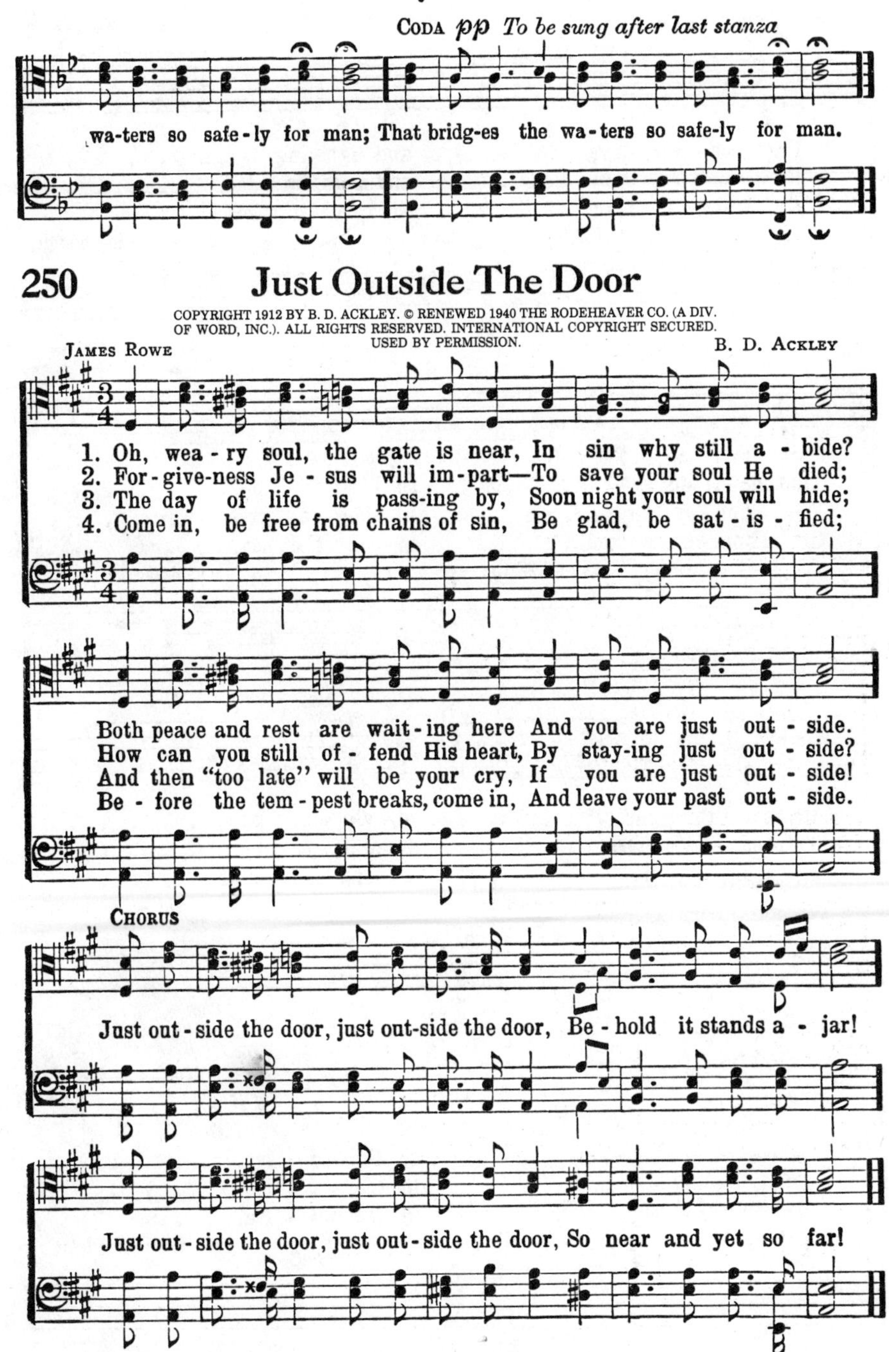
Coda pp To be sung after last stanza
waters so safe-ly for man; That bridg-es the wa-ters so safe-ly for man.
250
Just Outside The Door
James Rowe
B. D. Ackley
1. Oh, wea-ry soul, the gate is near, In sin why still a-bide?
2. For-give-ness Je-sus will im-part—To save your soul He died;
3. The day of life is pass-ing by, Soon night your soul will hide;
4. Come in, be free from chains of sin, Be glad, be sat-is-fied;
Both peace and rest are wait-ing here And you are just out-side.
How can you still of-fend His heart, By stay-ing just out-side?
And then "too late" will be your cry, If you are just out-side!
Be-fore the tem-pest breaks, come in, And leave your past out-side.
Chorus
Just out-side the door, just out-side the door, Be-hold it stands a-jar!
Just out-side the door, just out-side the door, So near and yet so far!

251 Memories Of Galilee

Robert Morris, L L.D. | Dr. H. R. Palmer

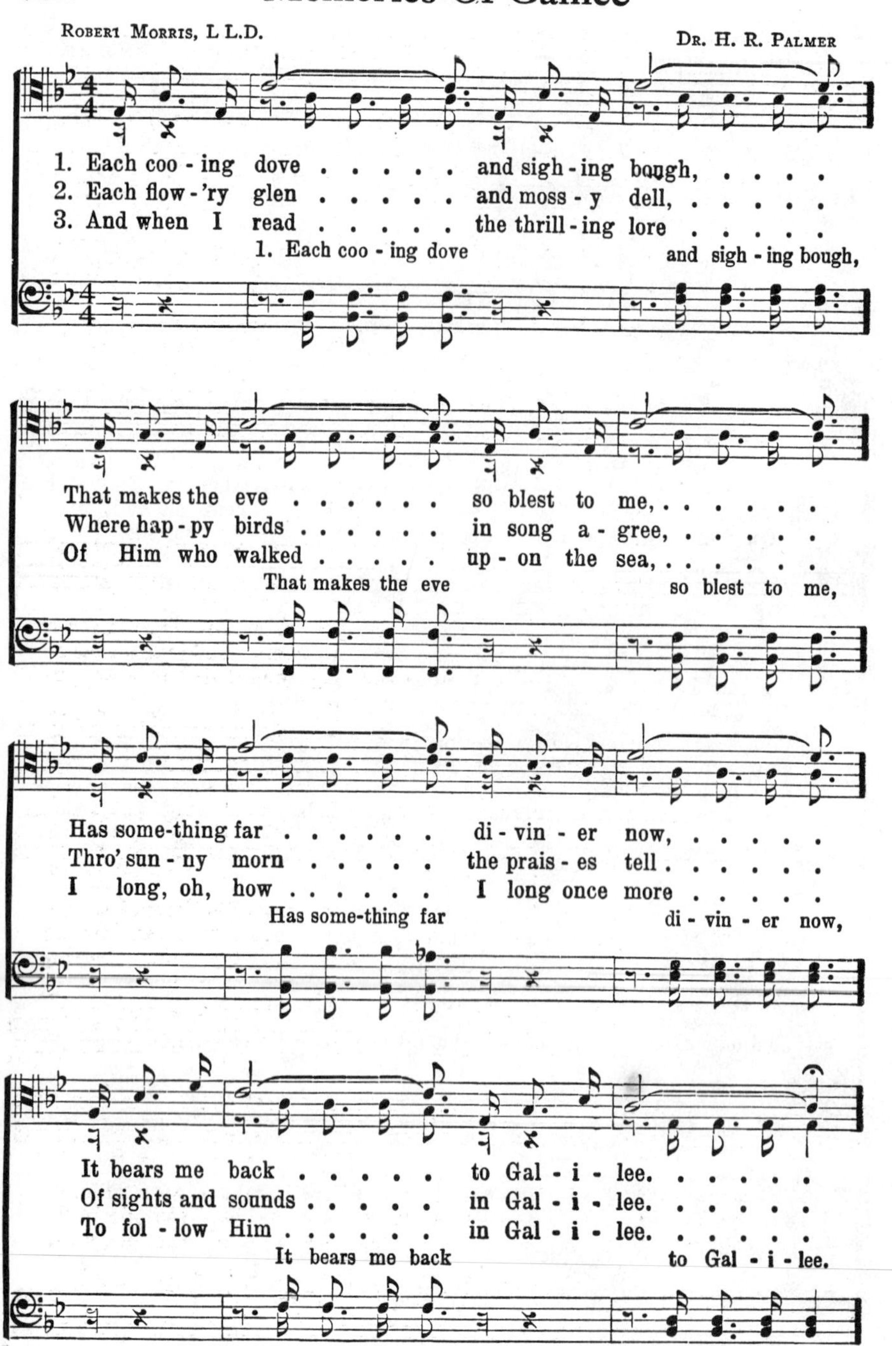

1. Each coo - ing dove . . . . . . and sigh - ing bough, ...
2. Each flow - 'ry glen . . . . . . and moss - y dell, ...
3. And when I read . . . . . . the thrill - ing lore . . . . . .
1. Each coo - ing dove and sigh - ing bough,
That makes the eve . . . . so blest to me, ...
Where hap - py birds . . . . in song a - gree, ...
Of Him who walked . . . . . . up - on the sea, ...
That makes the eve so blest to me,
Has some-thing far . . . . di - vin - er now, ...
Thro' sun - ny morn . . . . . . the prais - es tell . . . .
I long, oh, how . . . . I long once more . . . . . .
Has some-thing far di - vin - er now,
It bears me back . . . . . . to Gal - i - lee. . . . . . .
Of sights and sounds . . . . . . in Gal - i - lee. . . . . .
To fol - low Him . . . . . . in Gal - i - lee. . . . . . .
It bears me back to Gal - i - lee.

Memories Of Galilee

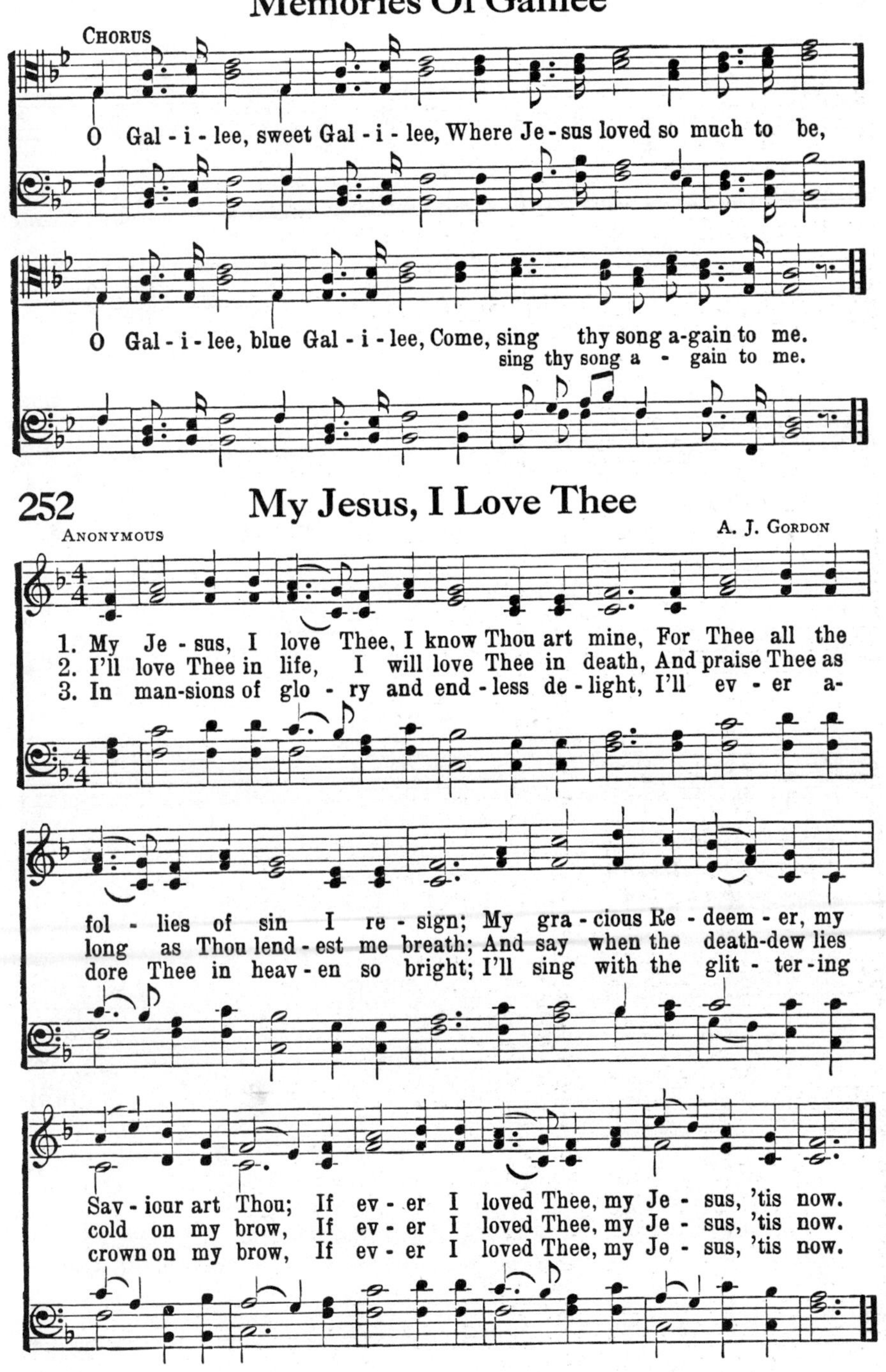
Chorus
O Gal - i - lee, sweet Gal - i - lee, Where Je - sus loved so much to be,
O Gal - i - lee, blue Gal - i - lee, Come, sing thy song a-gain to me.
sing thy song a - gain to me.
252
My Jesus, I Love Thee
Anonymous
A. J. Gordon
1. My Je - sus, I love Thee, I know Thou art mine, For Thee all the fol - lies of sin I re - sign; My gra - cious Re - deem - er, my Sav - iour art Thou; If ev - er I loved Thee, my Je - sus, 'tis now.
2. I'll love Thee in life, I will love Thee in death, And praise Thee as long as Thou lend - est me breath; And say when the death-dew lies cold on my brow, If ev - er I loved Thee, my Je - sus, 'tis now.
3. In man-sions of glo - ry and end - less de - light, I'll ev - er a - dore Thee in heav - en so bright; I'll sing with the glit - ter-ing crown on my brow, If ev - er I loved Thee, my Je - sus, 'tis now.

253

Steal Away!

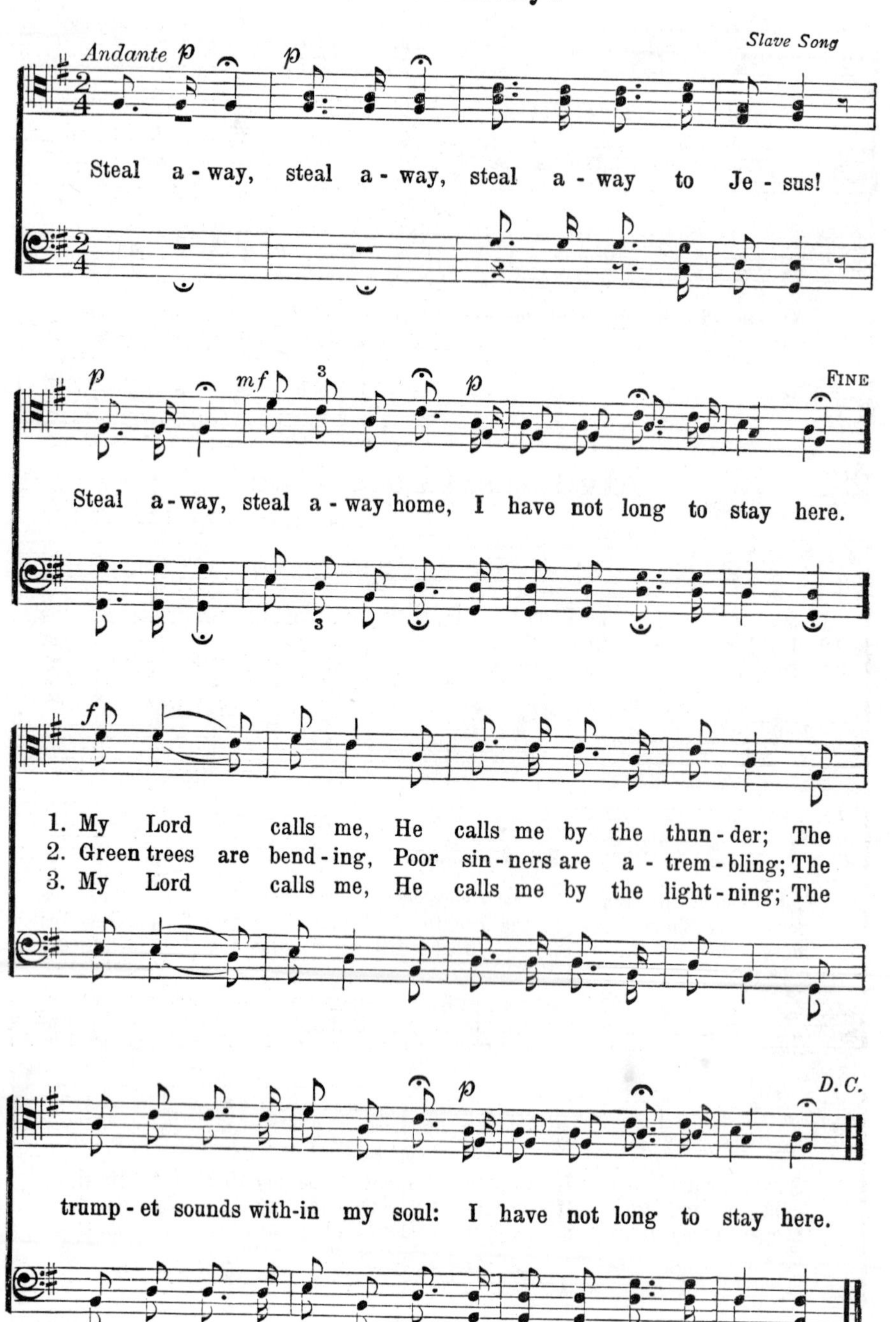

Andante
Slave Song
Steal a-way, steal a-way, steal a-way to Je-sus!
Steal a-way, steal a-way home, I have not long to stay here.
FINE
1. My Lord calls me, He calls me by the thun-der; The
2. Green trees are bend-ing, Poor sin-ners are a-trem-bling; The
3. My Lord calls me, He calls me by the light-ning; The
trump-et sounds with-in my soul: I have not long to stay here.
D. C.

254 Speed Away

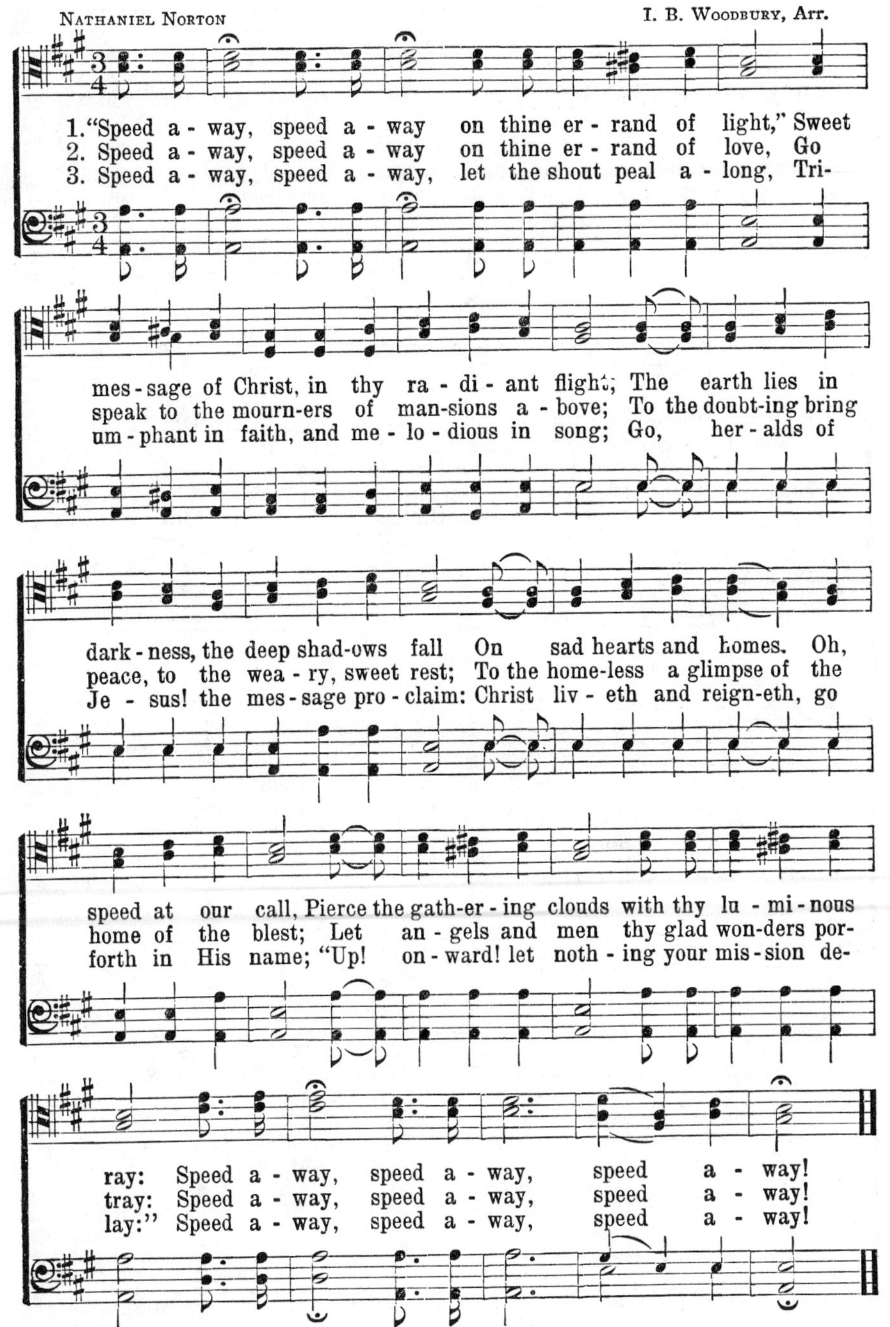

Nathaniel Norton
I. B. Woodbury, Arr.
1. "Speed a - way, speed a - way on thine er - rand of light," Sweet
2. Speed a - way, speed a - way on thine er - rand of love, Go
3. Speed a - way, speed a - way, let the shout peal a - long, Tri-
mes - sage of Christ, in thy ra - di - ant flight; The earth lies in
speak to the mourn-ers of man-sions a - bove; To the doubt-ing bring
um - phant in faith, and me - lo - dious in song; Go, her - alds of
dark - ness, the deep shad-ows fall On sad hearts and homes. Oh,
peace, to the wea - ry, sweet rest; To the home-less a glimpse of the
Je - sus! the mes - sage pro - claim: Christ liv - eth and reign-eth, go
speed at our call, Pierce the gath-er - ing clouds with thy lu - mi - nous
home of the blest; Let an - gels and men thy glad won-ders por-
forth in His name; "Up! on - ward! let noth - ing your mis - sion de-
ray: Speed a - way, speed a - way, speed a - way!
tray: Speed a - way, speed a - way, speed a - way!
lay:" Speed a - way, speed a - way, speed a - way!

255 Were You There?

256 Swing Low

Slow.
Swing low, sweet char - i - ot, Com - ing for to car - ry me
home; Swing low, sweet char - i - ot, Com-ing for to car - ry me home.
home; . . . .
FINE.
1. I looked o - ver Jor - dan, and what did I see,
2. If you get there be - fore I do,
3. I'm some - times up, I'm some - times down,
Com-ing for to car - ry me home? A band of an - gels
Com-ing for to car - ry me home; Tell all my friends I'm
Com-ing for to car - ry me home; But still my soul feels
com-ing af - ter me, Com - ing for to car - ry me home.
com - ing too, Com - ing for to car - ry me home.
heav-en - ly bound, Com - ing for to car - ry me home.
D. C.

257 I Know The Lord's Laid His Hands On Me
O I know the Lord, I know the Lord, I know the Lord's laid His
hands on me, O I know the Lord, I know the Lord, I know the Lord's laid His
hands on me.
1. Did ev - er you see the like be - fore?
2. O was - n't that a hap - py day,
3. — Some seek the Lord and don't seek Him right,
4. — My Lord's done just what He said,
I know the Lord's laid His hands on me; King Je - sus preach - ing
I know the Lord's laid His hands on me; When Je - sus washed my
I know the Lord's laid His hands on me; They fool all day and
I know the Lord's laid His hands on me; He's healed the sick and
to the poor! I know the Lord's laid His hands on me.
sins a - way? I know the Lord's laid His hands on me.
pray at night, I know the Lord's laid His hands on me.
raised the dead, I know the Lord's laid His hands on me.
D. C.

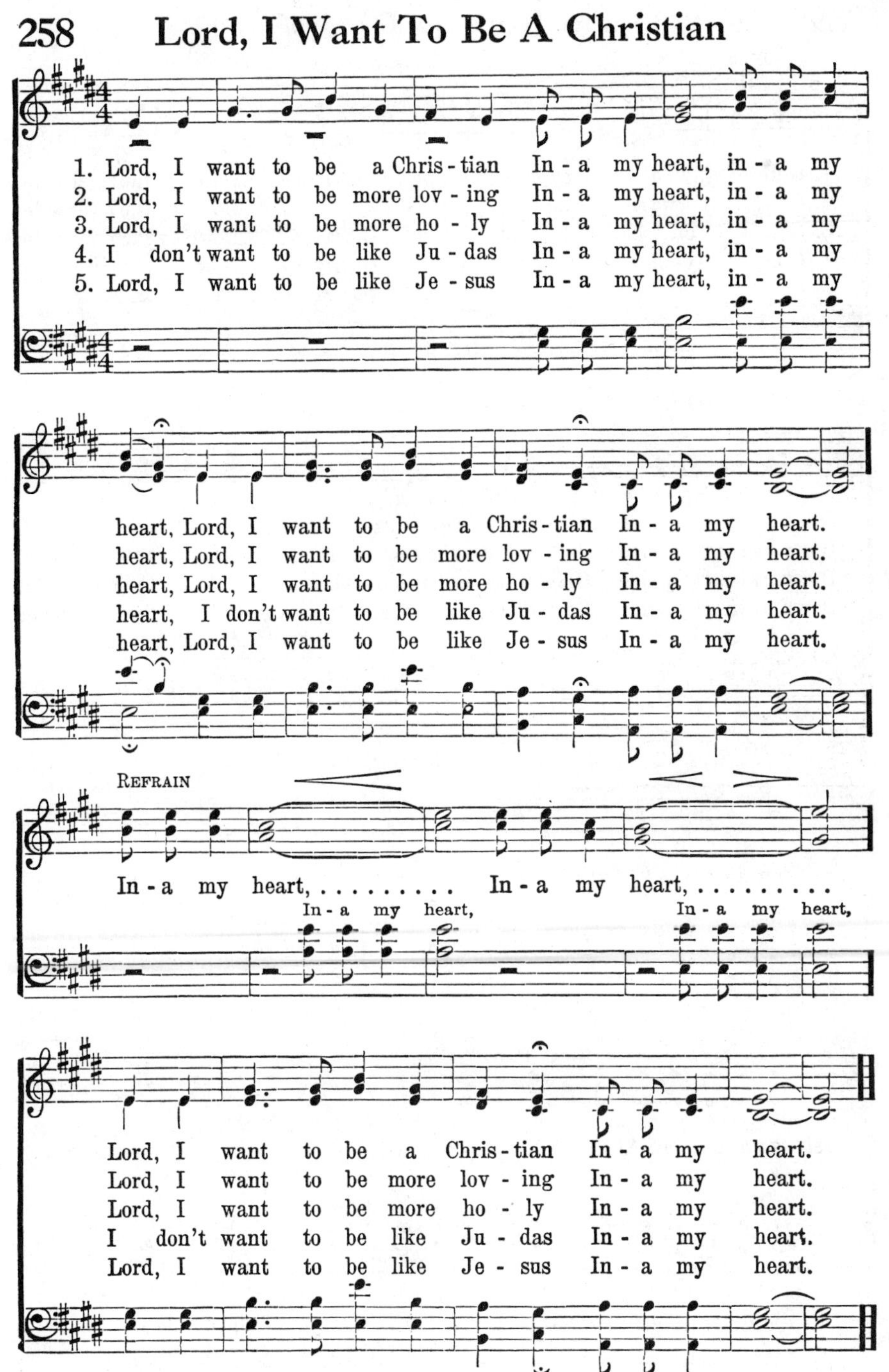
258 Lord, I Want To Be A Christian
1. Lord, I want to be a Chris-tian In-a my heart, in-a my heart, Lord, I want to be a Chris-tian In-a my heart.
2. Lord, I want to be more lov-ing In-a my heart, in-a my heart, Lord, I want to be more lov-ing In-a my heart.
3. Lord, I want to be more ho-ly In-a my heart, in-a my heart, Lord, I want to be more ho-ly In-a my heart.
4. I don't want to be like Ju-das In-a my heart, in-a my heart, I don't want to be like Ju-das In-a my heart.
5. Lord, I want to be like Je-sus In-a my heart, in-a my heart, Lord, I want to be like Je-sus In-a my heart.
REFRAIN
In-a my heart, ... In-a my heart, ...
In-a my heart, In-a my heart,
Lord, I want to be a Chris-tian In-a my heart.
Lord, I want to be more lov-ing In-a my heart.
Lord, I want to be more ho-ly In-a my heart.
I don't want to be like Ju-das In-a my heart.
Lord, I want to be like Je-sus In-a my heart.

Down By The River-Side

1. Goin't' lay down my burden, Down by the river-side, Down by the river-side,
2. Goin't' lay down my sword and shield, Down by the river-side, Down by the river-side,
3. Goin't' try on my long white robe, Down by the river-side, Down by the river-side,
4. Goin't' try on my starry crown, Down by the river-side, Down by the river-side,

Down by the river-side, Goin't' lay down my bur-den, Down by the river-side,
Down by the river-side, Goin't' lay down my sword and shield, Down by the river-side,
Down by the river-side, Goin't' try on my long white robe, Down by the river-side,
Down by the river-side, Goin't' try on my star-ry crown, Down by the river-side,

Goin' to stud - y war no more. Ain't goin't' study war no more, Ain't goin't'

study war no more, Ain't goin't' study war no more, . . . Ain't goin't: ‖ war no more.
goin't study war no more,

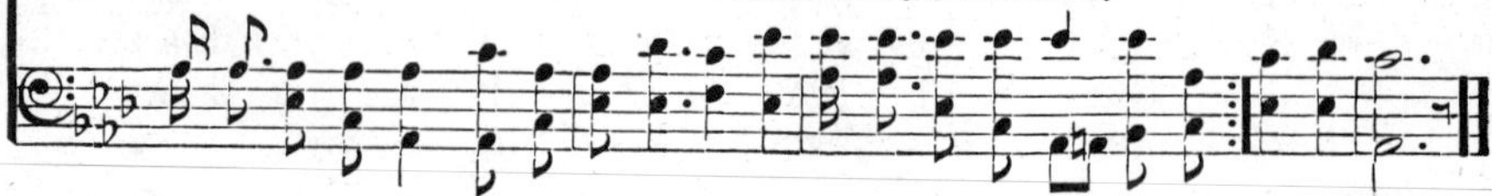

5. Goin't' meet my dear old mother.
6. Goin't' meet my dear old father.
7. Goin't' meet dem Hebrew children.
8. Goin't' meet my loving Jesus.

260

Through Love To Light

Richard W. Gilder, 1844-1909
Jean Sibelius, 1865-
Arr. for The Hymnal, 1932
Thro' love to light! O won-der-ful the way . . . . That leads from
dark-ness to the per-fect day; . . . From dark-ness and from
sor-row of the night . . . To morn-ing that comes sing-ing o'er the
sea! . . Thro' love to light, Thro' light, O God, to Thee, . . .
Who art the Love of love, th' e-ter-nal Light of light! . . A-men.

261 The Lord's Prayer

C. A. Wickes, ?
Our Father, who art in heaven, hallowed be Thy Name.
Give us this day our dai - ly bread;
And lead us not into temptation, but deliver us from evil;
Thy kingdom come. Thy will be done on earth, as it is in heaven.
And forgive us our trespasses as we forgive those who trespass a - gainst us.
For Thine is the kingdom, and the power,
and the glory, for ev - er. A - - men.
262
Sevenfold Amen
John Stainer, 1840-1901
A - men, A - - - - - - - - - men,
A - men, A - men, A - - - - men, A - - - - - - men, A - -
A - - - men, A - - - men,
A - - - - men,
- - - - - - - - men, A - - - - - - - - men, A - - men.
A - - - - men,

263 Saviour, Hear Us, We Pray

LUCY. 6. 6. 6. 6. with Refrain
W. W. Ellsworth, ?
Arr. from Johannes Brahms, 1833-1897
1. Sav - iour, hear us, we pray: Keep us safe thro' this day;
2. Be our Guard - ian and Guide; May we walk by Thy side
Keep our lives free from sin And our hearts pure with - in.
Till the eve - ning shades fall O - ver us— o - ver all.
Refrain
Je - sus, Lord, hear our prayer: May we rest in Thy care;
Je - sus, Lord, hear our prayer: May we rest in Thy care. A - men.
264 Dresden Amen
265 Threefold Amen
Danish
A - men, A - - - men.
A - men, A - men, A - - - - men.

266 Sanctus With Preface

COMPOSER UNKNOWN
Therefore with angels and arch-angels, and with all the company of heaven, We laud and magnify Thy glorious Name,
Ev-er-more prais-ing Thee, and say - ing: Ho - ly, ho - ly, ho - ly, Lord
God of Hosts, . . Heav'n and earth are full of . . . . Thy
glo - ry: Glo - ry be to Thee, O Lord, Most High. A - MEN.
267
Hear Our Prayer, O Lord
GEORGE WHELPTON, 1847-
Hear our prayer, O Lord, Hear our prayer, O Lord;

Hear Our Prayer, O Lord

In - cline Thine ear to us, And grant us Thy peace. A-MEN.

268 The Lord Bless Thee And Keep Thee

(NUM. 6: 24-26) LUCY RIDER MEYER

The Lord bless thee and keep thee! The Lord make His face shine up-

on thee, and be gra - cious un - to thee, . . And be

gra - cious un - to thee: The Lord lift up His coun - te-nance, His

And give thee peace. . . . .

coun - te-nance up - on thee, and give thee peace.

269 Lead Me Gently Home, Father

W. L. T. | W. L. Thompson

1. Lead me gen-tly home, Fa-ther, Lead me gen-tly home, When life's toils are
2. Lead me gen-tly home, Fa-ther, Lead me gen-tly home, In life's dark-est
end - ed, And part-ing days have come; Sin no more shall tempt me, Ne'er from
hours, Father, When life's troubles come; Keep my feet from wand'ring, Lest from
Thee I'll roam, If Thou'lt on - ly lead me, Fa-ther, Lead me gen-tly home.
Thee I'll roam, Lest I fall up-on the way-side, Lead me gen-tly home.
rit.
p
Chorus.
Lead me gen - tly home, Fa - ther, lead me gen - tly
Lead me gen - tly home, Fa - ther, Lead me gen - tly home, Fa - ther,

Lead Me Gently Home, Father
Lest I fall up - on the way - side, Lead me gen - tly home.
Lead me gen - tly, gen - tly home.
270
Sweet Home
David Denham
Henry Rowley Bishop
1. 'Mid scenes of con - fu - sion and creature complaints, How sweet to the
2. Sweet bonds that u - nite all the chil-dren of peace! And thrice pre-cious
3. While here in the val - ley of con - flict I stay, O give me sub-
4. I long, dear-est Lord, in Thy beau-ties to shine; No more as an
soul is com - mun - ion with saints; To find at the ban - quet of
Je - sus, whose love can-not cease! Tho' oft from Thy pres - ence in
mis - sion, and strength as my day; In all my af - flic - tions to
ex - ile in sor - row to pine; And in Thy dear im - age a-
mer - cy there's room, And feel in the pres - ence of Je - sus at home!
sad - ness I roam, I long to be - hold Thee in glo - ry, at home.
Thee would I come, Re - joic - ing in hope of my glo - ri - ous home.
rise from the tomb, With glo - ri - fied mil - lions to praise Thee at home.
Refrain
Home, home, sweet, sweet home; Pre-pare me, dear Savior, for heav-en, my home.

271

Awakening Chorus

Charlotte G. Homer
Chas. H. Gabriel
1. A-wake! a-wake! and sing the bless-ed sto-ry; A-
A-wake! a-wake!
2. Ring out! ring out! O bells of joy and glad-ness! Re-
Ring out! ring out!
wake! a-wake! and let your song of praise a-rise; A-wake! a-
A-wake! a-wake! A-wake!
peat, re-peat a-new the sto-ry o'er a-gain, Till all the
Re-peat, re-peat, Till all
wake! the earth is full of glo-ry, And light is beam-ing
a-wake! And light is beam-ing
earth shall lose its weight of sad-ness, And shout a-new the
the earth And shout a-new
Male Voices in Unison
from the ra-diant skies; The rocks and rills, the vales and hills re-sound with
glo-ri-ous re-frain; With an-gels in the heights sing of the great sal-
Full Harmony
glad-ness, All na-ture joins to sing the triumph song. The Lord Je-
va-tion He wrest-ed from the hand of sin and death.

Awakening Chorus
Unison
ho - vah reigns and sin is back-ward hurled! Re - joice! re-
sin is back-ward hurled!
joice! lift heart and voice, Je - ho - vah reigns!
Full Harmony
Pro-claim His sov-'reign pow'r to all the world, And let His
pow'r to all the world, And let His
glo - - rious ban-ner be un - furled! Je - ho - vah reigns!
grand and glo-rious ban - ner be un - furled! Je - ho - vah reigns! Je - ho - vah reigns!
Re - joice! re - joice! re - joice! Je - ho - vah reigns!
Re - joice! re - joice! re - joice!

272 All Hail, Immanuel

D. R. van Sickle — Chas. H. Gabriel

1. All hail to Thee, Im-man-u-el, We cast . . . our crowns be-fore Thee;
2. All hail to Thee, Im-man-u-el, The ran - somed hosts surround Thee;
3. All hail to Thee, Im-man-u-el, Our ris - - en King and Sav-ior!
Let ev-'ry heart o-bey Thy will, And ev - - - 'ry voice a-
And earth-ly mon-archs clam-or forth Their Sov - - 'reign King to
Thy foes are van-quished, and Thou art Om-nip - - - - o-tent for-
dore Thee. In praise to Thee, our Sav-ior King, The vi-brant
crown Thee. While those re-deemed in a-ges gone, As-sem-bled
ev - er. Death, sin and hell no lon-ger reign, And Sa-tan's
chords of Heav-en ring, And ech-o back the might-y strain:
round the great white throne, Break forth in-to im-mor-tal song:
pow'r is burst in twain; E-ter-nal glo-ry to Thy Name:
ff
All hail! all hail! All hail! all hail! Im-man-u-el!
All hail! all hail!

All Hail, Immanuel

CHORUS.
Hail! . . . . Im-man-u-el! Im-man-u-el! Hail! . . . . . .
Hail to the King we love so well! Hail! Im - man-u - el! Hail to the King we love so well!
Hail! . . . . . .
Im-man-u-el! Im-man-u-el!
Hail! Im - man - u - el! Glo-ry and honor and majesty, Wisdom and power be
Hail! . . . . Glo - - ry and maj-es-ty, Wis - dom be
rit. . . . . Hail! . . . . Im-
un - to Thee, Now and ev - er - more! . . . Hail to the King we love so well!
man-u-el! Im-man-u-el! Hail! . . . . Im-man-u-el! Im-man-u-el!
Hail! Im - man - u - el! Hail to the King we love so well! Hail! Im - man - u - el!
Hail! . . . . Hail! . . . .
King of kings and Lord of lords, All hail, Im - man - u - el! A-MEN.

273
Peace! Be Still!
Mary A. Baker
H. R. Palmer
1. Mas - ter, the tem-pest is rag - ing! The bil - lows are toss - ing high!
2. Mas - ter, with an-guish of spir - it I bow in my grief to - day;
3. Mas - ter, the ter - ror is o - ver, The el - e-ments sweet-ly rest;
The sky is o'er-shadowed with blackness, No shel - ter or help is nigh;
The depths of my sad heart are troub-led; O wak - en and save, I pray!
Earth's sun in the calm lake is mir - rored, And heaven's with-in my breast.
"Car - est Thou not that we per - ish?" How canst Thou lie a - sleep,
Tor-rents of sin and of an - guish Sweep o'er my sink - ing soul!
Lin - ger, O bless - ed Re - deem - er, Leave me a - lone no more;
When each moment so mad - ly is threat-'ning A grave in the an - gry deep?
And I per - ish! I per - ish, dear Mas - ter; O has - ten, and take con - trol!
And with joy I shall make the blest har - bor, And rest on the bliss - ful shore.

Peace! Be Still!

Refrain
p
pp
"The winds and the waves shall o - bey My will. Peace, . . be still! . . .
Peace, be still! peace, be still!
Wheth-er the wrath of the storm-tossed sea, Or de-mons, or men, or what-
cres - - - - - - - - cen - - - - - - - - do
ev - er it be, No wa - ter can swal-low the ship where lies The Mas-ter of
ff
o-cean and earth and skies; They all shall sweetly o - bey My will; Peace, be still!
p
p
pp
Peace, be still! They all shall sweet-ly o - bey My will; Peace, peace, be still!"

274 Holy, Holy, Holy

REGINALD HEBER
JOHN B. DYKES
Arr. for Chorus in six parts by
HAROLD HART TODD
I & II SOPRANOS
1. Ho - ly, ho - ly, ho - ly, Lord God Al - might - y!
2. Ho - ly, ho - ly, ho - ly! all the saints a - dore Thee,
ALTO
3. Ho - ly, ho - ly, ho - ly! tho' the dark - ness hide Thee,
I & II TENORS
4. Ho - ly, ho - ly, ho - ly! Lord God Al - might - y!
BASS
PIANO
Ear - ly in the morn - ing our song shall rise to Thee;.....
Cast - ing down their gold - en crowns a - round the glass - y sea;......
Tho' the eye of sin - ful man Thy glo - ry may not see;......
All Thy works shall praise Thy name, in earth, and sky, and sea;......

Holy, Holy, Holy

Ho - ly, ho - ly, ho - ly, mer - ci - ful and might - y,
Cher - u - bim and sera - phim fall - ing down be - fore Thee,

On - ly Thou art ho - ly; there is none be - side Thee,

Ho - ly, ho - ly, ho - ly, mer - ci - ful and might - y,

God in Three Per - sons, bless - ed Trin - i - ty.
Which wert, and art, and ev - er - more shall be. A - - MEN.

Per - fect in pow'r, in love, and pu - ri - ty. A - - MEN.

God in Three Per - sons, bless-ed Trin - i - ty. A - - MEN.

275 Jesus, Lover Of My Soul

CHARLES WESLEY

SIMEON B. MARSH
Arr. for Chorus in six parts by
HAROLD HART TODD

I & II SOPRANOS

1. Je - sus, Lov - er of my soul, Let me to Thy bos - om fly,
2. Oth - er ref - uge have I none, Hangs my help-less soul on Thee:

ALTO

3. Thou, O Christ, art all I want; More than all in Thee I find;

I & II TENORS

4. Plenteous grace with Thee is found, Grace to cov - er all my sin:

BASS

PIANO

While the near-er wa - ters roll, While the tem-pest still is high!
Leave, ah! leave me not a - lone, Still sup-port and com - fort me:

Raise the fall - en, cheer the faint, Heal the sick, and lead the blind.

Let the heal-ing streams a-bound; Make and keep me pure with - in.

Jesus, Lover Of My Soul

Hide me. O my Sav - ior, hide, Till the storm of life be past;
All my trust on Thee is stayed, All my help from Thee I bring;

Just and ho - ly is Thy name, I am all un - right - eous - ness;

Thou of life the foun - tain art, Free - ly let me take of Thee:

Safe in - to the ha-ven guide, O re-ceive my soul at last!
Cov - er my de - fense-less head With the shad-ow of Thy wing. A - MEN.

False and full of sin I am, Thou art full of truth and grace. A-MEN.

Spring Thou up with-in my heart, Rise to all e - ter - ni - ty. A-MEN.

Not Half Has Ever Been Told

JOHN BURCH ATCHINSON — O. F. PRESBREY

6/8
1. I have read of a beau - ti - ful cit - y, Far a-
2. I have read of bright man - sions in heav - en, Which the
3. I have read of white robes for the right - eous, Of bright
4. I have read of a Christ so for - giv - ing, That vile
way in the king-dom of God; I have read how its walls are of
Sav - ior has gone to pre - pare; And the saints who on earth have been
crowns which the glo - ri - fied wear, When our Fa - ther shall bid them "Come,
sin - ners may ask and re - ceive Peace and par - don for ev - 'ry trans-
jas - per, How its streets are all gold - en and broad: In the
faith - ful, Rest for - ev - er with Christ o - ver there; There no
en - ter, And My glo - ry e - ter - nal - ly share;" How the
gres - sion, If when ask - ing they on - ly be - lieve. I have

Not Half Has Ever Been Told

midst of the street is life's riv - er, Clear as crys - tal and pure to be-
sin ev - er en - ters, nor sor - row, The in - hab - it - ants nev - er grow
right-eous are ev - er-more bless - ed As they walk thro' the streets of pure
read how He'll guide and pro-tect us, If for safe - ty we en - ter His
hold, But not half of that city's bright glory To mortals has ev-er been told.
old; But not half of the wonderful sto - ry To mortals has ev-er been told.
gold; But not half of the wonderful sto - ry To mortals has ev-er been told.
fold; But not half of His goodness and mercy To mortals has ev-er been told.
Refrain
Not half has ev - er been told;.. Not half has ev - er been told;.. Not
been told;
been told;
half of that cit - y's bright glo - ry To mor-tals has ev - er been told.
Repeat the Refrain p

277 God Be With You

J. E. Rankin
W. G. Tomer
1. God be with you till we meet a-gain; By His counsels guide, uphold you,
2. God be with you till we meet a-gain; 'Neath His wings protecting hide you,
3. God be with you till we meet a-gain; When life's perils thick confound you,
4. God be with you till we meet a-gain; Keep love's banner floating o'er you;
With His sheep se-cure-ly fold you; God be with you till we meet a-gain.
Dai-ly man-na still pro-vide you; God be with you till we meet a-gain.
Put His arms un-fail-ing round you; God be with you till we meet a-gain.
Smite death's threat'ning wave before you; God be with you till we meet a-gain.
Chorus
Till we meet, ... till we meet, Till we meet at Je-sus' feet;
Till we meet, till we meet, till we meet;
Till we meet, ... till we meet, God be with you till we meet a-gain.
Till we meet, till we meet,

278 Friends Of All

COPYRIGHT, 1932, BY LAMAR & WHITMORE
Elizabeth McE. Shields
Grace Wilbur Conant
Briskly
Friends of all we'd like to be In our work and play; Each one giv-ing of his best,
Each one sharing with the rest In a friend-ly way, In a friend-ly way.
poco rit.
279
God Is Near
FROM WORSHIP AND CONDUCT SONGS
WORDS COPYRIGHT, 1927, BY ELIZABETH McE. SHIELDS. MUSIC COPYRIGHT, 1927, BY GRACE WILBUR CONANT
Elizabeth McE. Shields
Grace Wilbur Conant
Allegretto
1. Some-times when morn-ing lights the sky And glad-ness fills the air,
2. Some-times when flow-ers are in bloom And birds are sing-ing clear,
3. Some-times when trees are stand-ing tall With branches in the air,
4. Some-times when work and play are done And eve-ning stars ap-pear,
mf
poco rit.
I feel like tell-ing things to God, He seems so ver-y near.
I feel like sing-ing things to God, He must be ver-y near.
I feel like say-ing things to God, I know He must be near.
I feel like whisp'ring things to God, He is so ver-y near.
poco rit
p

280 Enter Into His Gates

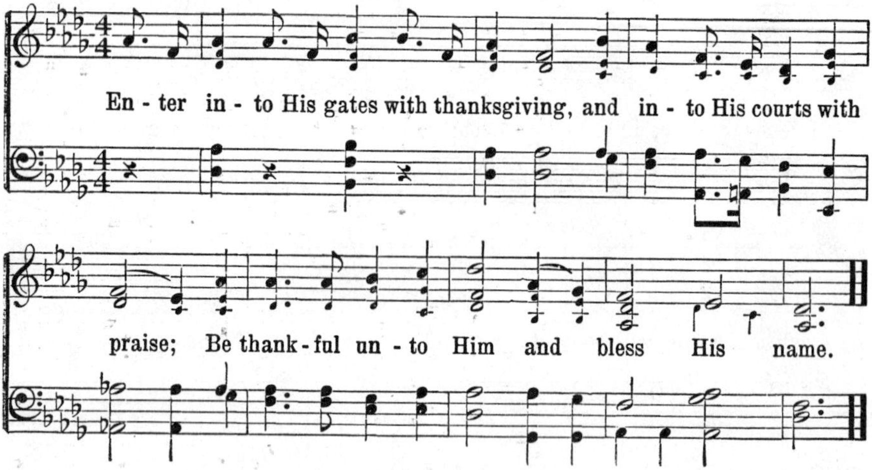

En - ter in - to His gates with thanksgiving, and in - to His courts with praise; Be thank - ful un - to Him and bless His name.

281 Father, We Thank Thee

MORNING HYMN

Rebecca J. Weston — D. Batchellor

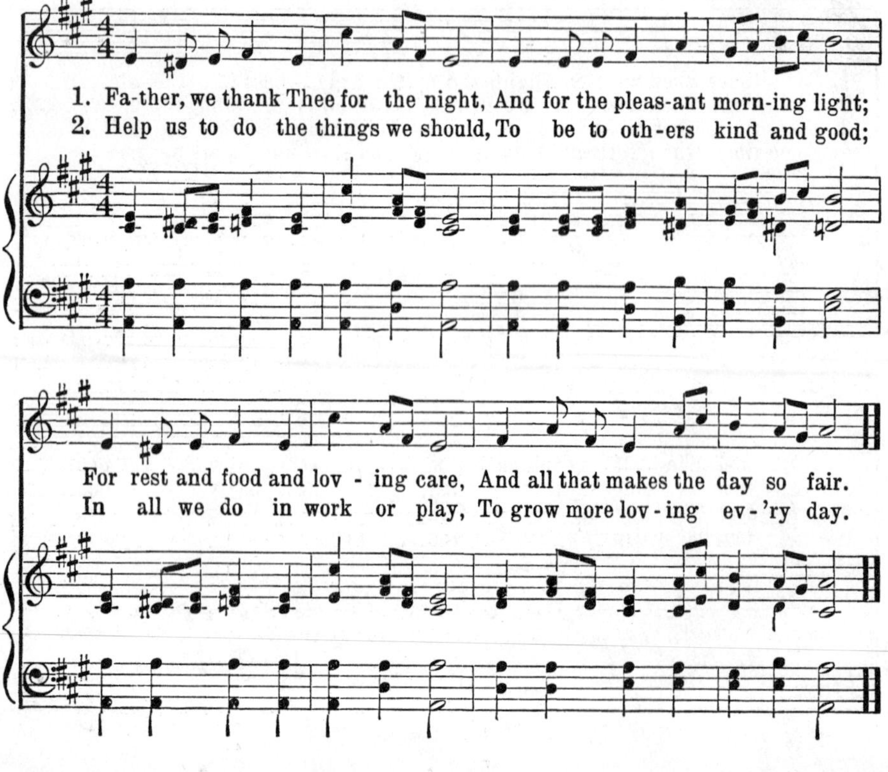

1. Fa-ther, we thank Thee for the night, And for the pleas-ant morn-ing light; For rest and food and lov - ing care, And all that makes the day so fair.

2. Help us to do the things we should, To be to oth-ers kind and good; In all we do in work or play, To grow more lov - ing ev - 'ry day.

282 All Things Bright And Beautiful

GOD'S WORK

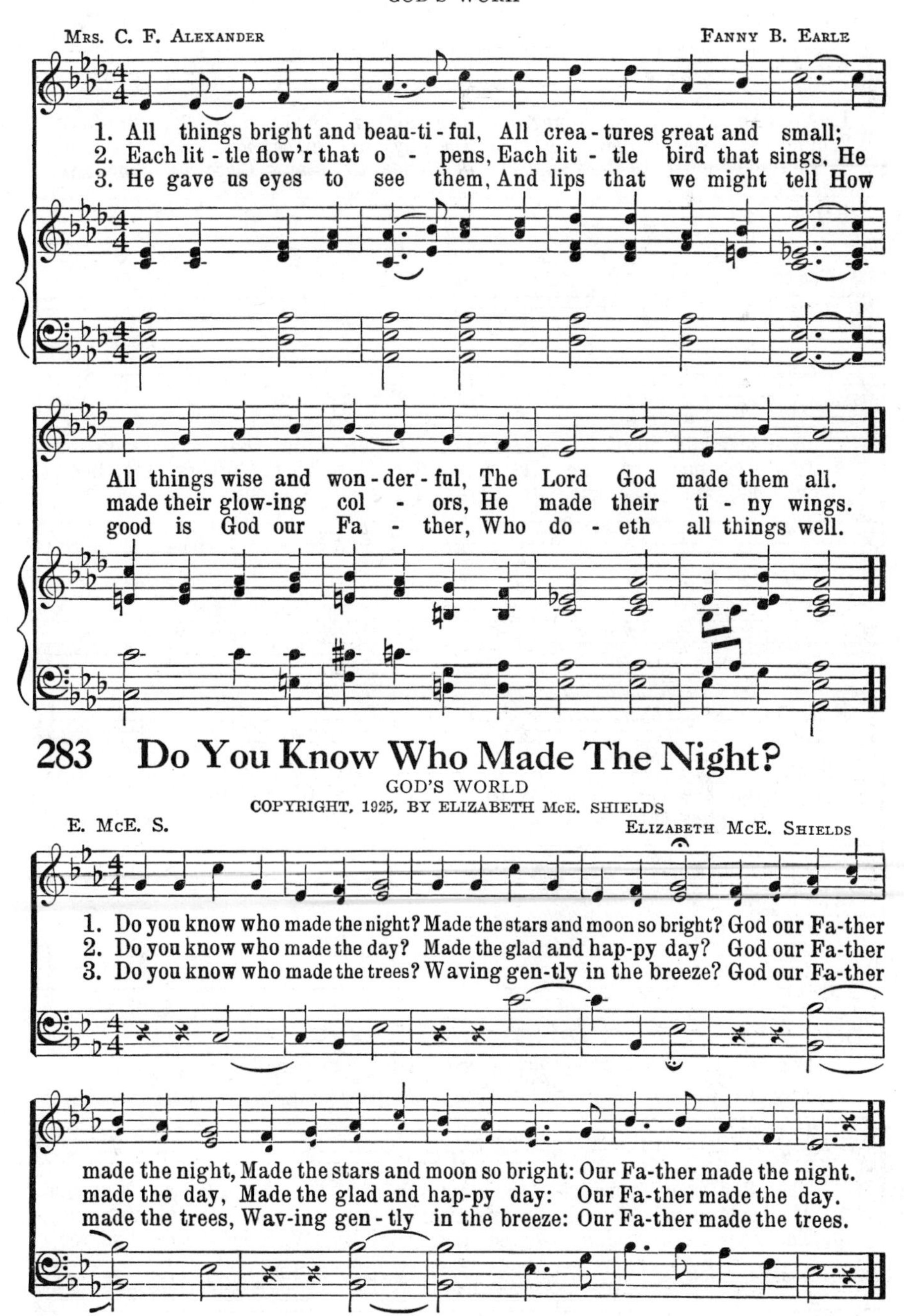
Mrs. C. F. Alexander
Fanny B. Earle
1. All things bright and beau-ti-ful, All crea-tures great and small;
2. Each lit-tle flow'r that o-pens, Each lit-tle bird that sings, He
3. He gave us eyes to see them, And lips that we might tell How
All things wise and won-der-ful, The Lord God made them all.
made their glow-ing col-ors, He made their ti-ny wings.
good is God our Fa-ther, Who do-eth all things well.
283 Do You Know Who Made The Night?
GOD'S WORLD
COPYRIGHT, 1925, BY ELIZABETH McE. SHIELDS
E. McE. S.
Elizabeth McE. Shields
1. Do you know who made the night? Made the stars and moon so bright? God our Fa-ther
2. Do you know who made the day? Made the glad and hap-py day? God our Fa-ther
3. Do you know who made the trees? Waving gen-tly in the breeze? God our Fa-ther
made the night, Made the stars and moon so bright: Our Fa-ther made the night.
made the day, Made the glad and hap-py day: Our Fa-ther made the day.
made the trees, Wav-ing gen-tly in the breeze: Our Fa-ther made the trees.

284
Away In A Manger
MÜLLER. 11. 11. 11. 11.
Anonymous
Carl Müller(?), ?
1. A-way in a man-ger, no crib for a bed, The lit-tle Lord Je-sus laid down His sweet head. The stars in the sky looked down where He lay, The lit-tle Lord Je-sus, a-sleep on the hay.
2. The cat-tle are low-ing, the Ba-by a-wakes, But lit-tle Lord Je-sus, no cry-ing He makes. I love Thee, Lord Je-sus, look down from the sky, And stay by my cra-dle till morn-ing is nigh.
3. Be near me, Lord Je-sus, I ask Thee to stay Close by me for-ev-er, and love me, I pray. Bless all the dear chil-dren in Thy ten-der care, And fit us for heav-en to live with thee there.
285
Nature's Message
FROM WORSHIP AND CONDUCT SONGS
COPYRIGHT, 1924, BY ELIZABETH McE. SHIELDS. USED BY PERMISSION
E. McE. S.
Elizabeth McE. Shields
1. The lit-tle flow'rs peep thro' the ground To say to peo-ple all a-round,
2. The birds come back each hap-py spring To say to peo-ple as they sing,
3. The trees are dressed in gowns so new; They say, "We have a mes-sage, too,

Nature's Message

"Your heav'n-ly Fa - ther sends His love To you and you and you."
"Your heav'n-ly Fa - ther sends His love To you and you and you."
Your heav'n-ly Fa - ther sends His love To you and you and you."

286 Tell Me The Stories Of Jesus

STORIES OF JESUS. 8. 4. 8. 4. 5. 4. 5. 4.

William H. Parker, 1845-1929 — Frederic A. Challinor, 1866-

Unison or Duet

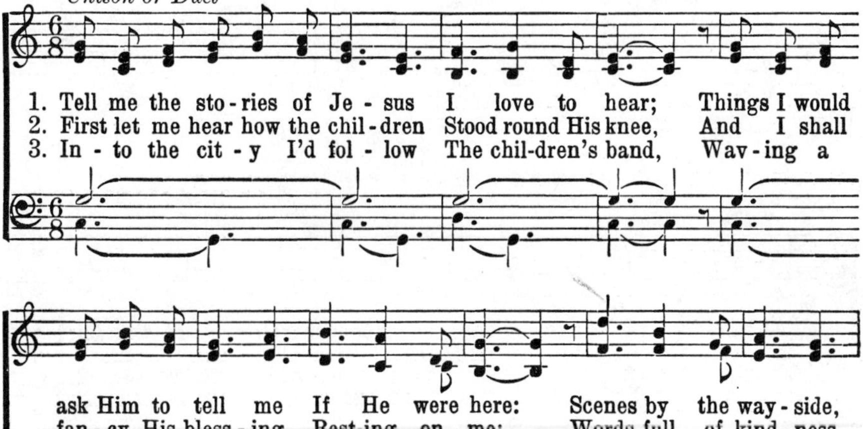

1. Tell me the sto - ries of Je - sus I love to hear; Things I would
2. First let me hear how the chil - dren Stood round His knee, And I shall
3. In - to the cit - y I'd fol - low The chil-dren's band, Wav - ing a

ask Him to tell me If He were here: Scenes by the way - side,
fan - cy His bless - ing Rest-ing on me; Words full of kind - ness,
branch of the palm-tree High in my hand; One of His her - alds,

Tales of the sea, Sto - ries of Je - sus, Tell them to me.
Deeds full of grace, All in the love - light Of Je - sus' face.
Yes, I would sing Loud-est ho - san - nas, "Je - sus is King!" A-MEN.

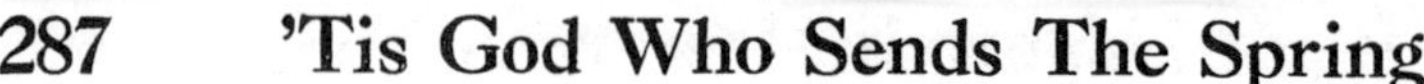

287 'Tis God Who Sends The Spring

Arranged from El Heerwart's Coll. MENDELSSOHN

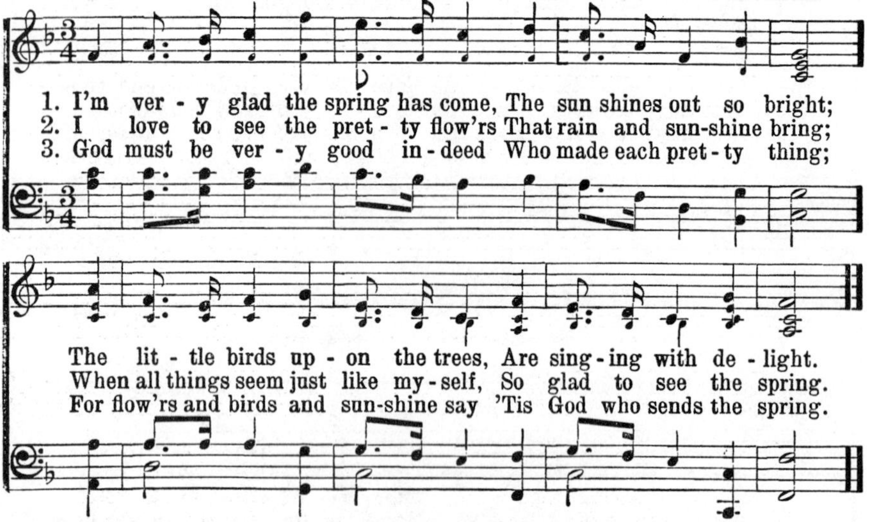

1. I'm ver - y glad the spring has come, The sun shines out so bright;
2. I love to see the pret - ty flow'rs That rain and sun-shine bring;
3. God must be ver - y good in - deed Who made each pret - ty thing;

The lit - tle birds up - on the trees, Are sing - ing with de - light.
When all things seem just like my - self, So glad to see the spring.
For flow'rs and birds and sun-shine say 'Tis God who sends the spring.

288 The Father's Care

Katharine Merrill A. B. Ponsonby

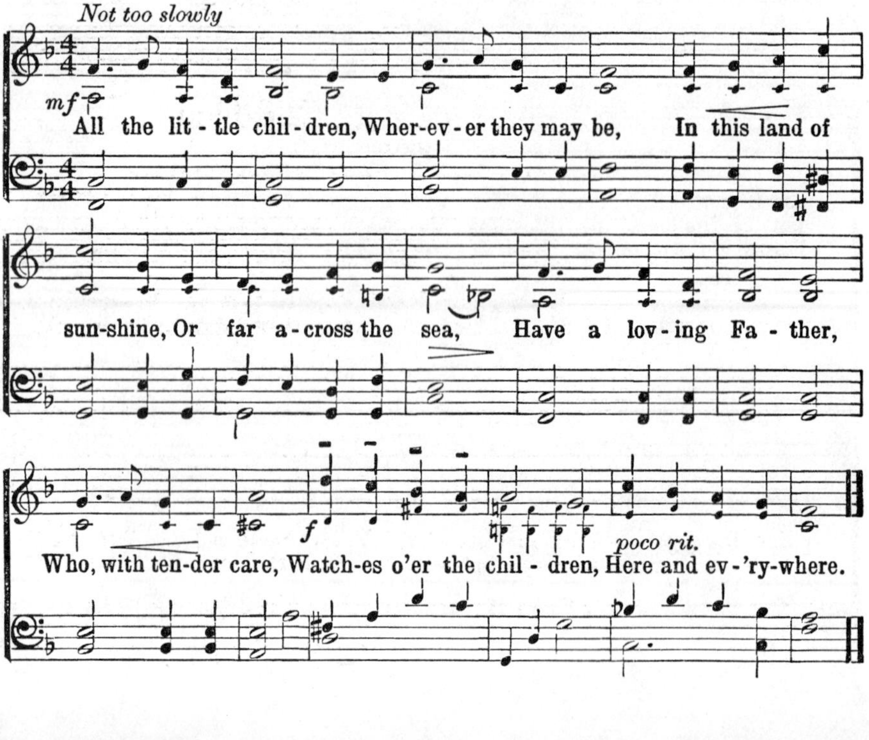

Not too slowly

mf

All the lit - tle chil - dren, Wher - ev - er they may be, In this land of sun-shine, Or far a - cross the sea, Have a lov - ing Fa - ther, Who, with ten - der care, Watch - es o'er the chil - dren, Here and ev - 'ry - where.

f *poco rit.*

289 Birds Singing In The Tree Tops

(SUMMER)
COPYRIGHT, 1916, BY IDA F. LEYDA, CHICAGO
FROM MELODIES, PERMISSION LEYDA PUB. CO.
I. F. L.
HAYDN
Arr. by H. M. B.
Cheerfully
1. Birds sing-ing in the tree tops, Flow'rs blooming in the grass,
2. Clouds floating high a - bove us, Boats sail - ing out to sea,
3. Hill, mountain, field and val - ley, Each one in beau-ty drest;
4. These all make hap-py sum-mer, God's gift—the great out-doors;
Close by the shad - y path - ways, Where children love to pass.
Far from the sand - y sea - shore, Where children love to be.
And all the spread-ing shade - trees, Where children love to rest.
He made the trees and flow - ers, The sea and sand - y shores.
290
Long Ago The Little Children
(THE CHILDREN'S FRIEND)
COPYRIGHT, 1920, BY JESSIE ELEANOR MOORE. USED BY PERMISSION
JESSIE ELEANOR MOORE
H. H. LEMMEL
1. Long a - go the lit - tle chil - dren Gath-ered close at Je - sus' knee,
2. Come and lis - ten to the sto - ry, Friend of chil-dren still is He;
For His kind - ly smile said gen - tly, "I love them and they love Me."
Lis - ten then and whis - per soft - ly, "I love Him and He loves me."

291 Every Morning Seems To Say

(SOMETHING HAPPY)
FROM THE CHILDREN'S YEAR, BY CONANT. USED BY PERMISSION OF MILTON BRADLEY CO.
HENRY VAN DYKE
B. PONSONBY
Ev - 'ry morn - ing seems to say, "There's some-thing hap - py
marcato
on the way, And God sends love to you!"
marcato
292 Jesus Loves Even Me
P. P. B.
P. P. BLISS
CHORUS
I am so glad that Je - sus loves me, Je - sus loves me, Je - sus loves me,
I am so glad that Je - sus loves me, Je - sus loves e - ven me.

293 Long Years Ago

(CAROL)
COPYRIGHT, 1930, BY LAMAR & WHITMORE
M. LANNING SHANE
MAY F. LAWRENCE
Not too fast
Long years ago Wise men with joy Brought birthday gifts To a small boy. From the
East they came, Thro' deserts wild, And they brought their best For a lit - tle child.
Long years have passed, And Christmas joys Fill the whole wide world For girls and boys.
294
The Stars Shone Bright
(CHRISTMAS CAROL)
COPYRIGHT, WHITMORE & SMITH
E. WEBSTER
M. E. KUNSMAN
1. The stars shone bright that Christmas night, When Je-sus lay on His bed of hay.
2. The shepherds came from far a - way To find the place where the ba - by lay.
3. The wise men brought their gifts of love; Led by the star that shone from a-bove.

295 Come, Let Us Worship

COPYRIGHT, LAMAR & WHITMORE

PSALM 95:6
PSALM 147:7

MAY F. LAWRENCE

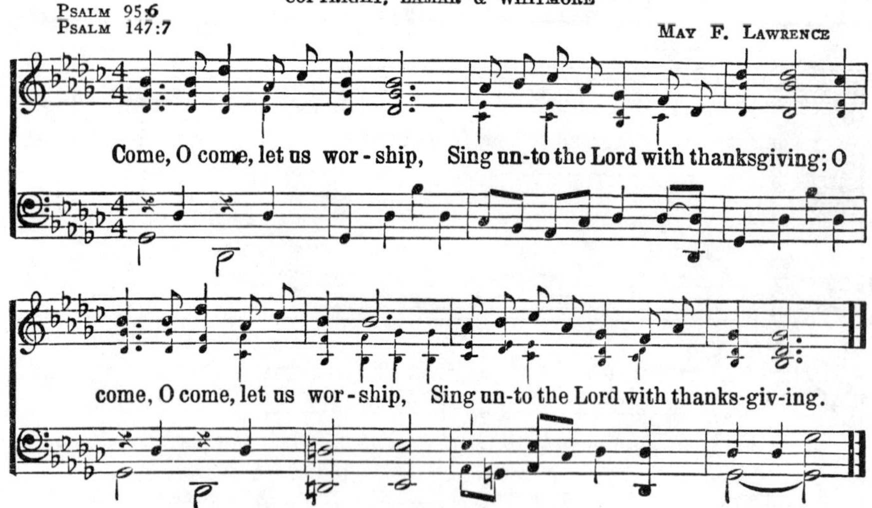
Come, O come, let us wor - ship, Sing un-to the Lord with thanksgiving; O
come, O come, let us wor - ship, Sing un-to the Lord with thanks-giv-ing.

296 I Was Glad

(A SONG OF GLADNESS)

COPYRIGHT, 1923, BY LAMAR & BARTON

I was glad when they said un - to me, Let us
go in - to the house of the Lord. I was glad when they said
un - to me, Let us go in - to the house of the Lord.

Responsive Readings

297 A Call to Worship

The Lord is in his holy temple:

Let all the earth keep silence before him.

The hour cometh, and now is, when the true worshippers shall worship the Father in spirit and truth: for the Father seeketh such to worship him.

God is a Spirit: and they that worship him must worship him in spirit and in truth.

O come, let us worship and bow down: let us kneel before the Lord our maker.

Enter into his gates with thanksgiving, and into his courts with praise.

I was glad when they said unto me, Let us go into the house of the Lord.

I went with them to the house of God, with the voice of joy and praise, with a multitude that kept holy day.

Seek ye the Lord while he may be found, call ye upon him while he is near.

As the hart panteth after the water brooks, so panteth my soul after thee, O God.

Great is the Lord, and greatly to be praised in the city of our God, in the mountain of his holiness.

Holy, holy, holy, is the Lord of hosts: the whole earth is full of his glory.

I will praise thee, O Lord, with my whole heart.

Let everything that hath breath praise the Lord.

298 The Presence of God

O Lord, thou hast searched me, and known me.

Thou knowest my downsitting and mine uprising, thou understandest my thought afar off.

Thou compassest my path and my lying down, and art acquainted with all my ways.

For there is not a word in my tongue, but, lo, O Lord, thou knowest it altogether.

Thou hast beset me behind and before, and laid thine hand upon me.

Such knowledge is too wonderful for me; it is high, I cannot attain unto it.

Whither shall I go from thy spirit? or whither shall I flee from thy presence?

If I ascend up into heaven, thou art there: if I make my bed in hell, behold, thou art there.

If I take the wings of the morning, and dwell in the uttermost parts of the sea;

Even there shall thy hand lead me, and thy right hand shall hold me.

If I say, Surely the darkness shall cover me; even the night shall be light about me.

Yea, the darkness hideth not from thee; but the night shineth as the day: the darkness and the light are both alike to thee.

Search me, O God, and know my heart: try me, and know my thoughts:

And see if there be any wicked way in me, and lead me in the way everlasting.

299 The Majesty of God

Be still, and know that I am God.

O worship the Lord in the beauty of holiness: fear before him, all the earth.

Before the mountains were brought forth, or ever thou hadst formed the earth and the world, even from everlasting to everlasting, thou art God.

For a thousand years in thy sight are but as yesterday when it is past, and as a watch in the night.

Of old hast thou laid the foundation of the earth; and the heavens are the work of thy hands.

They shall perish, but thou shalt endure: yea, all of them shall wax old like a garment; as a vesture shalt thou change them, and they shall be changed: but thou art the same, and thy years have no end.

Hast thou not known? hast thou not heard, that the everlasting God, the Lord, the Creator of the ends of the earth, fainteth not, neither is weary? There is no searching of his understanding.

He giveth power to the faint; and to them that have no might he increaseth strength.

The Lord hath prepared his throne in the heavens; and his kingdom ruleth over all.

Blessing, and glory, and wisdom, and thanksgiving, and honor, and power, and might, be unto our God for ever and ever.

300 The Sovereignty of God

The earth is the Lord's, and the fulness thereof; the world, and they that dwell therein.

For he hath founded it upon the seas, and established it upon the floods.

The Lord reigneth; let the earth rejoice; let the multitude of isles be glad thereof.

Clouds and darkness are round about him; righteousness and judgment are the habitation of his throne.

Thine eyes shall see the King in his beauty.

For the Lord is our judge, the Lord is our lawgiver, the Lord is our King.

Shall the axe boast itself against him that heweth therewith? or shall the saw magnify itself against him that shaketh it?

Nay but, O man, who art thou that repliest against God? Shall

the thing formed say to him that formed it, Why hast thou made me thus?

O the depth of the riches, both of the wisdom and knowledge of God!

How unsearchable are his judgments, and his ways past finding out!

For who hath known the mind of the Lord? or who hath been his counsellor?

For of him, and through him, and to him, are all things: to whom be glory for ever.

301 The Love of God

God commended his love toward us, in that, while we were yet sinners, Christ died for us.

He that spared not his own Son, but delivered him up for us all, how shall he not with him also freely give us all things?

Herein is love, not that we love God, but that he loved us, and sent his Son to be the propitiation for our sins.

For God so loved the world, that he gave his only begotten Son, that whosoever believeth in him should not perish, but have everlasting life.

Behold, what manner of love the Father hath bestowed upon us, that we should be called the sons of God.

Now are we the sons of God, and it doth not yet appear what we shall be: but we know that when he shall appear, we shall be like him.

If God be for us, who can be against us?

Nay, in all these things we are more than conquerors through him that loved us.

For I am persuaded, that neither death, nor life, nor angels, nor principalities, nor powers, nor things present, nor things to come,

Nor height, nor depth, nor any other creature, shall be able to separate us from the love of God, which is in Christ Jesus our Lord.

302 The Compassion of Christ

When he saw the multitudes, he was moved with compassion on them, because they fainted, and were scattered abroad, as sheep having no shepherd.

Surely he hath borne our griefs, and carried our sorrows.

Behold my servant, whom I uphold; mine elect, in whom my soul delighteth.

A bruised reed shall he not break, and the smoking flax shall he not quench.

Come unto me, all ye that labor and are heavy laden, and I will give you rest.

Take my yoke upon you, and learn of me; for I am meek and lowly in heart: and ye shall find rest unto your souls.

For we have not an high priest which cannot be touched with the feeling of our infirmities; but was in all points tempted like as we are, yet without sin.

Let us therefore come boldly unto the throne of grace, that we may obtain mercy, and find grace to help in time of need.

303 The Suffering of Christ

And when they were come to a place, which is called Calvary, there they crucified him, and the malefactors, one on the right hand, and the other on the left.

For it became him, for whom are all things, and by whom are all things, in bringing many sons unto glory, to make the captain of their salvation perfect through sufferings.

He was wounded for our transgressions, he was bruised for our iniquities: the chastisement of our peace was upon him; and with his stripes we are healed.

All we like sheep have gone astray; we have turned every one to his own way; and the Lord hath laid on him the iniquity of us all.

He was oppressed, and he was afflicted, yet he opened not his mouth:

He is brought as a lamb to the slaughter, and as a sheep before her shearers is dumb, so he openeth not his mouth.

He was taken from prison and from judgment: and who shall declare his generation?

For he was cut off out of the land of the living: for the transgressions of my people was he stricken.

Yet it pleased the Lord to bruise him; he hath put him to grief:

When thou shalt make his soul an offering for sin, he shall see his seed, he shall prolong his days, and the pleasure of the Lord shall prosper in his hand.

He was numbered with the transgressors;

And he bare the sin of many, and made intercession for the transgressors.

304 The Good Shepherd

The Lord is my shepherd; I shall not want.

He maketh me to lie down in green pastures: he leadeth me beside the still waters.

He restoreth my soul: he leadeth me in the paths of righteousness for his name's sake.

Yea, though I walk through the valley of the shadow of death, I will fear no evil: for thou art with me; thy rod and thy staff they comfort me.

He shall feed his flock like a shepherd:

He shall gather the lambs with his arm, and carry them in his bosom, and shall gently lead those that are with young.

I am the good shepherd: the good shepherd giveth his life for the sheep.

The hireling fleeth, because he is an hireling, and careth not for the sheep.

The thief cometh not, but for to steal, and to kill, and to destroy:

I am come that they might have life, and that they might have it more abundantly.

305 The Saviour

Thou shalt call his name Jesus: for he shall save his people from their sins.

For God sent not his Son into the world to condemn the world; but that the world through him might be saved.

This is a faithful saying, and worthy of all acceptation, that Christ Jesus came into the world to save sinners.

For the Son of man is come to seek and to save that which was lost.

For there is one God, and one mediator between God and men, the man Christ Jesus;

Who gave himself a ransom for all.

Ye know that ye were not redeemed with corruptible things, as silver and gold, from your vain conversation received by tradition from your fathers;

But with the precious blood of Christ, as of a lamb without blemish and without spot.

God forbid that I should glory, save in the cross of our Lord Jesus Christ, by whom the world is crucified unto me, and I unto the world.

The blood of Jesus Christ his Son cleanseth us from all sin.

306 The Son of God

Philip saith unto him, Lord, show us the Father, and it sufficeth us.

Jesus saith unto him, Have I been so long time with you, and yet hast thou not known me, Philip? he that hath seen me hath seen the Father.

Who is he that overcometh the world, but he that believeth that Jesus is the Son of God?

He that believeth on the Son of God hath the witness in himself.

Hereby know ye the Spirit of God: Every spirit that confesseth that Jesus Christ is come in the flesh is of God:

And every spirit that confesseth not that Jesus Christ is come in the flesh is not of God.

And we have seen and do testify that the Father sent the Son to be the Saviour of the world.

Whosoever shall confess that Jesus is the Son of God, God dwelleth in him, and he in God.

Wherefore God also hath highly exalted him, and given him a name which is above every name:

That at the name of Jesus every knee should bow, of things in heaven, and things in earth, and things under the earth; and that every tongue should confess that Jesus Christ is Lord, to the glory of God the Father.

In him dwelleth all the fulness of the Godhead bodily.

He must reign, till he hath put all enemies under his feet.

307 The Christian's Guide

I will pray the Father, and he shall give you another Comforter, that he may abide with you for ever.

The Comforter, which is the Holy Ghost, whom the Father will send in my name, he shall teach you all things, and bring all things to your remembrance, whatsoever I have said unto you.

Whom the world cannot receive, because it seeth him not, neither knoweth him:

But ye know him; for he dwelleth with you, and shall be in you.

I have yet many things to say unto you, but ye cannot bear them now.

Howbeit when he, the Spirit of truth, is come, he will guide you into all truth.

But as it is written, Eye hath not seen, nor ear heard, neither have entered into the heart of man, the things which God hath prepared for them that love him.

But God hath revealed them unto us by his Spirit: for the Spirit searcheth all things, yea, the deep things of God.

Now we have received, not the spirit of the world, but the spirit which is of God; that we might know the things that are freely given to us of God.

Which things also we speak, not in the words which man's wisdom teacheth, but which the Holy Ghost teacheth.

308 The Christian's Assurance

Hereby we know that we dwell in him, and he in us, because he hath given us of his Spirit.

Now if any man have not the Spirit of Christ, he is none of his.

For as many as are led by the Spirit of God, they are the sons of God.

For ye have not received the spirit of bondage again to fear; but ye have received the Spirit of adoption, whereby we cry, Abba, Father.

The Spirit itself beareth witness with our spirit, that we are the children of God:

And if children, then heirs; heirs of God, and joint-heirs with Christ.

We glory in tribulations also: knowing that tribulation worketh patience;

And patience, experience; and experience, hope:

And hope maketh not ashamed;

Because the love of God is shed abroad in our hearts by the Holy Ghost which is given unto us.

309 Repentance

Behold, the Lord's hand is not shortened, that it cannot save; neither his ear heavy, that he cannot hear:

But your iniquities have separated between you and your God, and your sins have hid his face from you, that he will not hear.

Have mercy upon me, O God, according to thy lovingkindness:

According unto the multitude of thy tender mercies blot out my transgressions.

For I acknowledge my transgressions: and my sin is ever before me.

Against thee, thee only, have I sinned, and done this evil in thy sight.

Hide thy face from my sins, and blot out all mine iniquities.

Create in me a clean heart, O God; and renew a right spirit within me.

Let the wicked forsake his way, and the unrighteous man his thoughts:

And let him return unto the Lord, and he will have mercy upon him; and to our God, for he will abundantly pardon.

If we say that we have no sin, we deceive ourselves, and the truth is not in us.

If we confess our sins, he is faithful and just to forgive us our sins, and to cleanse us from all unrighteousness.

310 Faith

Therefore being justified by faith, we have peace with God through our Lord Jesus Christ:

By whom also we have access by faith into this grace wherein we stand, and rejoice in hope of the glory of God.

He that believeth on him is not condemned:

But he that believeth not is condemned already, because he hath not believed in the name of the only begotten Son of God.

For ye are all the children of God by faith in Christ Jesus.

That no man is justified by the law in the sight of God, it is evident: for, The just shall live by faith.

But what things were gain to me, those I counted loss for Christ.

Yea doubtless, and I count all things but loss for the excellency of the knowledge of Jesus Christ my Lord: for whom I have suffered the loss of all things, and do count them but refuse, that I may win Christ,

And be found in him, not having mine own righteousness, which is of the law, but that which is through the faith of Christ, the righteousness which is of God by faith:

That I may know him, and the power of his resurrection, and the fellowship of his sufferings.

I know whom I have believed, and am persuaded that he is able to keep that which I have committed unto him against that day.

For me to live is Christ, and to die is gain.

311 Confession

The word is nigh thee, even in thy mouth, and in thy heart: that is, the word of faith, which we preach;

That if thou shalt confess with thy mouth the Lord Jesus, and shalt believe in thine heart that God hath raised him from the dead, thou shalt be saved.

For with the heart man believeth unto righteousness; and with the mouth confession is made unto salvation.

I am not ashamed of the gospel of Christ: for it is the power of God unto salvation to every one that believeth.

Whosoever therefore shall confess me before men, him will I confess also before my Father which is in heaven.

But whosoever shall deny me before men, him will I also deny before my Father which is in heaven.

I will bless the Lord at all times: his praise shall continually be in my mouth.

My soul shall make her boast in the Lord: the humble shall hear thereof, and be glad.

O magnify the Lord with me, and let us exalt his name together.

I sought the Lord, and he heard me, and delivered me from all my fears.

O taste and see that the Lord is good: blessed is the man that trusteth in him.

The Lord redeemeth the soul of his servants: and none of them that trust in him shall be desolate.

312 Obedience

Hath the Lord as great delight in burnt offerings and sacrifices, as in obeying the voice of the Lord?

Behold, to obey is better than sacrifice, and to hearken than the fat of rams.

Hate the evil, and love the good, and establish justice in the gate.

Wash you, make you clean; put away the evil of your doings from before mine eyes.

Not every one that saith unto me, Lord, Lord, shall enter into the kingdom of heaven;

But he that doth the will of my Father which is in heaven.

Many will say to me in that day, Lord, Lord, have we not prophesied in thy name? and in thy name have cast out devils? and in thy name done many wonderful works?

And then will I profess unto them, I never knew you: depart from me, ye that work iniquity.

Therefore whosoever heareth these sayings of mine, and doth them, I will liken him unto a wise man, which built his house upon a rock:

And the rain descended, and the floods came, and the winds blew, and beat upon that house; and it fell not: for it was founded upon a rock.

And every one that heareth these sayings of mine, and doth them not, shall be likened unto a foolish man, which built his house upon the sand:

And the rain descended, and the floods came, and the winds blew, and beat upon that house; and it fell: and great was the fall of it.

313 Prayer

When thou prayest, enter into thy closet and when thou hast shut thy door, pray to thy Father which is in secret;

And thy Father which seeth in secret shall reward thee openly.

But when ye pray, use not vain repetitions, as the heathen do: for they think that they shall be heard for their much speaking.

Be not ye therefore like unto them: for your Father knoweth what things ye have need of, before ye ask him.

Ask, and it shall be given you; seek, and ye shall find; knock, and it shall be opened unto you:

For every one that asketh receiveth; and he that seeketh findeth; and to him that knocketh it shall be opened.

Or what man is there of you, whom if his son ask bread, will give him a stone? Or if he ask a fish, will he give him a serpent?

If ye then, being evil, know how to give good gifts unto your children, how much more shall your father which is in heaven give good things to them that ask him?

The effectual fervent prayer of a righteous man availeth much.

The eyes of the Lord are upon the righteous, and his ears are open unto their cry.

In nothing be anxious; but in every thing by prayer and supplication with thanksgiving let your requests be made known unto God.

And the peace of God, which passeth all understanding, shall keep your hearts and minds through Christ Jesus.

314 The Bible

Thy word is a lamp unto my feet, and a light unto my path.

Order my steps in thy word: and let not any iniquity have dominion over me.

The law of the Lord is perfect, converting the soul:

The testimony of the Lord is sure, making wise the simple.

The statutes of the Lord are right, rejoicing the heart:

The commandment of the Lord is pure, enlightening the eyes.

The fear of the Lord is clean, enduring for ever:

The judgments of the Lord are true and righteous altogether.

More to be desired are they than gold, yea, than much fine gold:

Sweeter also than honey and the honeycomb.

Moreover by them is thy servant warned:

And in keeping of them there is great reward.

I commend you to God, and to the word of his grace, which is able to build you up, and to give you an inheritance among all them which are sanctified.

The entrance of thy words giveth light; it giveth understanding unto the simple.

All flesh is as grass, and all the glory of man as the flower of grass.

The grass withereth, and the flower thereof falleth away: But the word of the Lord endureth for ever.

315 Integrity

Lord, who shall abide in thy tabernacle? who shall dwell in thy holy hill?

He that walketh uprightly, and worketh righteousness, and speaketh the truth in his heart.

He that backbiteth not with his tongue, nor doeth evil to his neighbor, nor taketh up a reproach against his neighbor.

In whose eyes a vile person is condemned; but he honoreth them that fear the Lord.

He that sweareth to his own hurt, and changeth not.

He that putteth not out his money to usury, nor taketh reward against the innocent.

He that hath clean hands, and a pure heart; and hath not lifted up his soul unto vanity, nor sworn deceitfully.

He hath showed thee, O man, what is good; and what doth the Lord require of thee, but to do justly, and to love mercy, and to walk humbly with thy God?

316 Steadfastness

Be not carried about with divers and strange doctrines. For it is a good thing that the heart be established with grace.

A double minded man is unstable in all his ways.

Be strong in the Lord, and in the power of his might.

Put on the whole armor of God, that ye may be able to stand against the wiles of the devil.

For we wrestle not against flesh and blood, but against principalities, against powers, against the rulers of the darkness of this world, against spiritual wickedness in high places.

Wherefore take unto you the whole armor of God, that ye may be able to withstand in the evil day, and having done all, to stand.

Stand therefore, having your loins girt about with truth, and having on the breastplate of righteousness;

And your feet shod with the preparation of the gospel of peace;

Above all, taking the shield of faith, wherewith ye shall be able to quench all the fiery darts of the wicked.

And take the helmet of salvation, and the sword of the Spirit, which is the word of God:

Praying always with all prayer and supplication in the Spirit,

And watching thereunto with all perseverance and supplication for all saints.

317 Purity

Blessed are the pure in heart: for they shall see God.

Blessed are the undefiled in the way, who walk in the law of the Lord.

Keep thy heart with all diligence; for out of it are the issues of life.

A good tree cannot bring forth evil fruit, neither can a corrupt tree bring forth good fruit.

Let no corrupt communication proceed out of your mouth, but that which is good to the use of edifying, that it may minister grace unto the hearers.

Neither filthiness, nor foolish talking, nor jesting, which are not befitting.

Know ye not that ye are the temple of God, and that the Spirit of God dwelleth in you?

If any man defile the temple of God, him shall God destroy; for the temple of God is holy, which temple ye are.

Whatsoever things are true, whatsoever things are honest, whatsoever things are just, whatsoever things are pure, whatsoever things are lovely, whatsoever things are of good report;

If there be any virtue, and if there be any praise, think on these things. . . . And the God of peace shall be with you.

318 Forbearance

He that is slow to anger is better than the mighty; and he that ruleth his spirit than he that taketh a city.

Pride goeth before destruction, and a haughty spirit before a fall.

If any man be overtaken in a fault, ye which are spiritual, restore such an one in the spirit of meekness; considering thyself, lest thou also be tempted.

Bear ye one another's burdens, and so fulfil the law of Christ.

Do all things without murmurings and disputings.

Let nothing be done through strife or vainglory; but in lowliness of mind let each esteem other better than themselves.

Let all bitterness, and wrath, and anger, and clamor, and evil speaking, be put away from you, with all malice:

And be ye kind one to another, tenderhearted, forgiving one another, even as God for Christ's sake hath forgiven you.

319 Contentment

Godliness with contentment is great gain.

For we brought nothing into this world, and it is certain we can carry nothing out.

And having food and raiment let us be therewith content.

But they that are minded to be rich fall into temptation and a snare, and into many foolish and hurtful lusts, which drown men in destruction and perdition.

For the love of money is the root of all evil:

Which while some coveted after, they have erred from the faith, and pierced themselves through with many sorrows.

But thou, O man of God, flee these things;

And follow after righteousness, godliness, faith, love, patience, meekness.

I have learned, in whatsoever state I am, therewith to be content.

I know both how to be abased, and I know how to abound:

Every where and in all things I am instructed both to be full and to be hungry, both to abound and to suffer need.

I can do all things through Christ which strengtheneth me.

320 Brotherly Love

Love your enemies, bless them that curse you, do good to them that hate you, and pray for them which despitefully use you, and persecute you;

That ye may be the children of your Father which is in heaven: for he maketh his sun to rise on the evil and on the good, and sendeth rain on the just and on the unjust.

Therefore if thou bring thy gift to the altar, and there rememberest that thy brother hath ought against thee;

Leave there thy gift before the altar, and go thy way; first be reconciled to thy brother, and then come and offer thy gift.

If ye forgive men their trespasses, your heavenly Father will also forgive you:

But if ye forgive not men their trespasses, neither will your Father forgive your trespasses.

Whoso hath this world's goods, and seeth his brother have need, and shutteth up his compassion from him, how dwelleth the love of God in him?

Let us not love in word, neither in tongue; but in deed and in truth.

He that loveth not his brother whom he hath seen, how can he love God whom he hath not seen?

And this commandment have we from him, That he who loveth God love his brother also.

By this shall all men know that ye are my disciples, if ye have love one to another.

Behold, how good and how pleasant it is for brethren to dwell together in unity!

321 The Tongue

A soft answer turneth away wrath: but grievous words stir up anger.

Whoso keepeth his mouth and his tongue keepeth his soul from troubles.

These six things doth the Lord hate: yea, seven are an abomination unto him:

A proud look, a lying tongue, and hands that shed innocent blood,

An heart that deviseth wicked imaginations, feet that be swift in running to mischief,

A false witness that speaketh lies, and he that soweth discord among brethren.

Keep thy tongue from evil, and thy lips from speaking guile.

If any man among you seem to be religious, and bridleth not his tongue, but deceiveth his own heart, this man's religion is vain.

322 Joy

O come, let us sing unto the Lord: let us make a joyful noise to the rock of our salvation.

Let us come before his presence with thanksgiving, and make a joyful noise unto him with psalms.

Be glad in the Lord, and rejoice, ye righteous: and shout for joy, all ye that are upright in heart.

Because thou hast been my help, therefore in the shadow of thy wings will I rejoice.

The Lord hath done great things for us; whereof we are glad.

Our help is in the name of the Lord, who made heaven and earth.

Your joy no man taketh from you.

We glory in tribulations also . . . because the love of God is shed abroad in our hearts by the Holy Ghost which is given unto us.

Rejoice in the Lord alway: and again I say, Rejoice.

Arise, shine; for thy light is come, and the glory of the Lord is risen upon thee.

323 Service

I heard the voice of the Lord, saying, Whom shall I send, and who will go for us?

Then said I, Here am I; send me.

Ye know that the princes of the Gentiles exercise dominion over them, and they that are great exercise authority upon them.

But it shall not be so among you: but whosoever will be great among you, let him be your minister;

And whosoever will be chief among you, let him be your servant;

Even as the Son of man came not to be ministered unto, but to minister, and to give his life a ransom for many.

Let us not be weary in well doing: for in due season we shall reap, if we faint not.

As we have therefore opportunity, let us do good unto all men, especially unto them who are of the household of faith.

He hath sent me to heal the brokenhearted, to preach deliverance to the captives, and recovering of sight to the blind, to set at liberty them that are bruised.

For whosoever shall give you a cup of water to drink in my name, because ye belong to Christ, verily I say unto you, he shall not lose his reward.

324 Humility

Blessed are the poor in spirit: for theirs is the kingdom of heaven.

Humble yourselves therefore under the mighty hand of God, that he may exalt you in due time.

For thou desirest not sacrifice; else would I give it: thou delightest not in burnt offering.

The sacrifices of God are a broken spirit: a broken and a contrite heart, O God, thou wilt not despise.

For I say, through the grace given unto me, to every man that is among you, not to think of himself more highly than he ought to think.

If a man think himself to be something, when he is nothing, he deceiveth himself.

Be kindly affectioned one to another with brotherly love; in honor preferring one another.

Mind not high things, but condescend to men of low estate. Be not wise in your own conceits.

God resisteth the proud, and giveth grace to the humble.

Pure religion and undefiled before God and the Father is this, To visit the fatherless and widows in their affliction, and to keep himself unspotted from the world.

325 The Church

The Lord loveth the gates of Zion more than all the dwellings of Jacob.

Lord, I have loved the habitation of thy house, and the place where thine honor dwelleth.

Pray for the peace of Jerusalem: they shall prosper that love thee.

Peace be within thy walls, and prosperity within thy palaces.

Our feet shall stand within thy gates, O Jerusalem.

Thou shall call thy walls Salvation, and thy gates Praise.

Now ye are the body of Christ, and members in particular.

For as the body is one, and hath many members, and all the members of that one body, being many, are one body: so also is Christ.

That there should be no schism in the body; but that the members should have the same care one for another.

And whether one member suffer, all the members suffer with it; or one member be honored, all the members rejoice with it.

Christ also loved the church, and gave himself for it; that he might sanctify and cleanse it with the washing of water by the word,

That he might present it to himself a glorious church, not having spot, or wrinkle, or any such thing; but that it should be holy and without blemish.

326 The Christian Home

A worthy woman who can find? for her price is far above rubies.

She looketh well to the ways of her household, and eateth not the bread of idleness.

Her children rise up, and call her blessed; her husband also, and he praiseth her.

Favor is deceitful, and beauty is vain: but a woman that feareth the Lord, she shall be praised.

And, ye fathers, provoke not your children to wrath: but bring them up in the nurture and admonition of the Lord.

If any provide not for his own, and specially for those of his own house, he hath denied the faith, and is worse than an infidel.

Children, obey your parents in the Lord: for this is right.

Honor thy father and mother; which is the first commandment with promise; that it may be well with thee, and thou mayest live long on the earth.

A wise son maketh a glad father: but a foolish son is the heaviness of his mother.

Train up a child in the way he should go: and when he is old, he will not depart from it.

And these words, which I command thee this day, shall be in thine heart:

And thou shalt teach them diligently unto thy children, and

thou shalt talk of them when thou sittest in thine house, and when thou walkest by the way, and when thou liest down, and when thou risest up.

327 Missions

Ye shall receive power, after that the Holy Ghost is come upon you:

And ye shall be witnesses unto me both in Jerusalem, and in all Judaea, and in Samaria, and unto the uttermost part of the earth.

There is no difference between the Jew and the Greek: for the same Lord over all is rich unto all that call upon him.

I am debtor both to the Greeks, and to the Barbarians; both to the wise, and to the unwise.

For whosoever shall call upon the name of the Lord shall be saved.

How then shall they call on him in whom they have not believed? and how shall they believe in him of whom they have not heard? and how shall they hear without a preacher?

Go ye into all the world, and preach the gospel to every creature.

How beautiful are the feet of them that preach the gospel of peace, and bring glad tidings of good things!

328 Duty to the State

Let every soul be subject unto the higher powers.

For there is no power but of God: the powers that be are ordained of God.

Whosoever therefore resisteth the power, resisteth the ordinance of God.

For rulers are not a terror to good works, but to the evil . . . do that which is good, and thou shalt have praise of the same.

I exhort, therefore, that, first of all, supplications, prayers, intercessions, and giving of thanks, be made for all men;

For kings, and for all that are in authority; that we may lead a quiet and peaceable life in all godliness and honesty.

Render therefore to all their dues:

Tribute to whom tribute is due; custom to whom custom; fear to whom fear; honor to whom honor.

Submit yourselves to every ordinance of man for the Lord's sake.

For so is the will of God, that with well doing ye may put to silence the ignorance of foolish men.

329 Justice

Woe to him that buildeth a town with blood, and stablisheth a city by iniquity!

Woe unto them that call evil good, and good evil; that put darkness for light, and light for darkness.

They hate him that rebuketh in the gate, and they abhor him that speaketh uprightly.

They afflict the just, they take a bribe, and they turn aside the poor in the gate from their right.

The Lord is righteous in all his ways, and holy in all his works.

He that justifieth the wicked, and he that condemneth the just, even they both are abomination to the Lord.

Hear, O heavens, and give ear, O earth: for the Lord hath spoken.

Cease to do evil; learn to do well; seek justice, relieve the oppressed, judge the fatherless, plead for the widow.

Bring no more vain oblations; incense is an abomination unto me; the new moons and sabbaths, the calling of assemblies, I cannot away with; it is iniquity, even the solemn meeting.

Let justice roll down as waters, and righteousness as a mighty stream.

330 Temperance

Look not upon the wine when it is red, when it giveth his color in the cup.

At the last it biteth like a serpent, and stingeth like an adder.

Who hath woe? who hath sorrow? who hath contentions? who hath babbling? who hath wounds without cause? who hath redness of eyes?

They that tarry long at the wine; they that go to seek mixed wine.

Wine is a mocker, strong drink is raging: and whosoever is deceived thereby is not wise.

Be not deceived: neither . . . thieves, nor covetous, nor drunkards, nor revilers, nor extortioners, shall inherit the kingdom of God.

It is not for kings to drink wine; nor for princes strong drink:

Lest they drink, and forget the law, and pervert the judgment of any of the afflicted.

Woe unto them that rise up early in the morning, that they may follow strong drink; that continue until night, till wine inflame them!

They regard not the work of the Lord, neither consider the operation of his hand.

Woe unto them that are mighty to drink wine, and men of strength to mingle strong drink: which justify the wicked for reward, and take away the righteousness of the righteous from him!

And have given a boy for an harlot, and sold a girl for wine, that they might drink.

Woe unto him that giveth his

neighbor drink, that puttest thy bottle to him, and makest him drunken also!

That no man put a stumbling block or an occasion to fall in his brother's way.

331 World Peace

And there shall come forth a rod out of the stem of Jesse, and a Branch shall grow out of his roots:

And the spirit of the Lord shall rest upon him, the spirit of wisdom and understanding, the spirit of counsel and might, the spirit of knowledge and of the fear of the Lord;

And shall make him of quick understanding in the fear of the Lord: and he shall not judge after the sight of his eyes, neither reprove after the hearing of his ears:

But with righteousness shall he judge the poor, and reprove with equity for the meek of the earth: and he shall smite the earth with the rod of his mouth, and with the breath of his lips shall he slay the wicked.

And righteousness shall be the girdle of his loins, and faithfulness the girdle of his reins.

The wolf also shall dwell with the lamb, and the leopard shall lie down with the kid; and the calf and the young lion and the fatling together; and a little child shall lead them.

And the cow and the bear shall feed; their young ones shall lie down together: and the lion shall eat straw like the ox.

And the suckling child shall play on the hole of the asp, and the weaned child shall put his hand on the cockatrice' den.

They shall not hurt nor destroy in all my holy mountain: for the earth shall be full of the knowledge of the Lord, as the waters cover the sea.

And he shall judge among the nations, and shall rebuke many people: And they shall beat their swords into plowshares, and their spears into pruning hooks: nation shall not lift up sword against nation, neither shall they learn war any more.

O house of Jacob, come ye, and let us walk in the light of the Lord.

Put up again thy sword into his place: for all they that take the sword shall perish with the sword.

332 Brotherhood in God

Of a truth I perceive that God is no respecter of persons:

But in every nation he that feareth him, and worketh righteousness, is accepted with him.

And hath made of one blood all nations of men for to dwell on all the face of the earth, and hath determined the times before ap-

pointed, and the bounds of their habitation;

That they should seek the Lord, if haply they might feel after him, and find him, though he be not far from every one of us.

If ye fulfill the royal law according to the scripture, Thou shalt love thy neighbor as thyself, ye do well:

But if ye have respect to persons, ye commit sin, and are convinced of the law as transgressors.

For there is no difference between the Jew and the Greek: for the same Lord over all is rich unto all that call upon him.

The rich and the poor meet together: the Lord is the maker of them all.

333 Daily Provision

Therefore I say unto you, be not anxious for your life, what ye shall eat, or what ye shall drink; nor yet for your body, what ye shall put on. Is not the life more than meat, and the body than raiment?

Behold the fowls of the air: for they sow not, neither do they reap, nor gather into barns; yet your Heavenly Father feedeth them. Are ye not much better than they?

Which of you by being anxious can add one cubit unto his stature?

And why take ye thought for raiment? Consider the lilies of the field, how they grow; they toil not, neither do they spin:

And yet I say unto you, That even Solomon in all his glory was not arrayed like one of these.

Wherefore, if God so clothe the grass of the field, which today is, and tomorrow is cast into the oven, shall he not much more clothe you, O ye of little faith?

Therefore be not anxious, saying, What shall we eat? or, What shall we drink? or, Wherewithal shall we be clothed?

(For after all these things do the Gentiles seek:) for your heavenly Father knoweth that ye have need of all these things.

But seek ye first the kingdom of God, and his righteousness; and all these things shall be added unto you.

Be not therefore anxious for the morrow: for the morrow shall be anxious for the things of itself. Sufficient unto the day is the evil thereof.

334 Guidance

Trust in the Lord with all thine heart; and lean not unto thine own understanding.

In all thy ways acknowledge him, and he shall direct thy paths.

Be not afraid of sudden fear, neither of the desolation of the wicked, when it cometh.

For the Lord shall be thy con-

fidence, and shall keep thy foot from being taken.

Thou art my rock and my fortress; therefore for thy name's sake lead me, and guide me.

The path of the just is as the shining light, that shineth more and more unto the perfect day.

Thus saith the Lord that created thee, O Jacob, and he that formed thee, O Israel, Fear not: for I have redeemed thee, I have called thee by thy name; thou art mine.

When thou passeth through the waters, I will be with thee; and through the rivers, they shall not overflow thee:

When thou walkest through the fire, thou shalt not be burned; neither shall the flame kindle upon thee.

I will bring the blind by a way they knew not; I will lead them in paths that they have not known.

He calleth his own sheep by name, and leadeth them out.

And when he putteth forth his own sheep, he goeth before them, and the sheep follow him: for they know his voice.

335 Comfort

Blessed are they that mourn: for they shall be comforted.

The Lord is nigh unto them that are of a broken heart; and saveth such as be of a contrite spirit.

Many are the afflictions of the righteous: but the Lord delivereth him out of them all.

The Lord redeemeth the soul of his servants: and none of them that trust in him shall be desolate.

My tears have been my meat day and night, while they continually say to me, Where is thy God?

Yet the Lord will command his lovingkindness in the daytime, and in the night his song shall be with me, and my prayer unto the God of my life.

They that sow in tears shall reap in joy.

He that goeth forth and weepeth, bearing precious seed, shall doubtless come again with rejoicing, bringing his sheaves with him.

Why art thou cast down, O my soul? and why art thou disquieted within me?

Hope thou in God: for I shall yet praise him, who is the health of my countenance, and my God.

336 A Refuge

God is our refuge and strength, a very present help in trouble.

Therefore will not we fear, though the earth be removed, and though the mountains be carried into the midst of the sea;

Though the waters thereof roar and be troubled, though the mountains shake with the swelling thereof.

There is a river, the streams whereof shall make glad the city of God, the holy place of the tabernacles of the most High.

God is in the midst of her; she shall not be moved:

God shall help her, and that right early.

The heathen raged, the kingdoms were moved: he uttered his voice, the earth melted.

The Lord of hosts is with us; the God of Jacob is our refuge.

Come, behold the works of the Lord, what desolations he hath made in the earth.

He maketh wars to cease unto the end of the earth; he breaketh the bow, and cutteth the spear in sunder; he burneth the chariot in the fire.

Be still, and know that I am God: I will be exalted among the heathen, I will be exalted in the earth.

The Lord of hosts is with us; the God of Jacob is our refuge.

337 Our Helper

I will lift up mine eyes unto the hills, from whence cometh my help.

My help cometh from the Lord, which made heaven and earth.

He will not suffer thy foot to be moved: he that keepeth thee will not slumber.

Behold, he that keepeth Israel shall neither slumber nor sleep.

The Lord is thy keeper: the Lord is thy shade upon thy right hand.

The sun shall not smite thee by day, nor the moon by night.

The Lord shall preserve thee from all evil: he shall preserve thy soul.

The Lord shall preserve thy going out and thy coming in from this time forth, and even for evermore.

338 The Dignity of Man

When I consider thy heavens, the work of thy fingers, the moon and the stars, which thou hast ordained:

What is man, that thou art mindful of him? and the son of man, that thou visitest him?

For thou hast made him a little lower than the angels, and hast crowned him with glory and honor.

Thou madest him to have dominion over the works of thy hands; thou hast put all things under his feet.

And God said, Let us make man in our image, after our likeness.

So God created man in his own image, in the image of God created he him.

For I reckon that the sufferings of this present time are not worthy to be compared with the glory which shall be revealed in us.

Because the creature itself also

shall be delivered from the bondage of corruption into the glorious liberty of the children of God.

Likewise the Spirit also helpeth our infirmities.

And we know that all things work together for good to them that love God.

339 Continuing Life

If a man die, shall he live again?

We know that if our earthly house of this tabernacle were dissolved, we have a building of God, an house not made with hands, eternal in the heavens.

Jesus said unto her, I am the resurrection, and the life: he that believeth in me, though he were dead, yet shall he live:

And whosoever liveth and believeth in me shall never die.

Behold, I show you a mystery; We shall not all sleep, but we shall all be changed.

For this corruptible must put on incorruption, and this mortal must put on immortality.

O death, where is thy sting? O grave, where is thy victory?

Thanks be to God, which giveth us the victory through our Lord Jesus Christ.

I have fought a good fight, I have finished my course, I have kept the faith:

Henceforth there is laid up for me a crown of righteousness, which the Lord, the righteous judge, shall give me at that day:

And not to me only,

But unto all them also that love his appearing.

340 Judgment

For we must all appear before the judgment seat of Christ;

That every one may receive the things done in his body, according to that he hath done, whether it be good or bad.

When the Son of man shall come in his glory, and all the holy angels with him, then shall he sit upon the throne of his glory:

And before him shall be gathered all nations: and he shall separate them one from another, as a shepherd divideth his sheep from the goats:

And he shall set the sheep on his right hand, but the goats on the left.

Then shall the King say unto them on his right hand, Come, ye blessed of my Father, inherit the kingdom prepared for you from the foundation of the world.

Then shall he say also unto them on the left hand, Depart from me, ye cursed, into everlasting fire, prepared for the devil and his angels.

And these shall go away into everlasting punishment: but the righteous into life eternal.

Blessed are they that do his commandments, that they may have right to the tree of life, and may enter in through the gates into the city.

For without are dogs, and sorcerers, and whoremongers, and murderers, and idolaters, and whosoever loveth and maketh a lie.

I Jesus have sent mine angel to testify unto you these things in the churches.

I am the root and the offspring of David, and the bright and morning star.

341 The Heavenly Home

Let not your heart be troubled: ye believe in God, believe also in me.

In my Father's house are many mansions: if it were not so, I would have told you. I go to prepare a place for you.

And if I go and prepare a place for you, I will come again, and receive you unto myself;

That where I am, there ye may be also.

And God shall wipe away all tears from their eyes;

And there shall be no more death, neither sorrow, nor crying, neither shall there be any more pain: for the former things are passed away.

And I saw no temple therein: for the Lord God Almighty and the Lamb are the temple of it.

And the city had no need of the sun, neither of the moon, to shine in it: for the glory of God did lighten it, and the Lamb is the light thereof.

And the nations of them which are saved shall walk in the light of it: and the kings of the earth do bring their glory and honour into it.

And the gates of it shall not be shut at all by day: for there shall be no night there.

And they shall bring the glory and honour of the nations into it.

And there shall in no wise enter into it any thing that defileth, neither whatsoever worketh abomination, or maketh a lie: but they which are written in the Lamb's book of life.

342 Palm Sunday

Hosanna to the son of David:

Blessed is he that cometh in the name of the Lord; Hosanna in the highest.

Behold, thy King cometh unto thee,

Meek, and sitting upon an ass, and a colt the foal of an ass.

The kings of the earth set themselves, and the rulers take counsel together, against the Lord, and against his anointed.

Yet have I set my king upon my holy hill of Zion.

I will declare the decree: the Lord hath said unto me, Thou art my Son; this day have I begotten thee.

Ask of me, and I shall give thee the heathen for thine inheritance, and the uttermost parts of the earth for thy possession.

Be wise now therefore, O ye kings: be instructed, ye judges of the earth.

Blessed are all they that put their trust in him.

343 Good Friday

Is it nothing to you all ye that pass by?

Behold, and see if there be any sorrow like unto my sorrow.

He saith unto the Jews, Behold your King!

But they cried out, Away with him, away with him, crucify him.

Pilate saith unto them, Shall I crucify your King?

The chief priests answered, We have no king but Caesar.

Then delivered he him therefore unto them to be crucified.

And they took Jesus, and led him away.

And he bearing his cross went forth into a place called the place of a skull, which is called in the Hebrew Golgotha:

Where they crucified him, and two other with him, on either side one, and Jesus in the midst.

The stone which the builders rejected, the same is become the head of the corner.

For there is none other name under heaven given among men, whereby we must be saved.

344 Easter Day

Why seek ye the living among the dead?

He is not here, but is risen.

Him, being delivered by the determinate counsel and foreknowledge of God, ye have taken, and by wicked hands have crucified and slain:

Whom God hath raised up, having loosed the pains of death: because it was not possible that he should be holden of it.

And if Christ be not risen, then is our preaching vain, and your faith is also vain.

And if Christ be not raised, your faith is vain; ye are yet in your sins.

Then they also which are fallen asleep in Christ are perished.

If in this life only we have hope in Christ, we are of all men most miserable.

But now is Christ risen from the dead, and become the firstfruits of them that slept.

For as in Adam all die, even so in Christ shall all be made alive.

Blessed be the God and Father of our Lord Jesus Christ, who hath blessed us with all spiritual blessings in heavenly places in Christ.

Who hath abolished death, and hath brought life and immortality to light through the gospel.

345 Thanksgiving Day

O give thanks unto the Lord; for he is good: because his mercy endureth for ever.

Let Israel now say, that his mercy endureth for ever.

He hath not dealt with us after our sins; nor rewarded us according to our iniquities.

For as the heaven is high above the earth, so great is his mercy toward them that fear him.

Thou crownest the year with thy goodness.

The pastures are clothed with flocks; the valleys also are covered over with corn; they shout for joy, they also sing.

What shall I render unto the Lord for all his benefits toward me?

I will take the cup of salvation, and call upon the name of the Lord.

I will offer to thee the sacrifice of thanksgiving, and will call upon the name of the Lord.

I will pay my vows unto the Lord now in the presence of all his people, in the courts of the Lord's house, in the midst of thee, O Jerusalem.

Bless the Lord, O my soul, and forget not all his benefits.

Bless the Lord, all his works in all places of his dominion: bless the Lord, O my soul.

346 Christmas

Behold, I bring you good tidings of great joy, which shall be to all people.

For unto you is born this day in the city of David a Saviour, which is Christ the Lord.

Glory to God in the highest, and on earth peace, good will toward men.

For he that is mighty hath done to me great things; and holy is his name.

In him was life; and the life was the light of men.

And the light shineth in darkness; and the darkness comprehended it not.

For God, who commanded the light to shine out of darkness, hath shined in our hearts,

To give the light of the knowledge of the glory of God in the face of Jesus Christ.

And of his fulness have we all received, and grace for grace.

For the law was given by Moses, but grace and truth came by Jesus Christ.

General Index

TITLES IN CAPITALS

FIRST LINES IN Lower Case

Index of Responsive Readings

Topical Index

GOD

GRACE AND MERCY

GUIDANCE

HOLY SPIRIT

HEAVEN AND HOME

INVITATION

LORD'S SUPPER

(See Responses—Holy Communion)

Nos. 260-268

LOVE

LOYALTY

MEN'S VOICES

MERCY

(See Grace and Mercy)

MISSIONARY AND BROTHERHOOD

MORNING

NATIONAL

OPENING

PEACE

PRAISE AND WORSHIP

PRAYER

QUARTETTES

(See Special Selections)

RESPONSES

REVIVAL

(See Invitation)

SERVICE

SOLOS

(See Special Selections)

SPECIAL SELECTIONS

Choruses:

Solos, Quartettes, etc.:

SPIRITUALS

TEMPERANCE

(Moral Reform)

THANKSGIVING

WORSHIP

(See Praise and Worship)

YOUNG PEOPLE